MW00466516

FIRE YOURSELF

FIRE
YOURSELF
[daily]

365 DEVOTIONALS
WILLY STEWART &
THERESA ALLEN

MILESTONE
PUBLISHING HOUSE

The **FIRE YOURSELF MOVEMENT** is about a new generation of believers rising up to demonstrate their strength through service and love. Firing yourself is simply the abandonment of an egotistical, controlling and self-centered life. When you fire yourself as your own higher power, you acknowledge that your life is submitted to God's authority and you are availing yourself, your life, and your work for the fulfillment of His purpose.

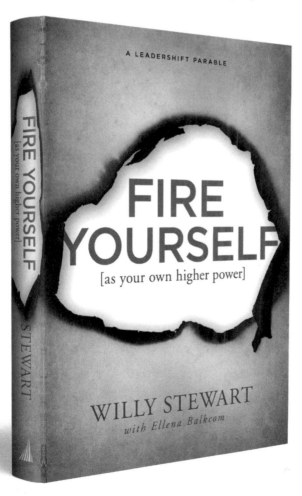

A LEADERSHIFT PARABLE

FIRE YOURSELF
[as your own higher power]

WILLY STEWART
with Ellena Balkcom

FIREYOURSELFMOVEMENT.COM

Published by Milestone Publishing House, Raleigh, North Carolina.

Cover & Interior Design by Roy Roper, www.wideyedesign.net
Cover Cross Illustration by Sherri Stewart, www.sherri-stewART.com

ISBN-10: 089893955
ISBN-13: 9780982839362

Printed in the USA

[acknowledgement]

Thank you for your purchase. Our hope is that the "Fire Yourself [daily]" book of devotionals will become a faithful travel companion as you live out your faith day to day. The journey may get hard sometimes, but we are never alone. With the Word of God as the Lamp to our feet and the Light to our path (Psalm 119:105), we can walk confidently trusting that Christ will never fail us! As for us failing Him…no worries! Salvation is Christ's work. He who called us to this journey will be faithful to complete the good work that He has begun in us (Philippians 1:6).

Proceeds from the "Fire Yourself [daily]" book of devotionals benefit the Haven of Rest Women's Ministry in Anderson, S.C. The Haven of Rest Women's Ministry is a long-term, faith-based residential program for women struggling with life-dominating problems. In a nurturing home environment, hurting women are exposed to the healing message of the Gospel, attend Christ-focused counseling sessions and instructional classes, and learn how to identify irrational thoughts and manage emotions. The program helps women rewrite their life scripts through goal setting; educational opportunities; and working closely with DSS case workers and the court system on their behalf. Through cultivating a personal relationship with Christ, developing new healthy coping skills, and access to constructive resources, women who were once stuck in a lifestyle of destruction and defeat can emerge as new creations, strong and confident in Christ. For more information about this 501c3 ministry, visit **www.havenofrest.cc**.

We encourage you to make today a fresh start. Fire Yourself as the CEO of your life! Give Christ the leadership position in your heart, and allow Him to live victoriously through you!

In Christ Alone,
Willy Stewart & Theresa Allen

[fire yourself]
JANUARY

January 1

A CHEERFUL HEART

Proverbs 17:22 (NIV): *"A cheerful heart is good medicine, but a crushed spirit dries up the bones."*

When was the last time you laughed? The last time you smiled . . . big? We live in a serious world with serious issues. Just read the newspaper or watch the news on television. Seldom is the information uplifting, and it often resets our minds with a more worldly perspective on life. Even as children of God filled with the hope found in Christ Jesus, we can get caught in this vortex of negativity and allow it to bring us down and dampen our spirits. However, we need to remember who we are in Christ . . . more than conquerors (Romans 8:37), the beloved of God (1 Thessalonians 1:4), and joint heirs with Jesus (Romans 8:16-18). Let us go into this world as witnesses of the good Word. Let us do it with a smile on our face radiating with the joy of God's love. Let us stand out because we are full of God's Spirit and because we know that His strength flows through us. Close your eyes; take a deep breath; feel God's love wash over you . . . now SMILE! What a great feeling! Let us take a cheerful heart into our homes, neighborhoods, and workplaces. After all, what do we have to be gloomy about? Our Lord has overcome the world, and the world could use a little "Christ perspective" on life (John 16:33).

Spread good cheer today!

January 2
ALL THINGS

Romans 8:28 (NIV): *"And we know that in all things God works for the good of those who love him, who have been called according to his purpose."*

I was asked the other day if I was going to heaven. I responded that without a shadow of a doubt, I was! I have been called for His purpose; He has become my salvation; and I will not perish.

When we trust in the Lord with all of our hearts, when we are absolutely certain of our faith, when we love Him more than we love anything else, when we are totally convinced of our salvation through Christ Jesus, then we can understand and accept that in ALL things God works for our own good. I will repeat it, "…that in ALL things God works for the good of those who love him…" The significance of that statement is far reaching. It did not say in some things. Pause for a second to absorb the magnitude of God's commitment to those who love Him. As we face uphill battles, when we question our own direction, when we are unsure about tomorrow, and when this world's challenges seem insurmountable, put your trust in the Lord. Do not be afraid, for He is our strength; He is our song; He will protect us; and He will be beside us. How do I know? God's Word said He would (Psalm 118). We just have to trust Him!

Praise God in All things today!

January 3
ALL YOUR HEART

Jeremiah 29:13 (NIV): *"You will seek me and find me when you seek me with all your heart."*

As we sail the ocean of life, let us set our coordinates on Christ and trust that He will guide us and protect us when we confront stormy seas. Let us seek Him and His wisdom with all of our heart and pray that He will comfort us in His everlasting arms always. We are so easily distracted, getting off course by our own ego and trying to maneuver through issues and problems on our own. The Lord clearly tells us to lean on Him and not on our own understanding. We have to seek God and trust Him with ALL of our heart. Step aside and let the Lord be the captain of your life's boat. He will lead you into quiet waters.

Let Christ set your course today!

January 4
AN ATTITUDE OF GRATITUDE

1 Thessalonians 5:16-18 (ESV): *"Rejoice always, pray without ceasing, give thanks in all circumstances; for this is the will of God in Christ Jesus for you."*

Too often, we save our gratitude for special days ... Thanksgiving, Christmas, Mother's Day. On these occasions, we make a conscious effort to express our appreciation or acknowledge our blessings in life. Thankfulness, however, should not be a novelty we put on once a year like our reindeer sweaters. Instead, we need to daily cultivate a heart of thanksgiving and a lifestyle that reflects thankfulness. Zig Ziglar said, "Of all the attitudes we can acquire, surely the attitude of gratitude is the most important and by far the most life changing."

This is something that most parents try to instill in children at a young age. We remind our kids of the two magic words...please and thank you. For some reason, though, the "please" tends to stick more than the "thank you." Why? The answer is simple. "Please" gets me what I want; it is for me and about me (I get something for it). "Thank you," on the other hand, is for someone else (the giver of the gift). It is so easy to always keep the focus on me.

Jesus set the perfect example of a thankful heart throughout His life on Earth. We read in the Gospels how He gave thanks before breaking bread with the disciples (Luke 22:19); He gave thanks before feeding the 5000 (Matthew 14:13-21); He gave thanks before raising Lazarus from the dead (John 11:1-57). In all things, the Son of God kept His focus on the Father. The result? He maintained an attitude of gratitude, and so should we!

You are blessed today!

January 5
BE STILL BEFORE THE LORD

Psalm 37:7 (NIV): *"Be still before the Lord and wait patiently for him; do not fret when men succeed in their ways, when they carry out their wicked schemes."*

Be still. This is a difficult task for most of us to accomplish. We have tasks on our "to do" lists that must get checked off. And, if we are completely honest, we only feel valuable or important if we are moving and doing. There are times, though, IMPORTANT times, when we must stop our busyness and wait for God. If we are to grow spiritually, we have to be connected with our Lord. We need to pause completely, clear the mind, open the heart, and bare the soul, so we can hear our Father's voice. We need to quiet the background noises of our lives, so we can tune into God's words and listen to His guidance. From the moment we wake up until we lay down exhausted at the end of the day, we typically do not stop working, multi-tasking, playing, leading, following, managing, parenting, exercising and so many more activities such that we are never truly still. We need to remember that busyness does not always mean we are being productive. We can fill our lives with a lot of good things and still miss the best thing. In the same way Jesus quieted the stormy seas, we should take time each day to quiet the commotion that steals our attention. This will allow us to deeply embrace the Almighty, allow His peace to permeate our soul, be completely showered in His abundant love, and experience the divine joy that comes from Him. So, let us be still in focused prayer, be thankful for the blessings we receive every day, and seek the Lord's guidance and protection in all we do.

Have a peace-filled day!

January 6
CALLED TO COMFORT

2 Corinthians 1:3-4 (ESV): *"Blessed be the God and Father or our Lord Jesus Christ, the Father of mercies and God of all comfort, who comforts us in all our affliction, so that we may be able to comfort those who are in any affliction, with the comfort with which we ourselves are comforted by God."*

Too many times we try to console or comfort people by quoting biblical scriptures at random. We tell people to "trust God" or "just give it to the Lord," and we have no clue how empty our words sound. Though our intent may be good, it is really just a hollow courtesy. Until we become broken ourselves and know what it is like to experience pain and suffering– until we have faced the seemingly premature death of a loved one or felt the intense betrayal of a trusted companion; unless we have battled the darkness of depression or struggled with an addiction and experienced the feelings of powerlessness and shame – until you and I have been wounded, we cannot feel genuine compassion. There is a reason why God's children go through troubles, trials, and heartaches in life… our wounds gives us the ability to authentically feel another person's pain.

Our own suffering brings us credibility to speak to other people in pain simply because we've been in their shoes. When we talk, broken people listen, because they know that we know how they feel. Jesus allows His children to be broken, but He does not leave us that way. Once we are broken, God comforts us, strengthens us, and fills our emptiness with something powerful…. a testimony of His persevering grace. Our lives become proof of God's strength, His grace, and His overcoming power! Look around, Beloved, and see the familiar hurt of others. Then, go and comfort with the same comfort that God the Father lavished on you.

Encourage someone today with the Hope you have in Christ Jesus!

January 7
CHRIST'S MIGHTY POWER

2 Corinthians 12:9 (NIV): *"But he said to me,
'My grace is sufficient for you, for my power is made perfect
in weakness.' Therefore I will boast all the more gladly
about my weaknesses, so that Christ's power may rest on me."*

We all have weaknesses … yes, all of us. In fact even our strengths, when overused or used inappropriately, can become a weakness. And it is in these weaknesses that we are vulnerable to sin allowing the devil to do his work and entrap us in his snares. But there is hope, for nothing is impossible with God! Christ says that His power is made perfect in weakness. It is when we fully acknowledge that we are completely incapable of fixing a situation or knowing a right answer apart from Christ's intervention that we make room for His mighty power to be displayed. Perhaps it is time to fire ourselves as our own higher power. Perhaps it is time to bow before the One True God, and through prayer and thanksgiving, allow Him to fill us with the Holy Spirit. Because God loves us, He will work in us and through us to accomplish great things. All we have to do is call out to Him.

Have a mighty day!

January 8

CLOTHED IN
THE VIRTUES OF GOD

Colossians 3:12-14 (NIV): *"Therefore, as God's chosen people,
holy and dearly loved, clothe yourselves with compassion, kindness,
humility, gentleness and patience. Bear with each other and
forgive whatever grievances you may have against one another.
Forgive as the Lord forgave you. And over all these virtues,
put on love, which binds them all together in perfect unity."*

Paul's instructions to the Colossians should be the theme for humanity. Imagine if humanity would clothe themselves with compassion, what a different world this would be! As children of God, however, we are being told to clothe ourselves with certain virtues, attitudes, and behaviors that are pleasing to the Lord:

- Compassion – genuine empathy and sympathy for the suffering of others.
- Kindness – goodness and charitable behavior; mild disposition; pleasantness.
- Humility – the quality of being modest and respectful.
- Gentleness – tenderness and concern for others.
- Patience – the state of endurance under difficult circumstances, which can mean persevering in the face of delay or provocation without acting on annoyance/anger in a negative way.
- Forgiveness – to grant free pardon and to give up all claim on account of an offense or debt.

We have been asked to pursue God's Kingdom with virtue, and "He who pursues righteousness and love finds life, prosperity and honor." (Proverbs 21:21).

Strive for unity today!

January 9
CONTENTMENT

Philippians 4:11-13 (NIV): *"... I have learned to be content*
whatever the circumstances. I know what it is to be in need,
and I know what it is to have plenty. I have learned
the secret of being content in any and every situation, whether
well fed or hungry, whether living in plenty or in want.
I can do everything through him who gives me strength."

Contentment . . . a feeling of deep comfort that comes from within, a feeling that is not affected or dependent upon external circumstances. This state of being happens when we are in Christ. It is not a mood; it has no cause; it just is. This true happiness provides the background color of your spiritual canvas. It permeates your soul, and it centers your life.

Jesus began His famous "Sermon on the Mount" in Matthew 5:1-12 with the beatitudes. The eight qualities He discusses are character traits of the true child of God; those who are blessed and a part of His Kingdom. The Greek word for "blessed" can be translated as happy, fortunate, and blissful. However, it is not the superficial kind of happiness that temporary pleasures offer or that is dependent upon circumstances. It is referring to a joy and inner peace that comes from abiding in Christ. It is an inner power that enables the child of God to bear up under the pressures, trials, and persecutions of life. Know that people and things will never completely satisfy. Contentment cannot be bought. Jesus Christ alone is the source of fulfillment that we all long for. He is the Living Water that never runs dry (Isaiah 58:11), and He will never fail you (Deuteronomy 31:6-8). Peace, joy, and genuine happiness are available to you today. Blessed are those who are in Christ (John 15:5).

Choose to be content today!

January 10
CREATED FOR GOD

Revelation 4:11 (NIV): *"You are worthy, our Lord and God, to receive glory and honor and power, for you created all things, and by your will they were created and have their being."*

God creating you for Himself proves your worth. He carefully designed your looks; your likes and dislikes; your strengths and weaknesses; what makes you laugh and what makes you cry. Every detail that makes you uniquely YOU came from the mind of God. There is only one like you…incomparable, rare and perfectly imperfect. God loves you deeply … so, love yourself. No matter when and where you were born, no matter what the circumstances were around your birth, you are not an accident, nor are you a surprise to God. Your life is intentional. You were created on purpose and for a purpose and were meant to exist with Him throughout all eternity. Do not settle for man's opinions. You are precious in God's eyes. Live your life for God, and you will discover true joy in living.

SMILE . . . and know that you are God's today!

January 11
DELIVERED FROM TROUBLES

Psalm 34:19 (NIV): *"A righteous man may have many troubles, but the Lord delivers him from them all...."*

Can you imagine your world without challenges, conflicts, issues, troubles, or stress? Can you imagine a world of peace and love and joy? If you can, GOOD! You are imagining heaven. In the meantime, this world, our world, will have troubles. The real question is how do we respond when fears, challenges, and conflicts rise up against us? What do we do when we walk through the valley of the shadow of death? Do we charge forward and try to tackle these issues on our own? Do we become an army of one ready for battle with all of our earthly weapons of retaliation, avoidance, and aggression? Do we wither and hide in our own cave of sorrow? Or do we trust that our Mighty Lord, who rejoices over us with singing and who loves us beyond our own comprehension, will deliver us from all of them? When fear creeps in, when despair starts to take over, look to God, the Author and Finisher of our faith (Hebrews 12:2). He will strengthen us and uphold us in His righteous right hand (Isaiah 41:10). When troubles come, keep your focus on God. In Him, we are victorious.

Walk confidently in Jesus Christ today!

January 12
DISPELLING DOUBT

Mark 9:23-24 (ESV): *"And Jesus said to him, 'If you can!
All things are possible for one who believes.' Immediately the father
of the child cried out and said, 'I believe; help my unbelief!'"*

Many of us are quick to profess our unwavering belief in God. But, do we? Do we truly believe? Listen closely to your speech. Doubt is a cunning foe. It can hide in the very words that we speak. Consider each of the following familiar statements: "I know God can do all things, but I don't know how I am going to pay this bill." or "God is loving, but I am so worried about this situation." Did you identify the doubt hiding in these seeming proclamations of faith? We need to start dispelling doubt. Do not give it a foothold in our hearts or in our words. Jesus said that ALL things are possible for the one who believes (Mark 9:23). Proverbs teaches that there is great power in the words we say. With our tongue we can speak life or death (Proverbs 18:21). So, let us become intentional about our words and start speaking life into our faith and over our circumstances: "I don't know how I am going to pay this bill, BUT I KNOW that God can do all things!" "I am worried about this situation, BUT I KNOW that God is loving, and His peace will comfort me." Remember, genuine faith is not based on the hope that somehow our circumstances may change BUT solely in the Almighty God that we serve!

Have a doubt-free day today!

January 13
DO OVER

Colossians 2:14 (NIV): *"having canceled the charge*
of our legal indebtedness, which stood against us
and condemned us; he has taken it away, nailing it to the cross."

Ever hear of a "do over?" It's the chance to start over again and face no penalty for the previous attempt. When my kids were small and learning to hit a baseball, if they swung and missed, they would yell, "Do over!" In other words, "I want to try again…that first swing does not count." Through the cross of Jesus Christ, we get a "do over" with God. When the blood of Jesus is applied to our sinful hearts, we get the chance to start a new life and face NO PENALTY for the previous attempt! Let that sink in. In Christ, the penalty for all of our mistakes, our unwise choices, our sinful thoughts, attitudes, and behaviors and our attempt at independence from God are all as though they never existed. Jesus gives us a brand new heart, one that has new desires, new hopes, new drive, and new dependence; one that is not fickle or easily tossed around by the winds and waves of the world, but is steadfast and purposeful. In Christ, the old has gone and the new has come (2 Corinthians 5:17). With the power of the Holy Spirit on the inside, our "do over" becomes an eternal home run!

Walk in freedom today!

January 14
ENGRAVED

Isaiah 49:16 (NIV): *"See, I have engraved you on the palms of my hands; your walls are ever before me."*

What a visual of God's love for us! Be careful not to read over this too quickly. It is worth an intentional look at each word. Soak in what our Blessed Father is saying to you and me:

See - The instruction here is to "pay attention, this is serious."

I – God, our Father…Creator of Heaven and Earth…The Author & Finisher of our faith.

Have – Past tense, it has been done.

Engraved - Permanent and painful. As we say, "written in stone".

You - You can insert your name here! God is speaking personally to you and me.

On the palms of my hands - In the softest part of both hands: the Right Hand of Blessing and the Left Hand of Judgment.

Your walls are ever before me - God knows absolutely everything about us.

There is NOTHING that can separate you from the love of God. We may move away from Him from time to time; but God is constant. He promises to never leave and never forsake you (Hebrews 13:5). Standing securely on the promises of God, you can have the confidence to face your everyday life, with its challenges and tribulations, and deal with whatever comes your way, because you know that the Lord is with you. He is guiding, protecting, and directing you always. Rest in Him. He has not forgotten you…You are loved!

Walk securely today!

January 15
FAITH

Hebrews 11:1 (NIV): *"Now faith is being sure of what we hope for and certain of what we do not see."*

There is no greater comfort in life than knowing that our faith is authored and perfected by our Lord Jesus Christ. Even though we do not see Him with our physical eyes, we know the God in Whom we believe is real and certain because we experience His power, His peace, and His joy in our spirits. There are three thoughts that come to mind in our understanding and embracing of this perfect faith: clarity, commitment, and service.

Clarity is the absolute understanding that this faith is given to us by grace and is the foundation of hope for an eternal life in Heaven with Christ and the Father. With this understanding comes our commitment to follow God's commandments: to love the Lord with all our being, to love others the way we are loved by the Lord, and to forgive as we have been forgiven. Then, the desire to serve God and others is a natural outpouring of the abundance of Christ's love in our hearts.

Faith in God is not a passive belief nor is it an uncertain journey. We walk steadfastly with assurance that each step leads us homeward. Faith is our "…hope of eternal life, which God, who does not lie, promised before the beginning of time…" (Titus 1:2).

Believe in Christ today!

January 16
FIRE YOURSELF

2 Corinthians 1:8-9 (NIV): *"We do not want you to be uninformed, brothers, about the hardships we suffered in the province of Asia. We were under great pressure, far beyond our ability to endure, so that we despaired even of life. Indeed, in our hearts we felt the sentence of death. But this happened that we might not rely on ourselves but on God, who raises the dead."*

The best advice I have heard, one that had a profound effect in changing my ways, was to "fire myself as my own higher power." It wasn't that I didn't believe in God and our Lord Jesus Christ, it was that I did not rely on Him in times of hardship and stress. I always needed to do it on my own and be in control. We are tested every day with challenging situations at home and at work. However, we are instructed to rely on God, to always give thanks even in moments of despair, and to ask for direction and protection. When feelings of stress or anxiety arise, just reach out to the Lord, the true Higher Power. Instead of being self-reliant and egotistical, let us be thankful that God is always with us and in us.

Do yourself a favor today . . . fire yourself! Submit to the authority of an Almighty God, and let Him do what He does best . . . be Sovereign over all things. Life is hard, but we have nothing to fear knowing that God is in control.

Fire yourself and rely on God today!

January 17

GOD'S PERFECT WAY

Psalm 18:30 (NIV): *"As for God, his way is perfect; the word of the Lord is flawless. He is a shield for all who take refuge in him."*

Have you ever come to a fork in the road — a crisis of decision — and struggled with which way to go? Sure, we all have. But do you realize that NEVER happens to God? He is never uncertain, never caught off guard, never left scratching His head stressed about what to do now. The Lord is flawless and His way is perfect. Although we are not perfect, God has given us His perfect Word to teach us, to equip us, and to show us the way . . . His way. There is tremendous security in knowing that God is always with us, holding us in His righteous right hand, and keeping us from the devil's snares (Isaiah 41:10). This assurance gives us courage to walk steadfastly on His path. Fear of the next step is abandoned in the Light of His love. Let us look to God's perfect ways for forgiveness, guidance, and strength. Let us take refuge in our God knowing that through Him, we can do all things (Philippians 4:13).

Trust that Christ is directing your steps today!

January 18
GRACE

Ephesian 2:8-9 (NIV): *"For it is by grace you have been saved, through faith—and this not from yourselves, it is the gift of God—not by works, so that no one can boast."*

Grace: *The freely given, unmerited favor and love of God.*

It is because of God's immense love for sinners that He has given us the unmeritorious gift of salvation. The gift comes, not as a result of our works or our goodness, but as a result of His work and His goodness. By transferring faith in self to faith in Christ Jesus alone, we are saved.

God is the Creator; we are His workmanship. He is the Good Shepherd; we are the sheep. Any work that we do comes through His hands and should be done for His glory, not ours. God has prepared a plan for your life and for mine. Each of us has a ministry to attend to. Through His grace, we can fulfill the beautiful purpose God has for our lives (Psalm 138:8).

Receive His grace today!

January 19
GRACIOUS WORDS

Proverbs 16:24 (NIV): *"Gracious words are a honeycomb, sweet to the soul and healing to the bones."*

Remember the chant on the schoolyard playground, "Sticks and stones may break my bones, but words will never hurt me"? Although the saying sounds good, no words were ever more wrong. The truth is that sticks and stones may bruise the body, but words can kill the soul (Proverbs 18:21). Fortunately, our words also have the power to speak life, healing, and encouragement into others. Wise King Solomon said that gracious words are sweet like honey and bring healing to a wounded spirit. There is a hurting world all around us—people who need healing; people with spirits that need resurrecting. Be gracious in your words today; love extravagantly, forgive freely, and laugh infectiously. Christ wants to love on others through the sweetness of you.

Speak life into others today!

January 20
HE IS RISEN!

Mark 16:6,19 (NIV): *"Don't be alarmed," he said. "You are looking for Jesus the Nazarene, who was crucified. He has risen! He is not here. See the place where they laid him. After the Lord Jesus had spoken to them, he was taken up into heaven and he sat at the right hand of God."*

For three years, Jesus ministered to people. He loved them and healed them. He told them about the Kingdom of God. Even still, those closest to Him did not completely understand the significance of His words. The final week of Christ's life started with cheers of "Hosanna!" from the crowd but ended with cries of "Crucify Him!" And on that faithful Friday, our Lord Jesus Christ laid down His life for you and for me. The earth shook; the veil tore; the devil danced with glee. Oh, but Sunday was coming!

Easter Sunday, the day of the resurrection of Jesus Christ, is the validation of our faith and the hope for salvation. There is no greater hope in our lives than knowing that Christ resurrected on the third day, fulfilling the prophesies from the Old Testament. And what's more, because He lives, we can live also. Jesus died to pay the penalty for our sins. He exchanged His life for ours. For those of us who believe in Him, we get credit for His righteousness and He takes responsibility for our sins. Because of Christ, we will never die but will have eternal salvation (John 3:16; 11:25-26).

Christ promised that He would rise, and He did! Christ has promised that He will come again so that we can be with Him forevermore, and He will (John 14:3)! In the meantime, The Apostle Peter encourages us with these words: "Though you have not seen him, you love him; and even though you do not see him now, you believe in him and are filled with an inexpressible and glorious joy, for you are receiving the goal of your faith, the salvation of your souls" (1 Peter 1:8-9).

Celebrate today . . . FOR HE IS RISEN!

January 21
HE KNOWS

1 Peter 3:12 (NIV): *"For the eyes of the Lord are on the righteous and His ears are attentive to their prayer, but the face of the Lord is against those who do evil."*

God knows what is in our hearts. He knows everything we do and think, even before we do it. That statement is worth repeating: God knows everything we do and think, even before we do it! We are commanded, throughout the Word, to be righteous and to do good for His Glory and for His namesake. God's children are to think and act in an upright and moral way. We are to be holy. As the Lord is good to those of us whose hope is in Him, likewise we are to be good to others. We are to be witnesses of the Word; we are to love our neighbor; we are to give back to our community; and we are to be Christian role models to those around us. Let's pray to our Lord, whose ears are attentive to our asking, for wisdom and guidance to help us make right decisions and to fill our hearts with His goodness so that we can pour Christ into the lives of others. We can only accomplish this when we seek Him, and our eyes are focused on Him.

Walk worthy today!

January 22

HIS CATHEDRAL

Psalm 32:8 (NIV): *"I will instruct you and teach you in the way you should go; I will counsel you and watch over you."*

Like any good parent, God is careful to teach and instruct His children. He does not save us, then leave us with the question: "Now what?" We can think about our lives as though we are building a Cathedral for God, one block at a time. Through His Word, God has revealed the blueprint that we must follow, and He will guide us and watch over us while we follow His instructions. The Holy Spirit is the Foreman of this effort, and although we have the blueprint to follow, only God knows what the final product will look like (Jeremiah 29:11). The future is His, and everything belongs to Him. Our job, then, is to live each day with a teachable and obedient heart, to study His Word, and to extend His love, peace, and joy to others. With God's counsel, little by little and day by day, we will become a Cathedral of righteousness for His Glory.

Allow Christ to take the lead today!

January 23
HIS WAYS

Isaiah 55:8-9 (NIV): *"For my thoughts are not your thoughts, neither are your ways my ways," declares the Lord. "As the heavens are higher than the earth, so are my ways higher than your ways and my thoughts than your thoughts."*

As intelligent beings, we often pride ourselves in being able to figure stuff out. We love to take on challenges and find workable solutions (that is why puzzles and mazes are so appealing to us). Conversely, it makes us very uncomfortable when we cannot logically resolve a problem or figure our way out of a situation. This is the point of crisis when we are reminded that we need a God. When all we can say is "WHY?" . . . He knows all. Through faith in Him, we can learn to stop trying to understand His ways or question His timing. Instead, we should embrace His love and take complete refuge in Him, for God is good. Frankly, this is not easy. It bruises our intellectual egos, but this kind of faith is possible if we are connected spiritually. The closer my relationship with God, the more I trust His heart and His handiwork in my life.

What is truly amazing is that when we abide in Him (John 15:5), His song is clearer; our fears dissipate; and we are able to have peace in the middle of our troubling circumstances (Philippians 4:7). Beloved, we are not gods, and we cannot know and understand all. God, however, is not human, and NOTHING is impossible for Him (Luke 1:37).

Trust His Ways today!

January 24
HOT DAYS

1 Peter 1:7 (ESV): *"...so that the tested genuineness of your faith—more precious than gold that perishes though it is tested by fire—may be found to result in praise and glory and honor at the revelation of Jesus Christ."*

Fire. What a powerful force. It can warm, purify, and purge. It can also burn, melt, and destroy. For Shadrach, Meshach, and Abednego, it was meant to be an executioner (Daniel 3). The three young men refused to compromise their belief in Jehovah God even under the most intense peer pressure. The result? A death sentence. Because the men would not bow to his man-made idol, King Nebuchadnezzar ordered that they be thrown into a fiery furnace...literally! What the king meant for harm, though, God meant for good. The biblical account goes on to explain how Christ was on the scene and walked with Shadrach, Meshach, and Abednego through their fiery trial. In the end, the men were taken out of the fire unharmed, glorifying God.

Much like Shadrach, Meshach, and Abednego, we go through hard times. There are days when it seems like everything and everyone is against us, and we just want to get out of the heat! When the fire you are in feels as though it will be your end, remember God can use it to purify you, to purge you, and to mold you (Romans 8:28-29). In the middle of your trial, God is there. Trust what He is doing in the fire, and may the test that you are facing today result in the praise and glory and honor of Jesus Christ.

Trust God in the heat of your day!

January 25

HUMILITY, WISDOM & INNOCENCE

Matthew 10:16 (NIV): *"I am sending you out like sheep among wolves. Therefore be as shrewd as snakes and as innocent as doves."*

At first glance, Jesus seems to contradict Himself in this instruction to His disciples. However, just the opposite is true. In this command, Christ gave the disciples a battle strategy for successfully combating the enemy while sharing the Gospel. He gives you and I the same battle plan today. We, like sheep, need to have a spirit of humility and meekness coupled with a servant's heart that is willing to consider others before self (Philippians 2:1-3). We will never win the lost to Christ with a proud and haughty attitude. At the same time, however, we are ever watchful for the snares and pitfalls of the enemy. Keenly aware that the devil lurks around, we should be wise like the serpent whose senses are sharp and reflexes are quick. When temptations beset us, we allow the Holy Spirit to guide us quickly to the way of escape (1 Corinthians 10:13). Yet, in all we do, we should be as innocent as doves, not giving anyone a reason to accuse us of injustice or immorality. Christ calls us to risk all for the sake of His Gospel…like sheep among wolves. But, He gives us a battle strategy of using snake-like wisdom and dove-like innocence in order to be victorious in our mission. Remember, this is a good fight of faith, and we are more than conquerors through Christ Jesus!

Be confident in the Lord and in the power of His might today!

January 26
JARS OF CLAY

2 Corinthians 4:7-11 (NIV): *"We have this treasure in jars of clay to show that this all-surpassing power is from God and not from us. We are hard pressed on every side, but not crushed; perplexed, but not in despair; persecuted, but not abandoned, struck down but not destroyed. We always carry around in our body the death of Jesus, so that the life of Jesus may also be revealed in our body. For we who are alive are always being given over to death for Jesus' sake, so that His life may be revealed in our mortal body."*

"Jars of clay" is a perfect analogy. At the time Paul wrote this passage, clay pottery, dishes, and cookware were common. Jars of clay were also very brittle. Our minds and bodies are a lot like jars of clay. We are frail. We break. We crack and fall to pieces. Clay pots do not hold up very well under the pressures of extramarital affairs, depression, sickness, addiction, or bankruptcy. When the children of God manage to keep our lives intact when they should be scattered across the floor in millions of tiny pieces, we, and others around us, realize that something supernatural is holding us together. What is it? It is the indwelling power of the Holy Spirit. Christ is a life-giving Spirit, and He uses these bodies of flesh to glorify Himself (1 Corinthians 15:45).

Fear not, Beloved! We may be hard pressed on every side, persecuted, or struck down, but we will never be defeated! In Christ, we are victorious over sin, sickness, and even death (1 Corinthians 15:57).

Be confident in Christ's strength today!

January 27
KEEP MOVING FORWARD

James 1:2-3 (NIV): *"Consider it pure joy, my brothers, whenever you face trials of many kinds, because you know that the testing of your faith develops perseverance."*

When your mental, physical, and spiritual strength has been tested to its maximum, and everything inside of you is screaming, "Just sit down!" . . . perseverance is that inner drive that says, "Just keep moving forward." It is the ability to put one foot in front of the other, to keep looking ahead and not look back. It is running beyond your first wind into your second to finish the race — regardless of the odds against you!

Our life's race is not a leisurely jog. It is a grueling marathon. On this course we will face hurdles of decisions and obstacles of temptations. Our faith will be tested to its limits. Just as our muscles are strengthened under weight and strain, our faith muscles grow stronger with testing as well. Spiritual perseverance of faith empowers us to face the trials and challenges of life, knowing that God's right hand is there to protect us (Isaiah 41:10). We are never on this track alone. Christ is in us (Colossians 3:3); His Holy Spirit fuels us (Acts 1:8); God is overseeing us (Philippians 1:6); and there is a great crowd cheering us on to the finish line (Hebrews 12:1-3). Therefore, let us persevere through the trials of today and remain ever aware that each step forward is one step closer to our heavenly goal.

Keep moving forward today!

January 28
LIVE WORRY FREE

Luke 12:22,25-26 (NIV): *"Then Jesus said to his disciples: "Therefore I tell you, do not worry about your life, what you will eat; or about your body, what you will wear. Who of you by worrying can add a single hour to his life? Since you cannot do this very little thing, why do you worry about the rest?"*

Christ is so intimate with each one of us. He knows us so well. This is why He took time to specifically address a condition that plagues us all…worry. We are all struggling with questions that need answers, decisions that need to be made, and issues that need resolutions. Some of these unknown things are quite serious, and the idea of making a wrong choice fills us with fear. This is life; an existence filled with challenges, troubles, and the unknown. But Jesus Christ makes the difference between living a life of peace and abundance or a life of anxiety and stress. When we start trusting Christ with EVERY aspect of our lives, worry begins to subside. When we surrender our right to know all and understand all, our minds rest. When we trust - really trust- that the Sovereign Lord is not stumped by our problems and has the answers for all our questions, we face each day with confidence. When we have faith in the One who has overcome the world and is with us and will protect us, we start living an abundant life. The Bible teaches that God blesses obedience. So, let us be obedient children and stop worrying. Let us overflow with supernatural peace that can only come from the Lord; knowing that what is unknown to us is never unknown to Him. Jesus is a Lamp for our feet and a Light for our path (Psalm 119:105). Fix your eyes on Jesus Christ and stop worrying. We may not know the way, but He does!

Cast your cares on Christ today!

January 29
LOOKING PAST APPEARANCES

1 Samuel 16:7 (ESV): *"But the Lord said to Samuel, 'Do not look on his appearance or on the height of his stature, because I have rejected him. For the Lord sees not as man sees: man looks on the outward appearance, but the Lord looks on the heart.'"*

We all know the saying "looks can be deceiving," but how many of us have actually been deceived by our own eyes? Here's a simple example: Imagine that you were hungry and saw a banana and an apple. You look at the banana and see the skin has some black spots on the peeling. Its appearance makes you turn up your nose. The apple, on the other hand, is shiny and red. Immediately you pick the apple to eat, because its appearance is pleasing to the eye. As soon as you bite into it, reality sets in. Even though the apple looked good on the outside, on the inside it was rotten to the core! Look back at the banana. Outside there are blemishes, but take the time to peel back the layers of discolored skin and you find beautiful, sweet fruit on the inside just waiting to be discovered!

Don't let surface appearances lead you to quick judgments. Remember, when men looked at David, they saw a dirty little shepherd boy, but God saw a King (1 Samuel 16:11). When men looked at Rahab, they saw a worthless harlot, but God saw a hero and the grandmother of His Son (Joshua 6:25). When men looked at Jesus, they saw an unattractive carpenter with "pie in the sky" dreams, but God saw the flawless Lamb and Savior (Isaiah 53:2). Man looks at the outward appearance, but God looks on the heart. May our prayer forever be that we see others through the flawless viewpoint of Jesus Christ.

Focus on truth today!

January 30

LOVE IS... ARE YOU?

1 Corinthians 13:4-7 (NIV): *"Love is patient, love is kind. It does not envy, it does not boast, it is not proud. It is not rude, it is not self-seeking, it is not easily angered, it keeps no record of wrongs. Love does not delight in evil but rejoices with the truth. It always protects, always trusts, always hopes, always perseveres."*

Just pause for a moment and contemplate each word in this the powerful Scripture. Can you imagine what the world around us could be like? SHOULD be like? Think about your life and ask yourself these questions:

- Are you always patient with your loved ones and all the people around you?
- Are you always kind, even to the server at the restaurant who mixed up your order?
- Do you envy, even a little, those who have more talent or treasure than you?
- Do you boast about a success and take the glory away from the Lord?
- Does your pride get in the way of forgiveness?
- Are you rude sometimes?
- Do you self-seek without God in the plan?
- Are you easily angered by spilled milk?
- Are you keeping track of those who have done you wrong?
- Do you delight in the failure of those you do not like?
- Do you delight in the truth of the cross and rejoice in the Spirit?
- Are you asking for God's love to protect you?
- Do you trust with all your heart that He will?
- Are you hopeful of eternal life?

Are you persevering through afflictions, troubles and challenges because you know, without a shadow of doubt that the love of God will pull you through it all? Genuine love is all of these things. Are you? Let's pray that the abundant and gracious love of God will be in us and flow out of us.

Let God's love flow through you today!

January 31
NEW CLOTHES

Isaiah 61:10-11 (NCV): *"The Lord makes me very happy. All that I am rejoices in my God. He has covered me with the clothes of salvation and wrapped me with a coat of goodness, like a bridegroom, dressed for his wedding, like a bride dressed in jewels."*

As children of God, we have the right to enter the presence of our Heavenly Father. We do not have to go through another person or request permission from an Arch Angel. We can go boldly to the throne of God (Hebrews 4:16). How can imperfection and sin approach a Holy God? Well, just like mom made you drop the muddy clothes at the door before coming into the house, God instructs us to change our clothes! He clothes us in Christ. You see, apart from Christ, God is inaccessible to us. Christ said, "I am the way, the truth, and the life. The only way to the father is through me" (John. 14:6).

In Christ, however, we are covered with His goodness, His sinlessness, and His holiness. When we accept Jesus as our personal Savior, we get new clothes! Galatians 3:27 says, "For through faith you are all sons of God in union with Christ Jesus. Baptized into union with him, you have all put on Christ as a garment." When we are robed in Christ, we can come into the presence of God without question or fear. We are accepted and welcomed by our Father.

Rejoice ... Your garments are spotless in Christ today!

[fire yourself]
FEBRUARY

February 1
NO GREATER LOVE

John 15:3 (NIV): *"Greater love has no one than this: to lay down one's life for one's friends."*

Memorial Day . . . the day America stops to remember her military sons and daughters. Some are fallen, some maimed, some changed, but all heroic. The American soldier is a national symbol of love and sacrifice; the defender who valiantly fights for a right we hold dear...FREEDOM!

Today is the Day of Salvation (2 Corinthians 6:2). It is the day for which Jesus Christ so valiantly gave His life. Our Savior...the perfect symbol of love and sacrifice. Christ is the defender of ultimate freedom ... freedom from sin, from death, and from self. He offers life, liberty, and the attainment of joy forevermore.

Let us remember and never forget the great love extended to you and to me. Let us never cheapen their sacrifices.

Celebrate freedom today!

February 2
OUR COMFORTER

Hebrews 4:16 (NIV): *"Let us then approach the throne of grace with confidence, so that we may receive mercy and find grace to help us in our time of need."*

Our Heavenly Father is merciful and compassionate. Therefore, we should come to Him in our time of need so that we may be comforted in the same way a parent would comfort a small child. It is a blessing to know that we have someone to go to; someone who will listen to our plight; and, someone who will respond. We are not alone in this world. It is comforting to know that we can approach our loving Father with confidence, trusting that He will restore our soul. He will wipe away the tears of our heart, and He will make us whole again. Life is short. It is nothing but a mist of vapor that will quickly pass, so let us live in the present. Let us be present in our lives, and let us comfort others with the heavenly love that by grace we have been given. Rejoice today! As for tomorrow, it will take care of itself.

Find comfort in Christ today!

February 3
OUR ROCK

Psalm 61:2-4 (NIV): *"From the ends of the earth I call to you, I call as my heart grows faint; lead me to the rock that is higher than I."*

Wouldn't it be great if we could live a life of complete happiness and comfort? This, however, is wishful thinking! The Bible teaches that in this cursed world we live in, we are going to experience ups and downs, times of sadness and despair, feelings of being stressed or overwhelmed, and days when we are flat out exhausted. On many days, our strength may seem frail. It is during moments like these, however, that we can experience the supernatural strength that comes from the rock of our salvation. If you feel like your heart is faint and your feet are on sinking sand, do not believe what your circumstances are trying to tell you. Instead, focus on the truth of God's Word and choose to join the psalmist in this confident declaration:

"I love you, O Lord, my strength.
The Lord is my rock and my fortress and my deliverer,
my God, my rock, in whom I take refuge,
my shield, and the horn of my salvation, my stronghold.
I call upon the Lord, who is worthy to be praised,
and I am saved from my enemies" **(Psalm 18:1-3).**

Rest in His strength today!

February 4
PRAYER OF RELEASE

Luke 23:34 (ESV): *"And Jesus said, 'Father, forgive them, for they know not what they do.' And they cast lots to divide his garments."*

The supreme example of a prayer of release happened some 2,000 years ago. Jesus, the Son of God, came to seek and to save the lost. Evil men rejected Him and nailed Him to an old rugged cross. As Christ hung on that cross, beaten, betrayed and victimized, He could have become offended and bitter. Instead, He prayed these simple words… "Father, forgive them, for they know not what they do" (Luke 23:34).

The truth is that often when people hurt us, they have no clue as to the extent of what they are doing to our spirits. They do not think about how satan will take that offense, that betrayal, that wound and use it to entrap and imprison you and me. They are unaware that satan wants to use them to steal our joy, our peace, our hope, our souls. But God knows. In His great wisdom and loving sovereignty, He tells us to release others from a debt they cannot pay and allow Him, the only Just Judge, to be our vindication (Psalm 17:2; Isaiah 54:17).

If you have been rejected, misjudged, falsely accused, even forgotten by those you have befriended, do not become bitter, angry, or vengeful. If things have not worked out as you had hoped they would, do not lose heart. Put your life in God's hands. Trust Him, love Him, serve Him, and know that God is still working in your life to bring His glorious purposes to fulfillment (Romans 8:28).

Freely forgive today!

February 5
THE POWER OF SUBMISSION

James 4:7 (ESV): *"Submit yourselves therefore to God. Resist the devil, and he will flee from you."*

The Bible says that in Christ we have been freed from the power of sin (Galatians 5:1), but the presence of sin is still around us. Satan's greatest weapon against the Believer is a lie. If he can convince you and me that he is bigger and more powerful than God, he has had a successful day. Satan does this by coming against us with temptations—thoughts, feelings, beliefs, and actions that turn us away from Christ. Sometimes the lure seems so strong, and we feel so weak. Even in these times, though, we can be victorious over our enemy. How? By utilizing the greatest weapon that we have against him…the power of submission to our God. We confess our frailty; we recognize God's authority; and we dutifully bow a knee to God expecting Him to act on our behalf. With our full attention on God, we can resist the enemy. In that moment the supernatural power of the Holy Spirit will flex His mighty muscle, and the enemy will flee. Notice, though, the power isn't in you and me trying hard to withstand satan; instead, it is in you and me intentionally yielding to God! We do not have to be afraid when temptations come our way because, "He who is in [you and me] is greater than he who is in the world!" (1 John 4:4).

Submit your life to the authority of Jesus Christ today!

February 6
PRAYER

Hebrews 5:7 (ESV): *"In the days of his flesh, Jesus offered up prayers and supplications, with loud cries and tears, to him who was able to save him from death, and he was heard because of his reverence."*

Jesus was the most radical person the Jewish community had ever met. He was a man that walked with power and authority. He could do wondrous miracles. He could command demons. The words Christ used when he spoke could calm raging waters and howling winds, heal diseases and raise the dead, and cause men's jaws to drop in awe. As the disciples walked with Jesus daily, they saw that he actually LIVED what he believed, and He practiced what he preached.

One day, the disciples approached Christ with one request… teach us to pray. They did not ask for miracle-working powers. They did not ask for authority over demons. The disciples knew that all of these things had to come from a power source. The disciples watched the life of Christ. They saw that He would get up early in the morning to pray (Mark 1:35). He would stay up late at night to pray (Luke 6:12). Jesus often withdrew Himself from "good things" to do the best thing, which was spend time with the Father (Luke 5:15-16). Day-in and day-out, the disciples found that the common denominator in all that Jesus did was He prayed to God. So they asked…"teach us to pray like you do" (Matthew 6:5-15).

James said the fervent prayer of a righteous person has great power (James 5:16). Do you want to walk with power and authority; do you want God to use you miraculously; do you want victory in your day-to-day living? Then, do what Christ did…pray!

Meditate on God's Word today!

February 7
RUN WITH ENDURANCE

Hebrews 12:1 (NIV): *"Therefore, since we are surrounded by such a great cloud of witnesses, let us throw off everything that hinders and the sin that so easily entangles, and let us run with perseverance the race marked out for us."*

The Christian race is not a leisurely jog, instead it is a grueling marathon. In a marathon at the beginning of the race everyone starts out strong, but eventually some people start to fall along the sidelines. Some may get a cramp, twist an ankle, or pop a shoelace. Others may stay in the race but decide to start walking instead of continuing to run; somewhere along the way, they lose their joy for the race. Then, there are those who run with their whole hearts. They have trained and dedicated themselves for this very moment in time. Their singular mission is to cross that finish line, whatever it takes. They push through the pain and the cramps; and when the finish line comes into sight, they give their final lap their best effort.

For three years, Jesus ministered to people. Everything He did was to teach people about the love of God. His race was long and hard and filled with obstacles, but according to Hebrews, "He held on while wicked people were doing evil things to him" (Hebrews 12:3). How did Jesus find the strength to go on? The same way that we can find the strength to go on and develop our spiritual endurance, by focusing on "the joy that God had put before Him" (Hebrews 12:2). When our life's race becomes hard, let us focus on the goal and look homeward to the joy that God has put before us. Then we can join in the song of the victorious and say, "I have fought the good fight, I have finished the race, I have kept the faith. Henceforth there is laid up for me the crown of righteousness, which the Lord, the righteous judge, will award me on that Day, and not only to me but also to all who have loved His appearing" (2 Timothy 4:7-8).

Run with endurance today!

February 8
SHINING LIKE THE SON

Isaiah 60:1-3 (ESV): *"Arise, shine, for your light has come, and the glory of the Lord has risen upon you. For behold, darkness shall cover the earth, and thick darkness the peoples; but the Lord will arise upon you, and his glory will be seen upon you. And nations shall come to your light, and kings to the brightness of your rising."*

In the midst of a dark world, God enables His children to be luminaries of His light. He says, "[They] shall come to your light…." Our call is to be so close to the Son that we reflect the love and grace of an Almighty God. As children of God, our mission is not only to tell others about Christ but to walk alongside the hurting and allow them to experience Christ through us. This requires a daily death to self (Galatians 2:20)! With the focus off of self and firmly fixed on God, our priorities become clear: Christ first, others second. Love, joy, peace, patience, kindness, goodness, faithfulness, gentleness, and self-control become the ways we interact with others (Galatians 5:22-23). When people encounter us, it should not be natural…it should be supernatural! The Holy Spirit will pursue, convict, redeem, and resurrect. Our part is wherever we are — home, work, or the grocery store — to provide a well-lit environment for Him to work.

Shine like the Son today!

February 9
SPIRIT OF LIFE AND PEACE

Romans 8:6, 14 (NIV): *"The mind of sinful man is death, but the mind controlled by the Spirit is life and peace; . . . Because those who are led by the Spirit of God are sons of God."*

Paul is telling the Romans that we are either in the Spirit, which leads to life and peace, or in sin and spiritually dead. This is a powerful statement that is not mincing words. Either you are with the Lord and have life, or you are not. There is no in-between. He goes on to declare that those who are led by the Spirit of God are sons of God. We have been chosen and have been given the light of life so that we can shine that light for others to see. Through the power of the Holy Spirit, we illuminate the darkness around us, so that those who are spiritually dead can see Christ and turn to Him. It is easy to live according to this world and go along with the crowd, like Pontius Pilate did when he turned an innocent Jesus over to a blood-thirsty mob (Matthew 27:24). It takes boldness and consistent determination to swim against the current of this world and make a statement for our faith in Christ; to stand tall and be noticed while being humble with love and peace in our hearts and with our minds controlled by the Spirit of God. We have all been given a choice … life or death (Deuteronomy 30:29). We must each make our choice. "…As for me and my house, we will serve the Lord" (Joshua 24:15).

Choose life today!

February 10
SPIRITUAL ESTEEM

Psalm 37:7 (NIV): *"Be still before the Lord and wait patiently for him; do not fret when men succeed in their ways, when they carry out their wicked schemes."*

Too often, we get so caught up in our own drive for building a "successful life" that we forget whose glory we were created for. We look around and see how others seem to be exceling in what they are doing, and we feel inadequate or even envious. We get wrapped up in the need for position, possession, and power, mistaking these things for measures of value and self-worth. This is called performance-based esteem, and it is a joy-stealing trap. Self-worth that comes from external factors will always fail, because we live in an ever-changing world. Conversely, Christ teaches that our esteem should come from our identity in Him. This is an intrinsic value that NEVER changes. Our external success should glorify our Lord and minister to others, not make us feel more or less worthy. Remember, we are not measuring ourselves against man's standards. So, let's keep our focus on the real prize! Our stay in this world is very temporary, but salvation is eternal.

Glorify God today!

February 11
SPIRITUAL MATURITY

James 1:2-3 (NIV): *"Consider it pure joy, my brothers, whenever you face trials of many kinds, because you know that the testing of your faith develops perseverance."*

It is not whether we will face trials and tribulations. It is what will we do when we face them, because they are sure to come. Knowing this we should prepare ourselves with spiritual maturity, with complete faith in Christ knowing that He will see us through these moments. It is when our faith is tested that we grow in our Lord and we mature in His love. When we accept the challenges of this world with joy, with holy serenity, and with perseverance, God will bless us. In Him we can do everything and in His strength we can overcome anything, yes, anything! Trust God, and with spiritual joy, let us grow our faith in the face of adversity. Remember that if God is with us, nothing and no one can stand against us.

Be determined today!

February 12
STRENGTH

Ephesians 3:16-17 (NIV): *"I pray that out of his glorious riches he may strengthen you with power through his Spirit in your inner being, so that Christ may dwell in your hearts through faith."*

There are many giants in our life that make us feel weak or inferior. Challenges loom, people intimidate, and it becomes easy to want to simply blend into the background of life. Christ, however, has called us to be bold witnesses for Him like lights on a hill. With this call, He has also provided supernatural power through His Holy Spirit. And it is this strength that enables us to go boldly and tell the world of the good news of salvation; to love unconditionally; and to courageously face the giants in our lands. Out of His glorious riches, we are filled with the strength of God, and we will fear no evil!

Have a courageous day!

February 13
SURELY

Matthew 28:20 (NIV): *". . . And surely I am with you always, to the very end of the age."*

The word "surely" is an adverb. It is used to emphasize the speaker's firm belief that something is true, without doubt, and certain. When Jesus spoke these words of comfort to His disciples before His ascension to Heaven, He wanted them to know that they would never be alone. Although they would not see Him physically, the Spirit of God would be in them. This same Spirit that empowered the disciples to "go and tell" is the exact same Spirit that indwells Believers today. We have nothing to fear in this life, because He is always with us . . . guaranteed!

As confidently as Christ promised to be with His children to the end of the age, He has also promised to come again. Therefore, do not grow weary in well doing, Beloved, for in due time we will reap a harvest of abundance (Galatians 6:9). The Apostle John shared the revelation given to him about the beauty of heaven to encourage us to look homeward. John recorded Christ's final assurance to His children in Revelation 2:20, ". . . Surely I am coming quickly." What a blessed guarantee! With faithful hearts, let us join the cry of John and say, "Even so, come, Lord Jesus" (Revelation 2:20).

Walk surely in Christ today!

February 14
TEMPTATION

1 Corinthians 10:13 (NIV): *"No temptation has seized you except what is common to man. And God is faithful; he will not let you be tempted beyond what you can bear. But when you are tempted, he will also provide a way out so that you can stand up under it."*

Too often, we face temptations in this world and think, "Something must be wrong with me that I am being tempted like this." The truth is these types of battles are common for both the saved and unsaved. The principality over this earth roams around seeking someone to devour (1 Peter 5:8). The problem comes when we do not recognize the source of the temptation. It has been said that "the devil's greatest work has been convincing the world that he doesn't exist." We are tempted by greed, by sex, by money, by winning at all costs, by _____ (you fill in the blank). We are tempted by things that seem "okay" in this world, because society has become desensitized to moral absolutes. This quote explains it all. If the world believes that the devil does not exist, then there are no consequences for acting on our temptations, especially if the temptations faced are accepted in today's society. However, when we are in Christ and are students of His Word, the Holy Spirit helps us to discern the traps of sin; to know right from wrong; and to know what is pleasing in our Lord's eyes.

There is no doubt that we will be tempted while in this world, but we can have confidence that greater is He that is in us than he that is in the world (1 John 4:4)! Our Mighty God will counsel us (Psalms 32:8); He will hold us in His righteous right hand (Isaiah 41:10); and He will deliver us from evil (2 Thessalonians 3:3). Through Jesus Christ, we are overcomers!

Have a victorious day!

February 15
THE GREAT EXCHANGE

Ephesians 4:23-24 (ESV): *"...and to be renewed in the spirit of your minds, and to put on the new self, created after the likeness of God in true righteousness and holiness."*

The Apostle Paul is teaching believers in the Book of Ephesians and you and me today that we should think and act like Christ. He literally means that our hearts should be like that of Christ. Having a heart like Jesus, though, does not come simply from imitation; it has to come from inhabitation! We cannot "act" the part, we have to BECOME like Him.

But, good news! If you have accepted Christ as your personal Savior, then you have His heart. It is kind of like having electricity in your house. Even though you are wired for light, you are still in the dark until you flip the switch on. Turn your heart completely over to Christ; let Him fill it with His light. Throughout the year, we often exchange gifts with those we love – Mother's Day, Father's Day, birthdays, and Christmas. Today, Jesus wants to exchange gifts with you. He wants to give you HIS joy for your sorrow; HIS hope for despair; HIS comfort for pain; HIS patience for anger. He wants to give you the heart of Jesus for your heart. And, I guarantee you this, you won't find God standing in an exchange line the next morning waiting to trade you in for something better. Because, you see, you are the perfect size, the perfect color, the perfect fit.....YOU are EXACTLY what He's always wanted! God loves each one of us today, and He wants us to love one another. He wants us all to have hearts just like Jesus.

Exchange your way for God's way today!

February 16
TOTAL SURRENDER

Psalms 116:17-18 (NIV): *"I will sacrifice a thank offering to you and call on the name of the Lord. I will fulfill my vows to the Lord in the presence of all his people...."*

And my sacrifice offering to you, Lord, is . . . I surrender all.

In order for Christ's peace to permeate the soul, we must give up all self-effort and independence from God. We must wave the white flag of humility and acknowledge our need and dependency on God. To some, that may feel like an injury to one's pride. After all, mankind loves to brag on his ability to "pull himself up by his boot straps" and to "take care of self." When we surrender our all to God, however, we finally begin to experience true freedom. That means freedom from worry, fear, self-focus, and self-preservation. Through surrender, we find rest in Christ and our burden becomes light (Matthew 11:28-30). We are empowered to walk securely in consistent victory over familiar temptations and old foes (Psalms 18:33). When we give our hearts and minds to the Lord so that they are no longer ours, goodness happens unconsciously, righteousness takes control, and the Fruit of the Spirit ripens in our hearts. Do not offer God pieces of your life. Eagerly and with a thankful heart, commit every cell of your being to the Lord. Total surrender to Him is the key to victorious living!

Have a victorious day!

February 17
TRUST IN THE LORD

Proverbs 3:5-6 (NIV): *"Trust in the Lord with all your heart and lean not on your own understanding; in all your ways acknowledge him, and he will make your paths straight."*

We need to shift our spiritual knowledge from the brain to the heart in order to feel the fullness of the Word. Likewise, we have to trust in the Lord with all of our heart, and we have to acknowledge Him in all that we do. This intimate relationship with our Savior cannot happen in the mind; it is not intellectual, for we do not have the mental aptitude to understand His ways. We have to trust Him from the depth of our soul, from the innermost part of our being. We have to trust Him with all that we are. When we are in this state of connectivity, we start to understand the purpose He has for us; our eyes open to His path, to the truth, and to His teachings. When our heart is in the Lord, it all starts to make sense. When we lean on His understanding, our confidence grows. When we totally trust Him, there is a deep calm in our soul.

Lean on Christ today!

February 18
VICTORY SECURED

John 19:30 (NIV): *"When he had received the drink, Jesus said, 'It is finished.' With that, he bowed his head and gave up his spirit."*

With these three words, "It is finished," Jesus successfully fulfilled the plan of our redemption. He delivered us from sin, and He gave us the hope of salvation. Just picture Jesus on the cross as He looked down through the ages speaking directly to you and to me, "I came to fulfill the prophesies, to provide you with a blueprint of how to live a righteous life, to give you peace and love towards one another; and to give you eternal life with unrestricted access to the Father. And, now, all of this is yours!" Even more, through His death and resurrection, Christ gave us His Spirit – the Holy Spirit – to live in us. He will protect us and guide us. He will fight our battles and seal joy in our hearts. When Jesus said, "It is finished," He was securing our victory to overcome the world! This beautiful gift is available to all who believe (John 3:16).

Receive the finished work of the cross today!

February 19
WALK THE TALK

Philippians 4:9,13 (NIV): *"Whatever you have learned or received or heard from me, or seen in me—put it into practice. And the God of peace will be with you. I can do everything through Him who gives me strength."*

What a directive from Paul to the Philippians and to all of us who believe and follow Jesus Christ! In other words, "Look at my life. I am an example of someone abiding in the Spirit and one who is walking in step with Jesus. I am a witness of love and righteousness, of peace and humility, of mercy and forgiveness; embrace my teachings and put them into practice in your own life." Paul not only refers to his teachings but also to his actions and attitudes. He is offering his life as a walking example of what is pleasing to God from whom profound peace flows. Wow! So, how close are we to being able to join Paul and offer ourselves as role models to those around us? Are we recognized as followers of Jesus Christ? Are we witnesses of the Word and points of light in this world? Through Jesus Christ who gives us strength, we can have the confidence to say, "Do what I do" and the power within to "do as He did." We should devote every day to living totally surrendered to Christ, ever mindful that we are being watched.

Reflect Christ today!

February 20
CALLED FOR HIS PURPOSE

Romans 8:28 (NIV): *"And we know that in all things God works for the good of those who love him, who have been called according to his purpose."*

We have been called, chosen, predestined for a purpose…to bring glory to God! He has transformed us to become recipients of grace so that we become qualified witnesses of His grace to others. The Lord fills our hearts with love and patience, with peace and humility so that His image is accurately reflected in this world through us. It is then that we become beacons for others to follow. We thank God, knowing that all situations and circumstances will ultimately work together for our good and His glory. So let us pick up our palm branches in honor of our King. Lift His banner high. He is worthy to receive all praise. Let us fulfill our calling and glorify our LORD.

Hosanna to the King!

February 21
A HEART OF THANKSGIVING

Romans 8:38-39 (NIV): *"For I am convinced that neither death nor life, neither angels nor demons, neither the present nor the future, nor any powers, neither height nor depth, nor anything else in all creation, will be able to separate us from the love of God that is in Christ Jesus our Lord."*

Think of the powerful statement the Apostle Paul is making in this verse. He said, "I AM CONVINCED." What a safe place it is to be in Christ. When we truly believe that God is true and His Word is true, we will develop a genuine heart of thanksgiving. We will be grateful for the depth, breadth, and unconditional love of God for us through Jesus Christ, who willingly died on the cross for our sins so that we can be saved, so that we can live, love, and be loved, and so that we can uncover the true happiness within. We are so blessed.

Today and everyday, love big, love deep, forgive as we have been forgiven, and live with purpose and significance. Let us be genuinely thankful for God's immense grace and love.

Smile, you are loved by God today!

February 22
ALL IN

Matthew 22:37-38 (NIV): *"Jesus replied: `Love the Lord your God with all your heart and with all your soul and with all your mind.' This is the first and greatest commandment."*

"ALL" — This is a very encompassing word. It means "the whole", "the greatest possible amount". It means "using everything and anything". When Jesus told His disciples to love God "with all," He left no room for any part of their beings or lives to be excluded from this complete envelopment of love and service to God. The hearer who truly gets this will be transformed from a lukewarm relationship with the Lord and will cross the bridge from mediocrity to freedom in Jesus Christ, because the trappings of this world no longer come first.

When Jesus saves us, we are called to be "ALL IN" with the Lord. Nowhere in the Word does it say that it is ok to love the Lord some, or to trust Him some, or to fear Him some. We are all called to a life of righteousness, of goodness, and of complete connectivity with God. We are called to love God with all our being. Then, we are told to "Love your neighbor as yourself." Stop for a second and think about that. Unless we are completely filled with love for God and the love of God, we cannot hope to genuinely forgive others, overcome our prejudices, or put others ahead of ourselves. The Apostle James warns, "Do not merely listen to the word, and so deceive yourselves. Do what it says" (James 1:22). Listening and knowing is not enough; we must obey. But obeying the commandments of Christ will never come from our best efforts to try and do. Obedience will only be possible through the power of the Holy Spirit living this life for us. Immerse yourself in God today. Be fully surrendered to Him, and He will love this impossible kind of love … through you.

Give Christ your all today!

February 23
A THANK OFFERING

Psalm 116:17-18 (NIV): *"I will sacrifice a thank offering
to you and call on the name of the Lord. I will
fulfill my vows to the Lord in the presence of all his people...."*

What can I sacrifice to the Lord as a thank offering? Myself! In order for Christ's peace to permeate the soul, first, we must give up. We must wave the white flag of humility, and we must drop to our knees and thank the Almighty for His love. When we surrender, we live; when we surrender, we grow; when we surrender, we are victorious in holiness; when we surrender, we win! When we give our heart and mind to the Lord so that they are no longer ours, goodness happens unconsciously, righteousness takes control, and the fruit of the spirit ripens in our heart. So commit every cell in your being, eagerly and with perfect trust, to the Lord our God. He did first, through His Son!

Surrender your all to Christ today!

February 24
ASK, SEEK, KNOCK

Matthew 7:7 (NIV): *"Ask and it will be given to you; seek and you will find; knock and the door will be opened to you."*

This is one of my favorite verses in the Bible. It gives step-by-step instructions on how we, as believers, should approach the Father with our cares and needs.

ASK - God's word clearly states that if we ask, it will be given to us. Simply stated, God answers our prayers. He may not give us the answer we always want to hear or in the exact time we sometimes want, but He always looks after our best interests and answers our prayers.

SEEK - God tells us in His word that if we seek, we shall find. We must look for God in every area of our life. If we seek Him in all our thoughts and actions, He will not put more in our lives than we can handle. Seek Him by reading the Bible daily, and make prayer a major priority every day.

KNOCK - If we knock, the door will be opened for us. Through prayer, God will allow us to open the door of His resources to us. We have the power of His Holy Spirit to overcome any sin or temptation.

In reading God's word, we know the final outcome of this world … Christians win! Therefore, I want my thoughts and actions to be "Kingdom focused," not in man's way, but God's way!

God is willing to open His door to you today!

February 25
BE ACCOUNTABLE

James 5:16 (ESV): *"Therefore, confess your sins to one another and pray for one another, that you may be healed. The prayer of a righteous person has great power as it is working."*

Accountability is a word that people often shy away from. We do not like the idea of someone "watching over our shoulder" or telling us what we should or should not be doing. In the minds of many, accountability is only for the weak, the immature, or those who are prone to addiction or making chronic bad choices. Just the opposite, however, is true. Accountability is a discipline of the strong; it both builds and protects character. It is a practice of those who are living their lives with the intentional pursuits of righteousness and servitude to others. To submit to the guardianship of accountability is to follow the example of Jesus Christ, who submitted to the authority of His Father and maintained a constant connection for personal strength and guidance (John 5:19; 8:28).

We all need one another. Find a trusted friend with whom you can share your struggles and triumphs. Be the kind of person who others can look to for mentoring or safe counsel. This is the Body of Christ in action. Wise King Solomon wrote in the Book of Ecclesiastes, "If one falls down, his friends can help him up. But pity the man who falls and has not one to help him up" (4:10)! "Though one may be overpowered, two can defend themselves. A cord of three strands is not quickly broken" (4:12).

Be a supportive friend today!

February 26
BE ALERT

1 Peter 5:8-9 (NIV): *"Be self-controlled and alert.
Your enemy the devil prowls around like a roaring lion looking
for someone to devour. Resist him, standing firm
in the faith, because you know that your brothers throughout
the world are undergoing the same kind of sufferings."*

Be alert. Live in the present. Focus on what matters. The enemy is ready to exploit our weaknesses; to pounce when we are distracted; and to take us down when we lose control. The enemy sets traps to entangle us with anger, greed, and pride. He gets the upper hand when laziness, lust and envy steal our hearts away from service, love and goodwill. Satan wants to lure us away from the safety of the fold. This is why we need to surround ourselves with fellow believers who can encourage us and warn us when we seem to be going astray. Be on guard, Beloved, remain clothed in the full armor of God (Ephesians 6:10-17). Stand firm and fear not, for our Lord is mighty to save, and He has already defeated the wicked one.

Be vigilant today!

February 27
BE CAREFUL

Matthew 10:16 (NIV): *"I am sending you out like sheep among wolves. Therefore be as shrewd as snakes and as innocent as doves."*

This is one of the instructions Jesus gave to His disciples, which today still rings true. We, the believers, need to be humble with a loving heart but careful and on alert, for the devil lurks in unexpected places. As a brother in Christ once told me, the devil is not worried about those he already have, he is after those who God has. He is campaigning for our souls. This world has become so desensitized to sin that it is easy to get caught-up in disobedience and sin. Only in the Spirit can we find strength to stay the course in the direction of that which we have been called.

Let us pray and ask for wisdom, patience and perseverance to continue to do the work of the Lord, even when we are tired and unmotivated. Let us pray that Christ will be with us and protect us like the shepherd protects his sheep. Let us take a moment to meditate on the Lord's Prayer, pausing to clearly understand the significance of each word. It is the prayer Jesus taught us in his Sermon on the Mount. Be careful, dear children, but do not fear – through Christ we are victorious!

Glorify God today!

February 28

CHRIST-LIKE

Philippians 2:5 (NIV): *"Your attitude should be the same as that of Christ Jesus."*

Jesus Christ, the Son of God who had the glory with the Father before the world began, comes to this world in the flesh without sin to die on the cross for the forgiveness of our sins and to give us the hope of salvation. And we are told that our attitude should be the same as His. That is a tall order! We are instructed that our disposition, our demeanor, our feelings should be like those of Jesus. We are told to be humble, servant-like, kind, gentle, patient, loving, and forgiving, without anxiety or worries. We should be giving, honest, moral, ethical, just, and fair; and all these traits should be exemplified with a character of perseverance and honorable authority, as a teacher, a mentor, and a passionate leader. Whew! Sounds impossible. The bar is set high, so we must depend on Him. We will fall short, for we are humans, perfectly imperfect. Thankfully, the Holy Spirit dwells within the children of God. When we cannot, He can! The Holy Spirit is able to respond in Christ-likeness through you and me in any given situation and on any given day. Our part is to cooperate with His leading and guiding. How awesome to know that when God requires us to do something, He also provides the means and strength for us to carry it out.

Let others see Christ in you today!

[fire yourself]
MARCH

March 1
CLEAN HANDS

Psalm 24:3-4 (NIV): *"Who may ascend the hill of the LORD? Who may stand in his holy place? He who has clean hands and a pure heart, who does not lift up his soul to an idol or swear by what is false."*

Remember Mom's #1 rule before sitting at her dinner table? Clean hands! The same is true with our Heavenly Father. He invites us to come and dine and to partake of His goodness and mercies. He requires, though, that we have clean hands. We cannot feast on the blessings of God when our hands and hearts are dirty from anger, bitterness, or unforgiveness. God lovingly leads us to the Cross of Calvary and washes us clean from the residue of sin. We do not need to be afraid to come before God when our hands need to be washed. Like any good parent, His scrub brush is never far out of reach! With the weight of guilt and shame lifted, we can fully enjoy the blessings of God's goodness. His mercies are new every day (Lamentations 3:22-23).

Feast on the love of God today!

March 2
COVENANT KEEPER

1 Kings 8:23 (NIV): *"O Lord, God of Israel,
there is no God like you in heaven above or on earth below—
you who keep your covenant of love with
your servants who continue wholeheartedly in your way."*

Driving to a nearby city with my family recently, there was the most vibrant rainbow in the sky I had ever seen. Cars were literally stopping on the side of the mountain to take pictures of this breath-taking phenomenon. I guess in today's world where most people only hold up their end of a pledge as long as the other party is doing his or her part satisfactorily, it is a stunning spectacle to see a covenant kept regardless. For someone to actually do what he or she has committed to do regardless of another person's response borders on the supernatural. It makes me wonder ... Does the integrity of my life – the way I keep my covenants to God and others, regardless of what I'm getting in return –make people stop and take notice? May our goal for today and every day be that we are a stunning spectacle of a true covenant-keeper, like our Father, so that others may recognize His supernatural power at work in our lives.

Keep your promises today!

March 3
DEPTH OF HIS RICHES

Romans 11:33 (NIV): *"Oh, the depth of the riches of the wisdom and knowledge of God! How unsearchable his judgments, and his paths beyond tracing out!"*

This exaltation from Paul has overarching meaning as to the power of our Lord God, as he talks about the infinite depth of His riches, His wisdom, and His knowledge. The riches God gives us, undeservedly, are through His abundant blessings and mercies, the hope of salvation, the forgiveness of sins and the peace of the Gospel. All of these riches are given to all without discrimination through the grace of God. It is in His wisdom and mercy that we are saved through grace and not by our works. We cannot save ourselves through our own wisdom; He did that for us in Jesus Christ. He knows our thoughts before we think them and our words before we speak them! Therefore, His determination and plan cannot be fully understood by mere humans, though in time it shall all be revealed. In the meantime, we are charged with continuing the work of Christ. We are to always seek His wisdom and knowledge in all we do and continue on the path of salvation.

Meditate on the goodness of God today!

March 4
DO I TRUST MYSELF OF GOD?

Psalm 20:7 (NIV): *"Some trust in chariots and some in horses, but we trust in the name of the Lord our God."*

How much trust do we have in Jesus Christ our Lord? Interesting question, because so often I find myself trusting in my own cavalry (not to be confused with Calvary). In David's time, chariots and horses were the war machines, feared in battle and very effective in mowing down men. We go into the day relying on our own resources, trusting our egos, feeling self-sufficient and leaving God out of our daily battles. It is in our daily walk and in everything we do that we should trust Him...walking in the light out of the darkness; walking on the path of peace and love, knowing that through our trust in Him and through His Calvary, we are purified from all sins. So in all we do, let us trust the name of the Lord our God who shines His light on us and illuminates us with His Spirit. "But if we walk in the light, as he is in the light, we have fellowship with one another, and the blood of Jesus, his Son, purifies us from all sin." (1 John 1:7).

Trust God today!

March 5
DO NOT BE DISMAYED

Isaiah 41:10 (NIV): *"So do not fear, for I am with you; do not be dismayed, for I am your God. I will strengthen you and help you; I will uphold you with my righteous right hand."*

It is in the difficulties and challenges of this life that we build perseverance. Perseverance leads to character building, the spiritual foundation focused on the light of hope, knowing without a shadow of a doubt that we will not be desolate. Amid the difficulties of life, we find the spiritual strength afforded by our Creator. God assures us that He will not allow more to come upon us than we can take, and He promises to be with us always. Let us turn affliction into light, His light that illuminates our being, the light that clears the darkness of confusion, and the torch that illuminates His way. "For you were once darkness, but now you are light in the Lord. Live as children of light." (Ephesians 5:8-9).

Have no fear today!

March 6
DO NOT LOSE HEART

2 Corinthians 4:16-17 (NIV): *"Therefore we do not lose heart. Though outwardly we are wasting away, yet inwardly we are being renewed day by day. For our light and momentary troubles are achieving for us an eternal glory that far outweighs them all."*

It is so easy to become disheartened by circumstances. Bills come in the mail; friends move away; loved ones get sick. But be encouraged. This world is a temporary dwelling place. We are destined for a world of peace and joy and perfection. We are journeying to a land where there will be no more sorrow, no more suffering, no more separation. When darkness tries to dim your mind, turn your eyes Heavenward and look to the Light. Speak truth to yourself; then, speak truth to someone else. Chances are there are people around you who need this hope-filled reminder too. Share the joy of believing in what is not seen… yet. Allow God's will to be done on earth through you, knowing that eternal glory in heaven will far outweigh your light and momentary troubles of this world!

Allow the Holy Spirit to renew the joy of your salvation today!

March 7
EXTRAVAGANT GIVING

Luke 6:38 (NIV): *"Give, and it will be given to you.*
A good measure, pressed down, shaken together
and running over, will be poured into your lap.
For with the measure you use, it will be measured to you."

A component of spiritual balance is to give. Whether it is through monetary gifts, putting God-given talents to good use, or time spent mentoring, counseling and witnessing to those in need, we have all been called, as children of God, to do for others. God equips each of us with something to give. Are you using your time, talents, and treasures for the Glory of God? It is inspiring to know so many who are spending countless hours volunteering, giving of their time, and following the Lord's calling to serve Him selflessly. When we cooperate with God's work, we are blessed beyond words. Let us keep God present in all that we do in our daily walk. Let us follow our Father's example and be extravagant givers ... all for the Glory of God!

Give back to God by doing for others today!

March 8
FACE IN THE MIRROR

1 Corinthians 13:12 (NIV): *"Now we see but a poor reflection as in a mirror; then we shall see face to face. Now I know in part; then I shall know fully, even as I am fully known."*

In our walk with Christ, He is constantly revealing to us truths about who He is and who we are in Him. Little by little, our understanding increases as we discover the gifts and power He has given His believers. The mirror clears up ever so slightly as we embrace Christ's love; as we are blessed with His peace; and, as we walk in His footsteps. In this body of flesh, we will not be able to fully understand the depth, width, and intensity of God's love for us. Yet, by studying the Word, spending time in prayer, and moving forward in faith, we begin seeing with more and more clarity the purpose to which we have been called. This is a daily process. The Apostle Paul described it like this, "And we all, with unveiled face, beholding the glory of the Lord, are being transformed into the same image from one degree of glory to another. For this comes from the Lord who is the Spirit" (2 Corinthians 3:18). Transformation is inevitable when we are in Christ and He is in us. Watch closely as the face in the mirror begins to change. The once familiar image of "you" will slowly fade as His reflection is accurately reproduced in you day by day!

Take notice of Christ at work in your life today!

March 9
FAN INTO FLAME GOD'S GIFT

2 Timothy 1:6-7 (NIV): *"For this reason I remind you to fan into flame the gift of God, which is in you through the laying on of my hands. For God did not give us a spirit of timidity, but a spirit of power, of love and of self-discipline."*

We are charged with fanning into flame the gift of God, the Spirit of power we have been given, a humble spirit but not a weak one. We can do anything in God. We can overcome obstacles and valleys, through self-discipline and the power of God who provides the strength and the know-how. When God's Spirit of power is in us, we can talk to people about the transforming power of God, about His abundant love, and they will be mesmerized. When the Spirit within witnesses the Word without timidity and from a position of self-assurance and conviction, people will stop and listen. Today, people are searching for a purpose. People are looking, but most do not know exactly what it is they are searching for. Companies call it institutional logic, social responsibility, civic engagement, or community awareness. People, young and old alike, are getting engaged in helping others, and non-profits are being created everywhere, all in search of personal significance. But, it is time for the children of God to fan into flame the Spirit of God. It is time to educate and to witness that significance in this world comes when this work is done for His glory, not ours.

Light a fire for Christ today!

March 10
FOOTPRINTS

Matthew 28:19 (NIV): *"Therefore go and make disciples of all nations, baptizing them in the name of the Father and of the Son and of the Holy Spirit."*

No one has left a larger footprint in this world than our Lord, Jesus Christ. After His death and resurrection, Jesus commanded His disciples to teach and baptize all nations; and today we live because of Him. He gave life to everyone in this world indiscriminately. There is no stronger act, no larger mark or footprint. It is said that we will all be judged not so much in how much money we made or what kind of car we drove, but what we did with the talents and abilities bestowed upon us. The question then becomes, "What kind of footprint are you going to leave in this world?" Stop for a few seconds and think about that question. Are you leaving a footprint on the sands of this earth, on the sands of your community, of your family, your work? Are your actions changing lives, improving this world, nurturing loved ones, helping your neighbor or the less fortunate? What will your tombstone say? What will the ones you left behind say about you? These are lots of questions, but the answer for each of them lies within our own soul. We may not have control over much of what happens around us, but we certainly have control over the footsteps we create in our own lives.

Walk in step with Christ today!

March 11
FOR HIS GLORY

Exodus 20:4 (NIV): *"You shall not make
for yourself an idol in the form of anything in heaven above
or on the earth beneath or in the waters below."*

This can be a touchy subject to some, especially in these times of liberal thinking and attitudes of "live and let live." Being followers of Christ, who have been saved by grace and have the hope of salvation, the warning here is about the things that we can become obsessed with that are not from the Lord, like activities in our lives that throw our spiritual connection out of balance, that sometimes throw our entire life out of balance. The key word in the scripture is "anything." This means basically any addictive behavior that is detrimental to us, detrimental to our families, our friends, and above all, our time with the Lord. This idol can be in the form of work, where your job defines who you are, gives you the greatest satisfaction, and your esteem is dependent on it. This is what's called performance-based esteem. It can take the form of any obsession, whether it is exercising, accumulation of material things, or anything that gives a person a sense of grandiosity, of superiority and feeds the ego (edging God out). The Lord wants us to prosper, to use our God-given talents to the fullest; however, we must do it for His glory and not ours. Stay focused on what matters, for we are nothing but a wisp of vapor in this world … but salvation is eternal.

Glorify God today!

March 12
GLORIOUS JOY

1 Peter 1:8(NIV): *"Though you have not seen him,*
you love him; and even though you do not see him now, you believe
in him and are filled with an inexpressible and glorious joy."

Joy is not the same as happiness. Joy is sustainable. Happiness is a fleeting feeling. Joy comes from deep within. Happiness is surface level; it comes and goes as our circumstances change. Christ does not promise that we will always be happy, but He does offer us a deep-seeded joy that the circumstances of life can never take away!

Being filled with "inexpressible and glorious joy" is the state of our being filled with the Spirit of God. This is a true contentment that comes only from loving Him. It is a feeling that is beyond this world's comprehension and that captures the essence of knowing that we are abiding in Christ. It is what makes Christians so odd to this world. People look and see our circumstances: job loss, sickness, death of a loved one; but instead of falling to pieces, we manage to keep it together and persevere. It is a supernatural power that resides in us and empowers us to stand under the pressures of a cursed world. It is undeniable proof that testifies, "Christ in me!"

Let us worship Christ and rejoice in Him, in the splendor of His holiness, for He is a good God that loves us unconditionally. It is through our faith in Christ that we can walk in consistent peace. So, regardless of the challenges this day may bring, we can still rejoice in the Lord, because this is the day He has made!

Have a joyful day!

March 13
GOD TURNS DARKNESS INTO LIGHT

Psalm 18:28-30 (NIV): *"You, O Lord, keep my lamp burning; my God turns my darkness into light. With your help I can advance against a troop; with my God I can scale a wall."*

It is really comforting when confidence and self-assurance comes from the trust we have in the Lord. We can cast our anxieties aside knowing that remaining in Him will yield abundant fruit and with His light we can overcome challenges. With Him we can scale walls, move mountains, and soar with wings like eagles. As believers, we have the hope of salvation. While in this world, our successes and victories rest with the Lord, but we must cooperate with the Holy Spirit. We must be obedient by living a righteous life, following the commands clearly given to us in the Word. We should pray often and stay connected through the Spirit in all we do and be thankful for the opportunities awarded to us; we should plan to be the best that we can be using our God-given talents in all that we do. We should witness with confidence knowing that our Lord is with us, and we should persevere against all odds, for the Lord has a plan for us. God's ways are not our ways (Isaiah 55:8), so we should rely on His understanding and not our own (Proverbs 3:5-6).

Let the Light of Christ shine through you today!

March 14

GOSPEL IN THE GARDEN

Genesis 3:15 (NASB): *"And I will put enmity between you
and the woman, and between your seed and her seed;
He shall bruise you on the head, and you shall bruise him on the heel."*

Many people mistakenly believe that the idea of a Messiah, who would save mankind from our sins, did not enter the mind of God until the New Testament. The truth is, though, that the Gospel, which means "Good News," is first revealed in the Book of Genesis. Jesus dying on the cross for you and me was not God's "Plan B," implemented because man messed up. God knew from the beginning of time that we would need Jesus. So when satan launched his attack against God's own, in one powerful statement, God gave satan a lethal warning and made mankind a loving pledge – a Redeemer is coming! Through His death, burial, and resurrection, Christ fulfilled the words of His Father (John 19:30); sealed the fate of satan (Revelation 20:10); and joined you and me with Himself for all eternity (Ephesians 2:6).

Share the Good News of our Redeemer today!

March 15
GREEN PASTURES

Psalm 23:1-3 (NIV): "The Lord is my shepherd,
I lack nothing. He makes me lie down in green pastures,
he leads me beside quiet waters, he refreshes my soul...."

"There aren't enough hours in the day!" Does that statement sound all too familiar? Life is busy. It is easy to become overbooked, overworked, and overwhelmed! For this reason, Christ makes us lie down and rest. Notice the language in the passage from Psalm 23. It is not a request or a choice. Instead, the Good Shepherd places His had gently, but firmly, on our shoulder and says, "Now sit." And, oh, isn't it nice to just sit and rest sometimes? Our loving Savior longs to refresh our weary souls. He knows that we are such "doers," but there are times when He insists that we rest in what He has already "done." Thank goodness for the Cross; thank goodness for our Shepherd; and thank goodness for the green pastures of His tender mercies.

Rest in Christ's finished work of the Cross today!

March 16
HIDE AND SEEK

Luke 19:10 (NIV): *"For the Son of Man came to seek and to save the lost."*

The Garden of Eden was a place of perfection and complete freedom. Adam and Eve lived in peace. They knew no fear, shame, guilt, or hiding. The introduction of sin, however, changed all of that. Scripture reveals that when Adam and Eve disobeyed God, mankind went into hiding from God. Genesis records that God came looking for man in the cool of the day, and He called out for His children. Adam's response? "I heard you in the Garden, and I was afraid because I was naked; so I hid" (Genesis 3:10). This is the travesty of sin. It separates us from God and sends us into hiding from His holiness. God's great love for mankind, though, refuses to allow our story to end there. Even though we may hide, He is always seeking. God loves you today. No matter what your story is…no matter what your sins are, do not hide from the One who can help and heal you. Expose yourself to God, and He will clothe you in His righteousness and love.

Run to God today!

March 17
IT IS HIS PLAN

Habakkuk 3:17-18 (NIV): *"Though the fig tree does not bud and there are no grapes on the vines, though the olive crop fails and the fields produce no food, though there are no sheep in the pen and no cattle in the stalls, yet I will rejoice in the Lord, I will be joyful in God my Savior."*

It is easy to love when we are loved; it is easy to trust when it is all good; and it is easy to have faith in God when life is smooth sailing. The true test of our faith, love and trust in God is when we are challenged and when things are not going our way. We let the river of faith in our Lord dry up when our plans fail, when our last business deal falls through, when we are wronged by someone else, when we have challenges at home, at school, at work, and when our desires are not met. Instead, we should rejoice in the Lord just because of what He has already done for us. God loved you and me so much that He gave us Jesus to bridge the gap that divided us from Him. Whether anything else ever works out the way we hope or not, we have reason to rejoice because of Christ alone. We can trust the heart of our loving God and the plans He has for our lives.

Rejoice in the Savior today!

March 18
JOYFUL WORK

Colossians 3:23-24 (NIV): *"Whatever you do, work at it with all your heart, as working for the Lord, not for men, since you know that you will receive an inheritance from the Lord as a reward. It is the Lord Christ you are serving."*

Often parents will hear the argument from their children, "My friends don't have to do that." To that comes the wise response, "But you are my child." I think this would be God's response to us, His children, in regards to the way we fulfill our work obligations. It is so easy to have the attitude, "If I had a really good job, then I would give it my all." The truth is, though, since we are His children, there is a higher standard for all we do. Our efforts are not to impress men. Our work efforts and ethics are to point to Jesus; the One who created us, skilled us, and provided the opportunity for us. When we work for His Glory, we understand that it is not about how many titles or toys we accumulate in this world, but it is about making the most of each day wherever God has established us. Our work environment is more than a paycheck, it is a field that we are assigned to harvest for Him (Luke 10:2). Therefore, let us be passionate as we labor for the Lord! When we follow the path of life knowing that our rewards are eternal, He fills us with the joy of His presence. It is our Lord Christ we are serving!

Serve the Lord with gladness today!

March 19

LIVING WATER

John 7:38 (NIV): *"Whoever believes in me, as the Scripture has said, streams of living water will flow from within him."*

Jesus not only knows what we need, He is what we need. Christ never gives us something apart from Himself. The Living Water that He promises to fill our parched souls with is Himself. Christ wants to wash us in the river of His goodness and righteousness. When we are immersed in Christ, supernatural things begin to take place in our minds and hearts: anger lessens, fears subside, bitterness is released, and the weight of a barren soul is replaced with the healing ebb and flow of the Holy Spirit. As we experience the power and presence of Christ, His love overflows from the banks of our hearts onto others. We are never left wanting when we abide in the fullness of Christ.

Immerse yourself in Christ today!

March 20

LOVE YOUR NEIGHBOR

Matthew 22:37-39 (NIV): *"Jesus replied: 'Love the Lord your God with all your heart and with all your soul and with all your mind. This is the first and greatest commandment. And the second is like it: Love your neighbor as yourself.'"*

In Luke 10, a lawyer asked Jesus what he needed to do in order to receive eternal life. Jesus asked him what the Law required. The man responded that he should love God and his neighbors. Jesus replied, "That is correct, now go live it." The lawyer, however, looking for a loophole in the mandate, asked Jesus, "...who is my neighbor?" (Luke 10:29).

Now, some may think, "That sounds just like a lawyer! Always looking for a loophole." But the truth is, we are all like the lawyer to some degree. We seek answers from God, then we try to conform His answers to suit our own comfort level. Be aware ... Christ will not be conformed to us. Instead, we must conform to Him. The trials and challenges we face each day serve a purpose. They shake us out of our self-focused comfort zones and drive us toward Christ and others. We must realize that we will not receive eternal life on our own terms, picking and choosing who we will or will not love. We will only enter eternal life united with the Body of Christ – a Body comprised of many members (1 Corinthians 12:12-13). If loving all people is a challenge for you, ask God to fill you with His love so that it may supernaturally flow out of you onto whomever God places in your path. This is the second greatest commandment.

Be filled with God's love today!

March 21
MAKE THE MOST OF YOUR LIFE

Habakkuk 3:18-19 (NIV): *"...yet I will rejoice in the Lord, I will be joyful in God my Savior. The Sovereign Lord is my strength; he makes my feet like the feet of a deer, he enables me to tread on the heights."*

In the grand scheme of eternity, life on earth is short. Knowing this, we should evaluate our lives to see if we are making the most of our time here. Do I start each day with a renewed spirit and "can do" attitude, ready to take on the opportunities or challenges that come my way? Or am I just going through the motions of living one more day? Life is not a dress rehearsal; there are no do-overs. The Bible teaches us that in this life we will have troubles, but when we trust that the Lord has a plan for us and is actively working out that plan, then we understand that these troubles are teaching moments that strengthen and shape us.

Make the most of your life! Allow the Holy Spirit to empower you and to propel you forward with purpose. Allow Him to put a skip in your walk and a smile in your soul. Be the person that others wonder and ask, "What's up with him/her?" Tread over your adversities knowing that God is your strength and EVERYTHING is under His feet.

Go "mountain climbing" with the Lord today!

March 23
MANNA

Matthew 4:4 (NIV): *"Jesus answered, 'It is written:*
Man does not live on bread alone,
but on every word that comes from the mouth of God.'"

Just as food and water are necessary for our physical sustenance, the Word of God is necessary for our spiritual life. It is the heavenly manna that nourishes our soul and provides the deep sense of comfort that leads to a holy life. The Word empowers us to live a self-controlled life with our focus on the cross and not on the things of this world. The Word encourages us with the hope of an eternity spent with Jesus Christ, our Savior. Knowledge of the Word is not enough. We must feast on God's manna through study, prayer, and meditation. Then, God's truths transfer from our heads into our hearts, and we start living in accordance to His ways. The Bread of Life fills us, and we are satisfied with His goodness.

Feast on God's Word today!

March 24

NEW DAY

Lamentations 3:22-23 (NIV): *"Because of the Lord's great love we are not consumed, for his compassions never fail. They are new every morning; great is your faithfulness."*

We have all heard the saying that yesterday is gone, tomorrow may not come, so enjoy the present. Too many people, though, get stuck in the past. We live under the weight of shame and guilt from choices we made yesterday. Maybe we are still walking in the consequences of yesterday's decisions, but our God has a way of making all things new. When we come to Him with the broken pieces of our life, the Master takes the tattered and old and divinely creates something breathtaking and new. Today is a new day. We have never lived it before. It is a clean slate, a fresh start to try something different than what we did yesterday. It is God's gift to us. His compassion towards us never fails. His love for us is relentless. His faithfulness is great. Because of God, yesterday will not consume us. To prove it, He lovingly presents to us today.

Praise God for His faithfulness to you today!

March 25
NO MORE ROLLERCOASTERS

Proverbs 16:32 (NIV): *"Better a patient man than a warrior,
a man who controls his temper than one who takes a city."*

If we are honest, there are many days when our emotions take us on a rollercoaster ride. We may get up in a decent mood, but by the end of the day, we have gone from laughing to crying, from comforting to cursing, from resting to raging. Days like this are evidence that our emotions are managing us, instead of us managing our emotions. It is as though we are swinging on an emotional pendulum. This is an uncontrolled life. God gave us our emotions so that we can fully experience life and relationships. He never intended for our emotions to enslave us, though. The Apostle James has an answer for uncontrolled emotions. He points us to God (James 1:5-8). We need to confess our inability to maintain our stability, and ask God to govern our responses to others, circumstances, and even our own thoughts. The Holy Spirit is a Wise Counselor. He will speak truth into our minds and hearts. He can help us to live by faith instead of feeling. And we can experience the fullness of emotion in soundness of mind instead of being taken on a wild ride!

Trust your feelings to God today!

March 26
NOT AGAIN!

Romans 7:15 (ESV): *"For I do not understand my own actions. For I do not do what I want, but I do the very thing I hate."*

Years ago, there was a pop-culture song that touted the expression "Whoops, I did it again!" Most of us can relate to this notion. We have good intentions, but somehow we lack the ability to follow through. It's not a matter of "want to;" it is more a matter of "power to." The Apostle Paul addressed this dilemma that is woven into the DNA of all mankind in Romans 7:15. Thankfully, the Scripture does not just state the obvious problem and leave us hopeless. It goes on to provide us with a solution…Christ Jesus (Romans 7:25)! Jesus is the answer for our weaknesses, our mistakes, and our patterns of habitual sin. He is the power that we lack on our own. In fact, it is in our weaknesses that His strength is gloriously displayed (2 Corinthians 12:9). So, the next time you find yourself "doing it again," instead of turning on yourself, turn to God. He is your strength and your overcoming power.

Rely on the strength of God today!

March 27
PRACTICE PEACE

Isaiah 26:3 (NIV): *"You will keep in perfect peace him whose mind is steadfast, because he trusts in you."*

PEACE, PEACE! We all want it. Most seldom experience it. Why? Because we lack self-discipline over our thought-life. The mind is the spiritual battlefield. Every argument, every lie, every feeling of anxiety, or rush of fear begins with a thought.

God gives us the recipe, however, in Philippians 4:8-9, to control our thought-life and experience true peace: "Finally, brothers, whatever is true, whatever is honorable, whatever is just, whatever is pure, whatever is lovely, whatever is commendable, if there is any excellence, if there is anything worthy of praise, think about these things. What you have learned and received and heard and seen in me — PRACTICE these things, and the God of peace will be with you." Practice a peace-filled day today!

Have a peaceful day!

March 28
REBALANCED

Matthew 14:13 (NIV): *"When Jesus heard what had happened, he withdrew by boat privately to a solitary place...."*

Have you ever ridden in a car with tires that are out of balance? You might get to where you want to go, but the trip will be anything but smooth! The same is true with our daily lives. God created mankind with a body, soul, and spirit. Too often, though, we get out of balance by neglecting one or more of these areas. What we need is to be rebalanced! Christ set the example of how to do this by withdrawing into times of solitude, where He could be alone with His Father and have His personal needs addressed. Don't you think you and I should do the same?

God gave us 24 hours in each day. He meant for some of that time to be spent on you taking care of you. How? Minister to your body by eating healthy meals and exercising regularly. Nourish your soul by spending quality time with family and friends. And, most importantly, energize your spirit by spending one-on-one time with God. Does this sound nice but impossible? Well, that's where God comes in. Ask for His help in rebalancing your life. What seems impossible to you is not too hard for God (Luke 1:37). He knows how to help us schedule our days so that everything He wants us to do can be accomplished. Be aware—this may mean that some "good stuff" we do must be surrendered for what is "best." Doing life God's way is fulfilling, productive, and balanced.

Take care of yourself today!

March 29
REJOICE!

Philippians 4:4 (NIV): *"Rejoice in the Lord always.*
I will say it again: Rejoice!"

It is appropriate that in the morning before we tackle the challenges of the day, we are reminded once again about God's command for us to rejoice in Him. To have delight and joy in Him, always; and that can be a challenge – to keep our focus on the goodness of God despite the day's circumstances. It is so easy to jump right back into the routine that leads to stress, negativity, and at times anger brought on by setbacks, problems, and issues that we face in our daily lives. We must deal with them, so let us pray to the Lord not only for wisdom, but let us also ask Him to fill our hearts with His strength and His song. We need a daily reminder; why not write the word REJOICE down where we can see it throughout the day? Why not? We do it for other things. Let us be intentional about rejoicing in the Lord, for He is awesome; salvation is ours.

Have a joyful day!

March 30
RENEWED

2 Corinthians 4:16-18 (NIV): *"Therefore we do not lose heart. Though outwardly we are wasting away, yet inwardly we are being renewed day by day."*

Problems, issues, conflicts, frustrations, troubles...we all have them; and unfortunately, sometimes we allow this negativity to suck the energy from us. It is so easy to get caught up in a state of self-pity, to lose heart, allowing temporary challenges to overwhelm us by fixing our eyes on what is seen ... our own storm. These issues can easily get magnified by our own natural behavioral tendencies, whether it is a lack of patience, low impulse control, low empathy, high independence and need to control, or just having an aggressive personality. All these behaviors, if not managed properly under stress, can get in the way of fixing our eyes on what is important; and that is to cast our anxieties on Him and to walk in His light. The Apostle Peter offers some good words of advice when dealing with troubles. He says to keep a humble attitude; to cast our cares on Christ; to remain self-controlled, because the enemy is waiting to pounce when we "lose it"; and to stand firm in our faith (1 Peter 5:6-9). When we follow this battle plan, "the God of all grace, who has called you to His eternal glory in Christ, will Himself restore, confirm, strengthen, and establish you" (1 Peter 5:10).

Let the Truth of God's Word renew your spirit today!

March 31
SOFT CLAY

Isaiah 64:8 (NIV): *"Yet, O Lord, you are our Father.
We are the clay, you are the potter; we are all the work of your hand."*

In order for the Lord our God to create a work of art out of us, we have to remain malleable and allow Him, the ultimate artist, to transform a mound of clay into something special. We are a work in progress with the Lord who smooths our jagged edges and polishes our rough surfaces. We have to maintain a warm heart and connect with Him through the Holy Spirit. After all, God is crafting the image of His son, Jesus, in us. Remain soft in His hands…humble and submissive to the Potter…for hardened clay is unusable. Let us pray for an open heart and mind; let us remain still and listen to His calling; let us allow the Lord to mold us into a beautiful vessel of honor. We are, after all, His special and unique creations.

Trust the hand of God in your life today!

[fire yourself]
APRIL

April 1

THE BEST IS YET TO COME

Romans 5:5 (NLT): *"And this hope will not lead to disappointment. For we know how dearly God loves us, because he has given us the Holy Spirit to fill our hearts with his love."*

Hope…sadly, too many people go through life without this vital perspective. The Bible encourages us with the fact that this earth, with all of its challenges, is not our home (Hebrews 13:14). As children of God, we are destined for a land of peace, joy, and perfect love. The distractions of this life that try to steal our attention and weigh heavy on our hearts do not need to become our life's focus. Instead, we should learn to turn our eyes homeward in moments of despair and focus on the joy that is set before us. That's exactly what Christ did! Hebrews 12:2 teaches us that Christ endured the cross by fixing His eyes on what lay ahead…the joy of Heaven. So, be of good cheer! Today may be less than stellar, but the best is yet to come! The momentary discomforts we experience in this life will quickly fade when we reach our heavenly home.

Be filled with the hope of glory today!

April 2
THE CREATOR

Genesis 1:1 (ESV): *"In the beginning, God created...."*

Many people may have good ideas and be known as problem solvers. Many people may work well with their hands and are able to repair, build, construct, form, or produce. But, the truth of the matter is there is only one Creator – God. All of the ideas and "creations" that mankind can offer come from thoughts or materials already in existence. God, however, gave birth to everything out of nothing. With His beautiful mind, He designed. With the power of His Word, He spoke. By the glory of His Majesty, all that exists came from God and is kept by God. How awesome to know that our Creator never wonders why or questions how. He is the author and sustainer of all things, and this Mighty Lord calls us His own. Take comfort in your Creator today. You are one of His best ideas, and He loves you.

God is keeping you today!

April 3
THE FLAWLESS WORD

Psalm 18:30 (NIV): *"As for God, his way is perfect; the word of the Lord is flawless. He is a shield for all who take refuge in him."*

To understand that there is perfection in God's word and way, we must first recognize that we are "perfectly imperfect" with numerous flaws and defects. God has given us His perfect Word to follow, to guide us, to show us the way, His way. There is tremendous reassurance knowing that if we do God's will and follow His way, He will be with us, holding us and keeping us from falling. Is the Lord delighted in your ways? Is your step firm, founded in faith, love, peace and righteousness? What would you do if you knew you would not fall doing it? Let us look to God's perfect ways for forgiveness, for guidance, and for strength. Let us take refuge in Him knowing that albeit we may stumble along the way, He will not let us fall. With this assurance, let us go out there and do some great work for His glory!

Take refuge in Christ today!

April 4

THE GOAL

Philippians 3:13-14 (NIV): *"Brothers, I do not consider myself yet to have taken hold of it. But one thing I do: Forgetting what is behind and straining toward what is ahead, I press on toward the goal to win the prize for which God has called me heavenward in Christ Jesus."*

What are you passionate about? What gives you energy when you do it, and you feel as if you could do it all day long? What are you working to obtain in this life? Paul's goal was crystal clear: eternal life in Heaven. He knew that in order to achieve that goal, he was going to have to forget past failures and regrets and charge forward with Christ Jesus. If you study the life of Paul, you will see that life was not easy for him, but his passion for Christ motivated him to press on.

Just as we set goals for our life on earth, whether these are business, educational, personal, or relational, we should also set goals in our spiritual life; such as read the Word daily, pray often, and obey God. Like Paul, we should fix our eyes on Christ and not keep looking back over our shoulders. Living passionately for Christ will motivate us to press on and keep moving forward towards the ultimate prize of Heaven. Then when this life's journey is over, we can say with confidence, "I have fought the good fight, I have finished the race, I have kept the faith. Now there is in store for me the crown of righteousness, which the Lord, the righteous Judge, will award to me on that day—and not only to me, but also to all who have longed for his appearing" (2 Timothy 4:7-8).

Press on today!

April 5
THE GREAT CALM

Mark 4:39 (ESV): *"And he awoke and rebuked the wind and said to the sea, "Peace! Be still!" And the wind ceased, and there was a great calm."*

Loud days, crazy days, "Calgon, take me away!" days… we all have them. Jesus had them. Just as the Apostle Mark recorded how Jesus quieted the stormy seas and howling winds with a sharp rebuke, we too should speak peace over our environments. Oftentimes, the peace in my environment begins with me and my reactions to my circumstances. When we choose not to explode, scream, or be shifted into "fire drill" mode, we can experience a calm in the middle of chaos. It is in this calm that the Holy Spirit renews our minds and provides clear direction. It is in this calm that we are reflections of the peace of our loving Savior who assures us that we are never alone (Deuteronomy 31:6).

Be the great calm in your environment today!

April 6
THE QUESTION

John 11:25-26 (NIV): *"Jesus said to her,*
'I am the resurrection and the life. He who believes in me
will live, even though he dies; and whoever
lives and believes in me will never die. Do you believe this?"

Do you believe this? Jesus asks this question so that if the answer is affirmative, it validates the Christian faith in you. First of all, accepting the fact that Christ resurrected and that He is life is the cornerstone of Christianity. It captures the meaning of our faith, the undeniable truth of an afterlife in God's presence. The promise of the question is the promise of eternal salvation to those who believe in Him. The next question we must answer is: Are we being obedient in our faith by following the commands clearly stated in the Word? It is in this obedience that we grow spiritually. When we love God above all, and we love others as the Lord loves us, we are acting on our faith and there is nothing greater than that. We are filled with glorious joy, because we have faith, because we know the truth, and because we are obediently sharing Christ with others through our daily walk.

Believe Christ today!

April 7
THE SPIRIT OF LIFE

Romans 8:1-2 (NIV): *"Therefore, there is now no condemnation for those who are in Christ Jesus, because through Christ Jesus the law of the Spirit of life set me free from the law of sin and death."*

Through Christ Jesus we have been set free! Before Christ, we were blind, but because of Him, now we see. We were children of the darkness, but now we are children of His Light. We were lost and alone, but now we are safe in His care. We were enslaved to sin and self, but now because of Christ Jesus, we are free to love, free to choose, free to live. The sensation of freedom through the Spirit is all encompassing; it is a feeling of deep tranquility in the soul. It opens our eyes to the awesomeness of God's handiwork, from the beauty of a flower to the majesty of the stars, and it ignites our souls with joy and contentment. This is what Jesus calls abundant life (John 10:10), and it is only a taste of what is to come. Glory to God!

Allow God's Spirit to transform you today!

April 8
THE VINE

John 15:5 (NIV): *"I am the vine; you are the branches. If a man remains in me and I in him, he will bear much fruit; apart from me you can do nothing."*

We are told that we need to be passionate about what we do in this world and to work as though we were working for the Lord (Colossians 3:23). He is the vine, the source of our energy and strength, and we are the branches, the bearers of His goodness. God the Father is the gardener, who carefully tends to this spiritual vineyard of life. He cuts off the branches that do not bear fruit and lovingly prunes those that do, so they can be more fruitful.

When we are in Christ and embrace the pruning process of the Father, the sky is the limit as to what we can accomplish for His glory. If we plan, prepare, execute and then share the success, we will bear much fruit. Let us pray that the Lord of the harvest will guide us and flow through us so that our branches are heavy with abundant fruit. Apart from Him, our branches will be bare.

Have a fruitful day!

April 9
THINK GREAT THOUGHTS

Jeremiah 29:11 (NIV): *"For I know the plans I have for you,"*
declares the LORD, "plans to prosper you and
not to harm you, plans to give you hope and a future."

Have you ever made the statement, "I am afraid to get my hopes up"? Too often, we are afraid to dream because we fear disappointment. We avoid asking God for big things in our lives, because deep on the inside we are not sure if He can or will answer our heart's desires. So we find ourselves settling for mediocre lives. What we need to understand, though, is Jehovah is a good God. He is an all-powerful God who not only enjoys displaying His majesty (Psalm 19:1), but He also delights in His children (Psalm 147:11). Likewise, God is pleased when we delight in Him (Psalm 37:4).

Look through Scripture. We see the results of people who dared to think great thoughts about what God could do in their lives. Solomon asked for wisdom, and today we still seek guidance (1 Kings 3:9-10). Elijah prayed that it would not rain, and God withheld the rain until Elijah prayed for the rains to return (1 Kings 18:41- 19:8). Moses was bold enough to ask to see God, and the Lord revealed His glory (Exodus 33:18-23). Our God is so much bigger than we allow Him to be. If you have a dream and wonder if God can or if He will, why not just ask Him? Our requests reveal the confidence that we have in a loving God (1 John 5:14).

Dream BIG today!

April 10
UP A TREE

Luke 19:5 (NIV): *"When Jesus reached the spot, he looked up and said to him, 'Zacchaeus, come down immediately. I must stay at your house today.'"*

I wonder what must have been going through the mind of Zacchaeus that faithful day. This man, who was a liar, a cheat, and despised by others because of his sinful lifestyle, had heard rumors about this Jesus. Stories about how the Christ could heal, deliver, and how He loved all must have captivated Zacchaeus's curiosity; so much so that he just had to see for himself what all the fuss was about. Could this Jesus possibly love someone like him? The Bible said that Zacchaeus was short in stature. So in order to get a good glimpse of Christ as He passed through the city, Zacchaeus climbed up in a tree … a place where he could see, but not be seen. When Jesus reached Zacchaeus's perch, He immediately called for him to come down. With compassion in His eyes and hope in His voice, Christ explained, "You are why I am here."

As clever as his hiding place seemed to be, Zacchaeus could not hide from Christ that day, and neither can we. Make no mistake, Christ sees through the veils and masks we hide behind. He knows the secret places of our hearts and minds. When everyone else judges and rejects, Jesus extends His open arms and bids you come just as you are. Today, as you read this devotion, listen to the voice of hope as He assures, "You are why I am here."

Spend time with Jesus today!

April 11

WE ARE ALIVE!

John 14:19 (NIV): *"Before long, the world will not see me anymore, but you will see me. Because I live, you also will live."*

We have been given the gift of life through Jesus Christ. We have been given the gifts of hope, peace, and love. It is in our commitment through these gifts that we can see Him; we can experience Him; and we can allow Him to do His work through us for the purpose that we have been called. God has called us to be witnesses in this world. We are to radiate the light of Christ to a dark world. When others see it, they should also see the Holy Spirit. We are God's children; we lead the way; we illuminate the path; and WE ARE ALIVE! Let us rejoice and let the world know that we live because of Him. All glory to God.

Celebrate life in Christ today!

April 12

WE HAVE BEEN CALLED

Romans 8:28 (NIV): *"And we know that in all things God works for the good of those who love him, who have been called according to his purpose."*

We have all been called, predestined, so that together, through God and for His glory, we can do the good work and be justified and glorified. We are being transformed not only to receive God's grace but also to become witnesses of His grace to others. Let us ask the Lord for guidance and wisdom, as we walk in this world carrying the torch for others to see. Let's ask that He will fill our hearts with love and patience and with peace and humility, so Christ's purpose in this world can be reflected through us, as channels for others to follow. We thank God knowing that good things will happen to His believers; He is with us holding us by our right hand, guiding us. Let us place our trust in Him, maker of heaven and earth, and believe that He works for the good of us.

Walk confidently in Christ today!

April 13

A FRIEND INDEED

Ecclesiastes 4:10, 12 (ESV): *"If one falls down, his friends can help him up. But pity the man who falls and has not one to help him up...Though one may be overpowered, two can defend themselves. A cord of three stands is not quickly broken."*

Many songs and poems have been written in honor of friendship. Did you know that the Scriptures teach us that friendship is an important and even necessary part of our lives? It's true. We were not meant to live this life in isolation, separated from others. Instead, God designed mankind with a need for relationships, an interdependency where you look out for me, and I look out for you. It is in this mindset that we are able to guard one another against the enemy of our souls. The Bible describes satan as a prowling lion seeking someone to devour (1 Peter 5:8). The person he usually attacks is the one that is trying to stand alone and be independent from others, not understanding there is strength in numbers. Try this experiment: take a twig from your yard and see how easy it is for you to snap it in half. Then find several more twigs of the same size and width, hold them together, and see how difficult it is for you to snap the bunch. A house of unity cannot be quickly overtaken, and a cord of three strands cannot easily be broken. Embrace healthy friendships. Brothers and sisters in Christ are to be faithful friends, looking out for the wellbeing of one another.

Be a true friend to someone today!

April 14
A LIFE OF LOVE

Ephesians 5:1-2 (NIV): *"Be imitators of God, therefore, as dearly loved children and live a life of love, just as Christ loved us and gave himself up for us as a fragrant offering and sacrifice to God."*

It is so easy to get caught up in living for extrinsic rewards of position, possessions and power that we forget to live wise in the Lord. We need to be careful about the external forces that pull at us every day and that try to convince us that sinning is okay sometimes. These forces try to shift our focus from the spiritual to the worldly and convince us that because most are doing it, it must be all right. Instead, we need to try to understand God's will for us, to pause and be still and listen to His whisper, listen to His direction, and embrace His love. We need to live a life of eternal significance; we need to live a life of love.

Live a Christ-focused life today!

April 15

A SINGLE OFFERING

Hebrews 10:14 (ESV): *"For by a single offering he has perfected for all time those who are being sanctified."*

The Bible teaches us that God so loved the world that He wanted to redeem sinful mankind back to Himself (John 3:16). In order to do that, there had to be a sacrificial offering of a perfect, spotless Lamb. Jesus Christ died a substitutionary death for you and me. The punishment that belonged to us for our sinfulness, He took on our behalf.

In the Old Testament times, the priests had to continuously go before God to offer sacrifices on behalf of sinful men and women. These sacrifices did not remove the sin, but simply pushed the sin problem ahead until the next offering was to be made. When Christ went to the cross, however, He completely satisfied the wrath of God against our sin once and for all. Colossians 2:14 teaches that Christ took our debt and nailed it to the cross, marking it PAID IN FULL. Now, those who come to Christ and accept this pardon are clothed in His righteousness and share in His eternal inheritance. Our new identity is seen as perfect and holy before God. While we may not always feel or behave holy, God sees the eternal truth of who we are, even as we are in the process of becoming that person. His patience with us is beautifully described in a little five- letter word called "grace." Even more, you and I once had no power over sin. But now, thanks to Jesus Christ, the power that set us free from sin is the power that keeps us free from sin.

Rejoice in the Savior who loves you today!

April 16
ALWAYS RIGHT

Deuteronomy 32:4 (NASB): *"The Rock!*
His work is perfect, For all His ways are just; A God of faithfulness
and without injustice, Righteous and upright is He."

Many people think that they are always right. But how many of us can honestly say that we are actually always right? The answer is easy: "None, not one!" (Romans 3:10). God, on the other hand, is not human. He knows no limits, and He is ALWAYS right. He does not do what is good and right some of the time or most of the time. He does what is good and right all of the time. What's more, He has no hidden agendas for what He does. The Scripture teaches that God is always working for the good of those who love Him and are called according to His purpose (Romans 8:28). He is a rock, a strong and stable foundation who we can always depend on. When you have fears, uncertainties or insecurities, take them to the Rock. He will always lead you in the good and right direction!

Rely on the Lord today!

April 17
AN HONORABLE MANAGER

Luke 16: 10 (ESV): *"One who is faithful
in a very little is also faithful in much, and one who is
dishonest in a very little is also dishonest in much."*

Managers have to be good stewards. They must be careful with the resources allotted to them; this includes time, people, materials, and money. An evil manager looks out for his own good and does not care if he has to abuse or misuse the resources entrusted to him. An honorable manager, on the other hand, is one who looks out for the good of all; who carefully considers his plans; and who wisely utilizes his resources. He is also one who makes those in his care feel safe and valued. How about you…are you an honorable manager? We have all been given responsibilities in some form or another over people or things. Are you trustworthy with the least of these? The Scriptures teach us that those of us who show that we can be faithful and honest in small things will be trusted with great things by God.

Be an honorable steward today!

April 18

BE TRANSFORMED

Romans 12:1-2 (NIV): *"Therefore, I urge you, brothers, in view of God's mercy, to offer your bodies as living sacrifices, holy and pleasing to God—this is your spiritual act of worship. Do not conform any longer to the pattern of this world, but be transformed by the renewing of your mind. Then you will be able to test and approve what God's will is—his good, pleasing and perfect will."*

To offer your bodies as living sacrifices? To be transformed by the renewing of your mind? Paul is writing about a personal transformation, about looking deep within ourselves and surrendering our life to the Lord. We are to look inside our own cup and truly embrace the love of Christ; we are to look inside our own walls, our own skin, and audit our own spiritual life. We are masters of auditing others around us, finding fault, and judging our brothers and sisters. We are masters of surrounding our lives with external stuff, some of it in the name of God, which intentionally keeps us from looking at the depth of our spiritual well being. We are masters at seeing, from across the room, a speck of dust in someone else's eye. But we shudder at the notion of looking deep within our own soul. We avoid stripping our layers to expose what is underneath the external boundaries we have so cleverly built. We need to get beyond just knowledge and transform our internal being by surrendering our life to Jesus Christ. We need to die on the cross in order to be renewed; we need to sacrifice our bodies in order to be transformed; and we need to renew our souls in order to produce fruit. Let us stop looking externally, and let us look deeply at our own life. Once we get that right, we will start understanding God's will for us.

Allow Christ to transform you today!

April 19
CALL UPON ME

Psalm 50:15 (NIV): *"And call upon me in the day of trouble; I will deliver you, and you will honor me."*

It seems that we are always reminded through the Word our need to call upon the Lord in moments of trouble, in moments of despair, and in the moments when we feel hopeless and need to be comforted. The Lord is not saying that He will just be there for us, He is promising that we will be delivered from our afflictions. It is a call to action...a statement of fact. We just have to have faith and believe!

When we experience a transformation through Christ — from sadness to gladness, or from trouble to freedom — we can then comfort others. We are then able to honor our glorious and benevolent Lord. Let us praise the Lord and thank Him for being there always, when everything is good and when troubles come. "Praise be to the God and Father of our Lord Jesus Christ, the Father of compassion and the God of all comfort, who comforts us in all our troubles, so that we can comfort those in any trouble with the comfort we ourselves have received from God" (2 Corinthians 1:3-4).

Call upon the Lord today!

April 20
COMMIT YOUR WORK

Proverbs 16:3 (ESV): *"Commit your work to the Lord, and your plans will be established."*

God is a good God. He wants to see His children succeed in life. However, mankind's definition of success oftentimes differs from God's definition. For the most part, man thinks of success as having a high profile career with a lucrative salary, a large home, fancy car, brand-name clothes, and the best toys and gadgets that money can buy. From God's perspective, though, these things can often be curses instead of blessings, because they distract us from our first love…God. The successful person in God's eyes is the one who puts God first and seeks His will in all things. The person who works hard to bless others and glorify God instead of promoting only self is the one that God takes joy in blessing. The Bible says, "Give and it shall be given to you. Good measure, pressed down, shaken together, running over, will be put into your lap" (Luke 6:38). We will never bless ourselves with more than what God can bless us with, and we will never give more away than God will return to us. So, let us be obedient children and commit all that we are and all that we have to Him. In doing so, God will delight in blessing our lives.

Commit your all to Christ today!

April 21
CONFESSION

1 John 1:9 (ESV): *"If we confess our sins, he is faithful and just to forgive us our sins and to cleanse us from all unrighteousness."*

Satan has power in the dark. The things we keep hidden and secretive gives the enemy power over our thoughts, emotions, and overall wellbeing. God, however, is Light. In the Light darkness flees. For this reason, we are encouraged to confess. Whether it is sins or insecurities, fears or failures, laziness or bitter spirits, when we bring these things to the Light by speaking them directly to God or a trusted brother or sister in Christ, the enemy loses his grip on us. Confession is our way of cooperating with the cleansing power of the Holy Spirit, who wants to free us from the stickiness of sin and negativity in our lives. Confession is nothing to be embarrassed about either, for we all have sinned and we all fall short of the glory of God (Romans 3:23). Therefore, let's be obedient children to our Father God and bring to Him our innermost thoughts and secrets, so we can walk in freedom and in Light.

Share your heart with Christ today!

April 22
ENDURANCE

Philippians 3:13-14 (NIV): *"I do not regard myself as having laid hold of it yet; but one thing I do forgetting what lies behind and reaching forward to what lies ahead, I press on toward the goal for the prize of the upward call of God in Christ Jesus."*

Endurance is the ability to stand up under pressures that would crush ordinary men and women. When we, God's children, bear up under the pains of divorce, job loss, sickness, and betrayals, others take notice that there must be something supernatural holding us together. An enduring spirit keeps placing one foot in front of the other and keeps moving forward. The strides may not be long and fast, but all that faith requires is a tiny step forward. Christ Himself gave us the example of how to endure through life's most difficult times. Hebrews 12:2 said that Jesus focused on the joy that was set before Him. This Scripture records that in Jesus' darkest, most painful hours, He looked heavenward; and so should we. The troubles we face in this world are quickly passing, as we reach forward to what lies ahead. The joys that await us will make suffering in this life seem like nothing. Press on! There is a glorious, eternal prize awaiting you.

Let the joy of the Lord be your strength today!

April 23
EVERY GOOD THING

James 1:17 (NIV): *"Every good and perfect gift is from above, coming down from the Father of the heavenly lights, who does not change like shifting shadows."*

Have you ever been deceived by shadows? Perhaps you see an object from a distance lying in the shadow. Could it be... a dollar?! Excited about your newfound riches, you move towards the object and realize upon closer inspection that it is only a crumpled leaf. The object concealed in the shadows promised something good, but delivered disappointment. These are the gifts that satan has to offer. He takes his destructive lies and camouflages them in the shadows, so at first glance they seem good, only to discover later that they bring hurt and disappointment. God, however, does not disguise His gifts or cover them with darkness. He does not make empty promises. Instead, God offers you and me love, forgiveness, grace, freedom, and eternal life. He wraps these promises in His glorious light and fulfills them to us through His Son, Jesus Christ... and He is a good and perfect gift (John 3:16)!

Accept the gift of Jesus today!

April 24
EVERY SPIRITUAL BLESSING

Ephesians 1:3 (ESV): *"Blessed be the God and Father of our Lord Jesus Christ, who has blessed us in Christ with every spiritual blessing in the heavenly places."*

When Christ died, we shared in His death (Romans 6:8). When Christ was buried, we shared in His burial (Romans 6:4). When Christ resurrected from the grave, we were resurrected with Him (Ephesians 2:6). Therefore, as Christ is the recipient of the blessings of God the Father, we too share in His blessed inheritance. Christ withholds nothing from you and me. He gave us Himself completely and He shares with us all of the divine resources that are at His disposal. Know this though; Christ will never give us anything apart from Himself. For it is in Him that we have love, grace, mercy, and eternal life. Jesus Christ encompasses all the blessings that God has to offer His children. We are saturated in the abundance of Christ.

You are blessed in Christ today!

April 25
GOD IS LIGHT

1 John 1:5-7 (NIV): *"This is the message we have heard from him and declare to you: God is light; in him there is no darkness at all. If we claim to have fellowship with him yet walk in the darkness, we lie and do not live by the truth. But if we walk in the light, as he is in the light, we have fellowship with one another, and the blood of Jesus, his Son, purifies us from all sin."*

When we decide to walk in the light and are actually doing it, not only do we know it, but we can also feel it. There is a sense of warmth that overtakes us when our fellowship with brothers and sisters in Christ starts with a faith discussion, or we are able to witness to strangers with our actions, deeds, and words. God's peace, which provides spiritual comfort, fills our soul when we practice what we have learned from Jesus' teachings. We should frequently study Christ's famous Sermon on the Mount (Matthew 5-7). It is powerful and provides the foundation of our faith and the recipe for our daily walk; basically, these are the teachings we must put into practice in order to walk in the light. God's Word teaches us that we are the light of the world, and we should let our light shine before men, that they may see our good deeds and praise our Father in heaven (Matthew 5:14-16).

Our Lord knows what is in our hearts. He knows our thoughts before we think them. He knows our actions before we do them, yet we have the free will to decide: light or darkness. There is no grey area; we either walk through the narrow gate and the road that leads to life, or we don't. A simple choice that has eternal implications!

Walk in the Light today!

April 26
GOD LIKES SPENDING TIME WITH YOU

Luke 10: 40-42 (ESV): *"But Martha was distracted with much serving. And she went up to him and said, 'Lord, do you not care that my sister has left me to serve alone? Tell her then to help me.' But the Lord answered her, 'Martha, Martha, you are anxious and troubled about many things, but one thing is necessary. Mary has chosen the good portion, which will not be taken away from her.'"*

For the most part, people are "doers." We have our checklists of the things we must get done in order to feel successful in a given day. We clean the house and feel a sense of accomplishment. We close a business deal and feel important. We read three chapters in our Bible each day and go to church on Sundays and feel spiritual. God, however, is not impressed by all of our busyness. Some of the things we complete in a day are good and even necessary. The most important thing we can do each day, though, is spend time with Him. God loves to just hang out with you. Include God in your day. Talk to Him while you are commuting in the car, sitting in your office, washing the dishes, or working out at the gym. Invite Him to permeate your thoughts and calm your spirit by meditating on His goodness often. Spending time with God does not need to be another item we check off on our "to do" lists. It should be the highlight of our day that energizes us for the challenges ahead.

Invite God to hang out with you today!

April 27
GOD-GIVEN TALENTS

Matthew 7:7 (NIV): *"Ask and it will be given to you; seek and you will find; knock and the door will be opened to you."*

Sometimes the dilemma is how hard we should try to succeed in this world and how hard we should try to reach our earthly goals. It is our duty to use our God-given talents to their maximum, as long as it is done in such a way that our success glorifies God, that we support others along the way, that we earn our success honestly, ethically and morally. It is also important that we give back to help those in need and to help spread the Word. We need to be a Christian inspiration to those around us. We need to let our light shine, as we are illuminated by the Spirit; and we need to be thankful always for the opportunities and the blessings that come from our Father. Let's ask the Father to glorify us, so that in turn, we can glorify Him.

Honor God with your talents today!

April 28
GOOD HOPE

2 Thessalonians 2:16-17 (NIV): *"May our Lord Jesus Christ himself and God our Father, who loved us and by his grace gave us eternal encouragement and good hope, encourage your hearts and strengthen you in every good deed and word."*

If we are God's children, there is never a reason for us to feel hopeless. Why? Because Jesus Christ Himself has given us good hope. The Apostle Paul wrote in Romans 15:4, "Whatever was written in former times was written for our instruction that by the endurance and encouragement of the scriptures we might have hope." The Bible was written to give you and me assurance in Christ Jesus. We are assured that suffering will not last. We are assured that our sins are forgiven. We are assured that our needs will be met. We are assured that God's purpose and plan for our lives is perfect. We are assured that Jesus Christ is coming again to gather His children to live with Him eternally. The Bible is a book of promises meant to strengthen and encourage each one of us. If you feel discouraged today, open the Bible and remind yourself of God's numerous thoughts towards you. Be filled with the love, grace, and good hope of our Savior.

Place your hope in Christ today!

April 29
GUARD YOUR MIND

Proverbs 4:23 (NIV): *"Guard your heart above all else,
for it determines the course of your life."*

The Apostle Paul teaches us that the mind is the venue for our spiritual battles (Ephesians 6:12). For this reason, it must be alert and protected. An unguarded thought life is a breeding ground for toxins, such as: fear, pride, judgmental attitude and a critical spirit, self-doubt and negative feelings about oneself, discontentment, sexual fantasy, jealousy and envy. Fear is a paralyzing enemy of our soul. The fear of failure or being seen as insignificant can cause us to think and behave wrongly. My fear of not having control may cause me to be overbearing. Likewise, a heart that is prone to pride, a judgmental attitude, or a critical spirit is more likely to speak words that suck life out of people rather than breathing life into them. Jealousy, discontentment, and negative feelings about self will keep my thoughts focused on me and what I need or what I don't have instead of focusing on God and the needs of others. Consequently, I will always be a taker or cause injury instead of a being a giver or healer. Therefore, we should guard our hearts and minds against anything that would hinder our walk with Christ or our ability to purely and positively serve others.

Guard your mind today!

April 30
GUILTLESS

Hebrews 10:10 (NIV): *"And by that will, we have been made holy through the sacrifice of the body of Jesus Christ once for all."*

If we are all honest, there are things in this life in which we have participated that make us feel ashamed. These are sins that linger in our memories and make us feel as though God is not quite happy with me. The enemy of our soul wants to keep us bound by feelings of guilt and despair, so we cannot walk in freedom and shine brightly for God. As long as we carry the weight of shame, we will feel "not good enough" to be truly loved by God, much less used by God. We need to remember, though, the FINISHED work of the Cross! Jesus went to Calvary for one reason…to pay the debt that we owe. The Apostle Paul wrote in Colossians 2:14, "…by canceling the record of debt that stood against us with its legal demands. This he set aside, nailing it to the cross." What does this mean exactly? It means for those of us who are in Christ Jesus, there is not even a record that shows we were ever in debt to God. Not only do we not need to feel guilty anymore, we ARE NOT guilty anymore. In Christ, we are guiltless.

Embrace the truth that in Christ you are guiltless today!

[fire yourself]
MAY

May 1
HOPE

Hebrews 10:23 (NIV): *"Let us hold unswervingly to the hope we profess, for he who promised is faithful."*

Stay the course, set your sight on the hope of salvation through Jesus Christ who is faithful, who died for us and resurrected to give us hope. Trust and believe with confidence that we will have an eternal life. Our faith has to be unswervingly built on rock, unmovable, solid, our soul unconquerable by the evil desires of this world. We will fear the Lord, the foundation of wisdom; we will stand in front of Him with awe and love, with trust and respect, with sovereign reverence, and with an unshakeable commitment to serve Him. He hears our cries and fulfills our desires. We just have to trust and believe!

Have a blessed day!

May 2
I BELIEVE

Matthew 19:26, 30 (NIV): *"Jesus looked at them and said, "With man this is impossible, but with God all things are possible."*

We often get caught in the rhetoric of interpreting the scripture and lose sight of the bigger picture. It is with God that ALL things are possible; it is with God that we can accomplish what we set out to do, and it is with God that we can live a righteous life. If we say that we believe, then we must accept that Jesus was born of a virgin. We must believe He performed numerous miracles including raising the dead, He was crucified, died and resurrected, and He ascended into heaven to be with the Father. If we say we believe and have faith in Jesus Christ, we should follow Him and His commandments, and we should trust His Word. It really is that simple, not easy, but simple. And the big picture is the hope of salvation!

Believe in Christ today!

May 3
IN HIS FOLD

Psalm 23:1 (NIV): *"The Lord is my shepherd, I lack nothing."*

A shepherd's job is never ending. He is responsible for the daily care of his sheep. He leads them to green pastures and clean waters. He corrals them back to himself when they start to stray. The shepherd must be sober-minded and alert, ready to guard and protect his fold from predators, which are always lurking in the shadows. The shepherd even sacrifices his own personal safety and comfort for the good of his sheep. Understanding the great commitment that a shepherd has to his sheep, how precious to know that Christ is the Good Shepherd, and we are the sheep of His fold. He pledges to take care of our daily needs (Philippians 4:19). He draws us close to His side when we wander astray. He is our protector and our vindicator; we have nothing to fear (Psalm 18:1-3). Christ suffered and died so that we could thrive and live (1 Thessalonians 5:10). Because Jesus is our Shepherd, we can go through our days with confidence knowing that He is lovingly and faithfully watching over us.

Rest peacefully…you are in the Shepherd's care today!

May 4

IN THE FIRE

Daniel 3:25 (ESV): *"...But I see four men unbound, walking in the midst of the fire, and they are not hurt; and the appearance of the fourth is like a son of the gods."*

Many of us are familiar with the Bible story of Shadrach, Meshach, and Abednego. These were three Hebrew teenagers who were taken into captivity in Babylon. King Nebuchadnezzar was the evil ruler in that land. One day the king had a large golden statue built and commanded that everyone in the land bow down and worship it. These three young men, however, were determined to worship the one true God only, and thus, were reported to the king. When the king received word that Shadrach, Meshach, and Abednego would not worship the idol, he had the men tied with strong cords and thrown into the fire.

When the king looked into the fiery pit, he was amazed to see FOUR men freely walking around. The king had Shadrach, Meshach, and Abednego pulled out of the fire. Upon close inspection, the men were unharmed and did not even smell like smoke. The only things burned were the cords that evil men tried to bind them with!

What happened to the fourth man? Well, He is still in the fire. When the enemy rages, when people try to ensnare you, or when life's circumstances try to consume you, do not be afraid. Jesus is in the heat of the blaze, and He will deliver you!

Be fearless in Christ today!

May 5
IN THE SHADOW

Psalm 17:8 (ESV): *"…hide me in the shadow of your wings…."*

Think of some place that makes you feel safe. Now, what is it about that place that gives you a feeling of safety? Is it well lit? Is it a strong building? Is it a place where other people are? Perhaps it is a place that is warm and comforting. Whatever the reasons that you can think of that make you feel safe, Christ is all of that and more! He is the lamp for our feet (Psalm 119:105). He is a strong tower (Proverbs 18:10). He is a friend that sticks closer than a brother (Proverbs 18:24). In Christ we find rest and comfort (2 Corinthians 1:3-4). What's more, He will hide us in the shadow of His wings and will guard us against any foe. In the shadow of our Lord, we can feel safe. He is a big and mighty God. There is none like Him. There is none who can defeat Him. In Christ, we are safe; we are loved; and we are victorious!

Rest in Christ today!

May 6
KING OF KINGS

Revelation 19:16 (ESV): *"On his robe and on his thigh
he has a name written, King of kings and Lord of lords."*

Jesus Christ came to this earth over 2000 years ago in humble form. He wrapped Himself in clothes of flesh and was born to a simple couple. He grew into manhood, and at the age of 30 years old began His earthly ministry. For three years He loved on and ministered to people. Then in one grand display of love, He surrendered His life on a cross, suspended between heaven and earth and paid the penalty of sin for you and me. After He died, was buried, and resurrected Himself from the grave, Jesus ascended to heaven. Before He left, He told His followers not to be upset, because He was only leaving in order to prepare the eternal home for His children. There will come a day, however, when this same Jesus will return to earth to gather His children and take us home. When He comes again, it will not be simple, it will not be quiet, and it will not go unnoticed by many like the first time. When Jesus comes the second time, He will return with a mighty shout of victory as King of Kings and Lord of Lords. The Bible says that all will bow their knees and proclaim once and for all that Jesus is LORD (Philippians 2:10)!

Jesus Christ: Born a baby; died a man; arose a Savior; returning a KING!

Honor the King of Kings today!

May 7
LIAR, LIAR

John 8:44 (ESV): *"You are of your father the devil, and your will is to do your father's desires. He was a murderer from the beginning, and does not stand in the truth, because there is no truth in him. When he lies, he speaks out of his own character, for he is a liar and the father of lies."*

The Bible teaches us that the devil is not just your run of the mill liar, but that he is the father of all lies. When he opens his mouth, he speaks his native tongue, which is lies. He cannot tell the truth, for truth is not in him. Understanding this, why is it that we are so prone to listen when the enemy speaks to us? We know that he wants to condemn us and leave us feeling unredeemed and saturated with guilt. We know that if he says something is good, it is just a smoke screen for an evil trap. Yet time and again, we find ourselves being drawn in by this toxic siren. Before we came to know Christ, the Bible says that we served satan. It seems easy to conclude then that our native tongue was lies too. Now that we are in Christ, however, we have a new heart and a new language; that language is Truth. We learn this new language the same way we learn any new language — by studying it, meditating on it, and practicing it until it becomes natural. The Word is our study guide to learning truth. Read it daily; meditate on it; then, put into practice the things that you read. As for the devil, well, he is a liar. And as the old saying goes, one day…his pants will be on fire!

Listen to the voice of Truth today!

May 8
LISTEN-FOLLOW

John 10:27 (NIV): *"My sheep listen to my voice;*
I know them, and they follow me."

Many hear the voice of Jesus but not everyone listens to it. To hear is just to perceive with your ears, but to listen is to pay attention to what you are hearing. We have to pay attention to his Word and we have to follow what we are listening to. The Lord's desire is that we listen to Him continually — not just in moments of troubles, not just on Sundays, not just in the mornings — but always. We need to pray, study the scripture, fellowship with others who listen to Jesus Christ, and put what we learn into action with a commitment to discipline and consistency. Believing is a way of life, the only way or path to eternal life. When we are in the Spirit, when we are listening, when we are in the Father's hand, we can't be taken away. We may stumble, but we won't fall, for the Lord is greater than all.

Follow Jesus today!

May 9
LIVING FOR ETERNITY

Philippians 3:7 (NIV): *"Whatever things were gain to me, those things I have counted as loss for the sake of Christ."*

What are you living for? Is it for family and friends? Is it for school or a career? Perhaps, you would say you are living for retirement; a time when you can finally be free to do whatever you want. This is a question, however, that we all must answer. Our lives are no accident. We were created on purpose and for a purpose. When we consider the short amount of time we are allotted in this temporary existence on earth compared to the vastness of an unending eternity, our priorities will change. Life is not about what we can accumulate for self. It is about what we can do to point others to Christ. Everything pales in value and worth in the light of Christ. When we make Jesus the reason we are living, then life makes sense. Without Him, there is superficial happiness, short-lived dreams, confusion and chaos. Examine yourself today. What are your motives for getting out of bed each day? Remember, today is the day to start living for eternity.

Dedicate your life to Christ today!

May 10
LIVING UNOFFENDED

Proverbs 19:11 (ESV): *"Good sense makes one slow to anger, and it is his glory to overlook an offense."*

The word offense comes from the Greek word "skandalon," which literally means a stick for bait. An offense is one way the enemy uses to entrap God's children. When we get angry and fight battles unwisely, we are the ones who typically suffer. By choosing to remain calm and not allow our emotions to manage us, though, we can outwit the devil at his own game. He wants to upset and enslave us, but we can walk in peace and freedom. Yes, there are times when our blood boils and our lips ache to attack someone who has wronged or wounded us. However, in those moments, we can trust God to be our vindicator (Psalm 9:4). His Holy Spirit will help us to walk in peace, and we can leave the offender in the hands of our Father. The Scripture says that this kind of behavior is just good sense!

Let the joy of the Lord be your strength today!

May 11

NONE LIKE GOD

Jeremiah 10:6 (ESV): *"There is none like you, O Lord;
you are great, and your name is great in might."*

Mankind likes to put things on a horizontal measurement. I compare myself to you, while you compare yourself to me or someone else. We make judgments about rights and wrongs, successes and failures, value and worthlessness on this horizontal rule of comparison. While it may be possible to compare oneself with another, when we do this it is harmful to our self-esteem and to our relationships with others. We, however, cannot even attempt to measure God by these same standards. There is no one like Yahweh, the one true living God. He cannot be compared to man, because no man can match His power, His wisdom, His majesty, or His love. When other people let you down, do not assume God will too. When other people cannot help, do not assume that God cannot help either. When others do not forgive completely or love unconditionally, do not assume God is limited to the same shortcomings as human beings. His love knows no boundaries, and His mercies are new every day. There is none like our God!

Worship the one true God today!

May 12
ONLY GOD

Exodus 20:3 (ESV): *"You shall have no other gods before me."*

When God gave the Law to Moses on tablets of stone in the Old Testament, He listed ten moral codes for the children of Israel to live by. The first rule He listed was that the people would not worship another god. Yahweh was to be revered as the one true God. Time and time again, though, the children of Israel broke this law and worshipped foreign gods. They even created idols made from wood, stone, or metals and worshiped them. None of these other gods were true; they were not even alive. In their disobedience and waywardness, the children of Israel brought much pain and suffering upon themselves. Let us be careful, though, lest we judge these people too harshly. Don't you and I still do the same thing today? Oh, we say with our lips that we serve God alone, but our hearts are far from Him. We do not make Him a priority in our days, and at night we just long for sleep. Our God is often neglected and forgotten. We live like independent orphans until we find ourselves in peril. Then, we cry out to Him and wonder how He could let such tragic things happen to "His children." Let us learn a lesson from the children of Israel and offer our allegiance to the Almighty. He alone is worthy of praise. He alone is the God who never slumbers nor sleeps (Psalm 121:4). He never grows tired or weary (Isaiah 40:28). Yahweh is the one true God. Let us give Him the honor He deserves.

Trust in the one true God today!

May 13
OUR GUARDIAN

Psalm 23:4 (ESV): *"Even though I walk through the valley of the shadow of death, I will fear no evil, for you are with me; your rod and your staff, they comfort me."*

There is nowhere that you or I can go and be away from the Presence of God. Think about that for a moment. God is with us when we are in the green pastures and beside the still waters. He is with us when we are on the mountaintops and when we are in the valleys; And God is with us during the darkest hours of our lives. Circumstances may seem bleak and fearful. The enemy may whisper haunting words to chill our spirits, but God is always with us. He is like a Guardian that goes before us and brings up the rear behind us. He encamps around His children (Psalm 34:7). We are protected by the covering of the Almighty. God tells us not be fearful and not to be dismayed, because He is our strength and our help, and He upholds us in His righteous right hand (Isaiah 41:10).

Rest easy…Christ is walking before you today!

May 14
OUR PROTECTOR

Psalm 32:7 (NIV): *"You are my hiding place; you will protect me from trouble and surround me with songs of deliverance."*

It is a natural instinct when we are down or in distress to go into our hiding place, our own cave. We retreat to that place where we can be with ourselves away from the world and away from trouble. Unfortunately, when we do this, we do it in a selfish way, for self-protection. The Lord is telling us that it is in Him where we can find protection from troubles; He is our hiding place. He is the light of the world. He is the one who will light up our darkness and our path; and He is the one who will sooth us, calm us, restore us with songs of deliverance and love, and with songs that bring peace to our soul. We don't have to go through life's troubles alone. We don't have to reach out far for help or assistance, because He is next to us. We just need to seek shelter in Him and be strengthened by our Father's abundant love.

You are safe in Christ today!

May 15
PURPOSE

Psalm 138:8 (ESV): *"The LORD will fulfill his purpose for me; your steadfast love, O LORD, endures forever. Do not forsake the work of your hands."*

Perhaps there are times when you have asked yourself the question, "Why was I born?" That is not uncommon. There is something in all of mankind that longs for a sense of purpose in life … a reason for being. The Bible teaches that everything that was made comes from God, is sustained by God, and is for God (Colossians 1:16). The Creator is so intentional about His creation that He planned out all the days of your life (Psalm 139:16). You can trust that God had a reason for making you. Even more, He will prepare you for His purpose. Be aware, though, you will not be able to fulfill His purpose for your life on your own. But when you have surrendered to God's will for your life, nothing (no man nor personal failures) can stop God's plan for you! How comforting to know that God can be trusted to finish the good work He started in you (Philippians 1:6).

Be surrendered to God's purpose for your life today!

May 16
REVIVAL

Psalm 51:12 (ESV): *"Restore to me the joy of your salvation, and uphold me with a willing spirit."*

King David wrote Psalm 51 as a prayer of repentance after he had committed a horrific moral failure in his life. He had committed adultery with Bathsheba. Then, when David found out she was pregnant, he had her husband killed to cover up his sin. In this psalm David is transparent before God and pleads to Him for revival of the Spirit in his life. Haven't we all been there? Maybe that is where you are right now. You feel as though you are in a barren desert far away from God. Your soul is parched and you ache for newness of life in your spirit. You need a revival. There are three things that we must do when we find ourselves in this place. First, we need to recognize our sin. Second, we need to repent or turn away from that sin. Third, we need to return to the Lord. He is waiting to breathe on you once again. You do not have to walk through this life feeling hopeless, weighted down, suffocating from the guilt or shame of sin. Instead, you can walk energized, hope-filled, and free from all condemnation … REVIVED!

Return to the Lord today!

May 17

SEEK HIS FACE

Psalm 27:7-8 (NIV): *"Hear my voice when I call, O Lord; be merciful to me and answer me. My heart says of you, 'Seek his face!' Your face, Lord, I will seek."*

When we seek the Lord's face, we attend His house, and in communion through Christ, we have His presence within us. His presence is in us through the light of the Spirit and we have a heart ready and willing to accept Him. When we are in the Lord, then the trappings of this world are insignificant; when we are in the Lord, the fruits of the Spirit control our mind and soul and reside within us. It is said that if you work hard when no one is watching, you will never have to worry when they are. If we are connected to Jesus Christ every day, if we are living and feeding our soul with the teachings of the Word, if we live according to His commandments and have walked through the narrow gate with the hope of salvation, then our performance in this world is for His glory, not ours. Because as the Scripture says, "The man who does the will of God lives forever" (1 John 2:17).

Seek the Lord today!

May 18
SELF-DECEPTION

Jeremiah 17:9 (ESV): *"The heart is deceitful above all things, and desperately sick; who can understand it?"*

Self-deception is often rooted in pride. The prophet Jeremiah pointed out that one of man's biggest problems is that the heart is deceitful. Mankind, at large, is blind to self and overly reliant on what we feel to be true about ourselves. We see ourselves through the lens of our own personal worldview, consisting of our experiences, our beliefs, and our expectations. The problem, too often, is that the lens we view ourselves through is distorted. Consequently, we base our thoughts, beliefs, and actions on distorted truths. Much like the distortion of a fun house mirror, the "self" we see is not always the "self" that we really are. Self-deception is the primary reason we need accountability from others. We may convince ourselves that we are right and good, but the fruit in our lives and its effects on other people will reveal the truth. Others serve as genuine mirrors for us to see our true selves.

Dare to look at yourself through the mirror of another today!

May 19
SERVE WITH GLADNESS

Psalm 100:1-2 (ESV): *"Make a joyful noise
to the Lord, all the earth! Serve the Lord with gladness!
Come into his presence with singing!"*

The Lord loves a cheerful heart. Why? Because a cheerful heart is one at rest, one that is trusting in the sovereignty of the Savior. God wants us to surrender our fears and worries to Him, and in His presence rejoice. When we can sing in times of sorrow or stress, we are serving God with gladness. When we can lift up His name in praise and adoration just because of who He is and not because of something He has done for us lately, we bring honor to the Almighty. Serving the Lord with gladness is an attitude of trust and a position of rest. When we serve Him this way, though, we find that our hearts are filled with joy unspeakable and our faith is strengthened.

Rejoice in the God of your salvation today!

May 20
SING PRAISES

Acts 16:25 (NIV): *"About midnight Paul and Silas were praying and singing hymns to God, and the other prisoners were listening to them."*

When all is right with the world, it is easy for us to whistle a happy tune. Let things begin to unravel in our lives, however, and the praises don't flow quite as easily. A "must know" fact about our God is that He loves for His children to sing praises (Read Psalms 64; 98; 147 – just to name a few!). Why? Because our songs of praise reveal the love, faith, and commitment we have in Him. When our praises go up even though circumstances are bringing us down, the heart of God is stirred into action. Paul and Silas were in the middle of a true crisis. Instead of fretting and worrying, they lifted their voices in honor to God and sung with all their hearts. God showed up, and He showed out! The shackles that bound the apostles did not stand a chance in the presence of the Almighty.

Be encouraged today—the same God that showed up for these men is just a praise away. So, when the weight of the world is on your shoulders … sing praises. When the boss is riding you hard and deadlines are coming due … sing praises. When the washing machine is overflowing and the baby is screaming … sing praises. When the traffic is bumper to bumper and you absolutely cannot be late for your appointment … sing praises. When you lift your voice in worship to the Almighty, He will show up for you!

Sing praises to the Lord today!

May 21
SPIRITUAL ROCK

Psalm 61:2-4 (NIV): *"From the ends of the earth I call to you, I call as my heart grows faint; lead me to the rock that is higher than I."*

It would be great if we could live a life of complete happiness and comfort; but we know that is not possible. We are going to have our ups and downs, moments of sadness and despair, moments of stress and disillusion, moments when we are flat out exhausted, and when our heart is overwhelmed. In these moments, we should trust the Lord, the rock of salvation, for He is our strength, our comfort and our beautiful song. When our heart is faint, lean on Christ, for He is our rock and is watching over us. 1 Corinthians 10:4 reads, "For they drank from the spiritual rock that accompanied them and that rock was Christ." Take comfort … if the Lord is with us, who can be against us?

Be strong in the Lord today!

May 22
TASTE AND SEE

Psalm 34:8 (ESV): *"Oh, taste and see that the Lord is good!
Blessed is the man who takes refuge in him!"*

"Try it; you'll like it!" Oh, how many times have we heard our loving mothers say this when we were young? In a desperate effort to expand our finicky diets of macaroni & cheese or peanut butter & jelly, they would plead with us to just give this new dish a try; a little taste test. It is in this same spirit that the Psalmists invite you and me to give Jesus a try. Just taste a little of His loving kindness; just sample the peace that passes all understanding; just brush your lips against the wellspring of living water ... try Him; you'll fall head over heels in love with Him! Not only that, but we will find that Christ is a safe refuge for us. He will guard us and keep us. We can find rest in Him. There is nothing that can snatch us from the hand of the Almighty (John 10:28-29). Our God is good, and we are blessed because of Him.

Allow Jesus to fill you with His Love today!

May 23
THE APPLE OF HIS EYE

Psalm 17:8 (ESV): *"Keep me as the apple of your eye...."*

Did you know that God smiles when He thinks of you? It's true. You are His most prized possession. God thinks about you continuously. The Bible says that His thoughts about you are as numerous as the sands on the seashore (Psalm 139:17-18). Not only that, He keeps careful watch over you. He knows how many hairs are on your head today, and He will know how many you are left with tomorrow (Luke 12:7)! There is no one like you who can fill His heart with joy, and there is no one like you who can cause His heart to ache. When you are sad, so is God. He sees every tear you cry and lovingly collects them (Psalm 56:8). God does not withhold anything good from you. There may be days when you think that God is not fair or that He is not good. This is not true. Remind yourself that the God who you serve is always looking out for your best interest. He sees the bigger picture, and He knows the end from the beginning. EVERYTHING He does, He does because of love. Trust the Lord. Take comfort in knowing that you are His child, the very apple of His eye!

Smile! You are loved today!

May 24
THE CHURCH

Hebrews 10:25 (ESV): *"...not neglecting to meet together, as is the habit of some, but encouraging one another, and all the more as you see the Day drawing near."*

The church is a family of believers who are committed to the mutual accountability of one another. Membership is a covenant to hold each other accountable to walk this life's journey in a manner that is pleasing to God and that will point others to Christ. There are some who choose not to go to church because they feel there are people there who are hypocritical. Please do not allow yourself to be lured into this trap. This is the enemy's scheme to keep you from the fortress that Christ has established for His children. The church is to be a place of worship and a place where brothers and sisters in Christ can mutually encourage one another with the truth of God's Word. The world can be a wearisome place. The enemy wants us to believe that church is not important. Christ, however, gave His life for the church. He loves each one of us, and He wants us to love one another. Do not allow sin or social discrepancies to keep you from your Father's house. And if there are some sitting on the pew next to you who are only "playing games," do not allow their behavior to discourage you. Instead, you be a positive role model for others to follow. Remember, there are young people looking to adults and seniors to teach them how to serve the Lord. Let us be that right example.

Find a church home today!

May 25
THE DEITY OF CHRIST

Colossians 2:9-10 (NIV): *"For in Christ all the fullness of the Deity lives in bodily form, and you have been given fullness in Christ, who is the head over every power and authority."*

The doctrine of the deity of Jesus Christ states the divine attributes that He, as God Himself, possesses. These attributes are omnipotence (John 14:9), omniscience (Luke 11:17), omnipresence (Matthew 18:20), immutability and eternality (Hebrews 13:8). And this Deity lived in its fullness in Jesus Christ when He walked the earth and is with Him after His resurrection and ascension.

The relevance of this information is that the same Christ who is all powerful and all knowledgeable, who is present everywhere and is eternal, is also our savior and our refuge, our teacher and our mentor, our guide and our rock, and our light and our truth. If we believe that Jesus Christ is the Son of God, then we believe in an all-powerful God who teaches humbleness, kindness, humility, and patience. He teaches love, peace and joy. He brings hope of salvation, hope of life, and He carries us through our worst moments. Jesus paid the ultimate price for our sins. We should now do our best to follow in His footsteps, to be the rays of sunshine in this world, and to proclaim His name and glorify Him with all that we do.

We have to remember that our Savior is an all-powerful, all-loving God. And when He is for us, no one and nothing can prevail against us (Romans 8:31).

Honor the Almighty today!

May 26
THE ONE JESUS LOVES

John 21:20 (ESV): *"Peter turned and saw the disciple whom Jesus loved following them, the one who had been reclining at table close to him and had said, 'Lord, who is it that is going to betray you?'"*

The Gospel of John is unique from the other three gospel accounts of the life of Christ. The author of this book wrote about the life of Jesus from the perspective that God is love. Everything we see about how Christ interacted with people, how He healed people, and how He shared truth with people revealed His heart. After reading his book, it is easy to see how this disciple was thoroughly convinced that Jesus loved him. So much so, that in his writing, the disciple simply refers to himself as "the one whom Jesus loved." Some people may take offense and think that John thought way too highly of himself. I disagree. I believe that John genuinely believed Christ. When you and I come to the place where we are convinced of Jesus' great love for us, then we too will look in the mirror and say with unbridled enthusiasm, "Now there is the one that Jesus loves!"

Jesus loves you today!

May 27

THIS LITTLE LIGHT OF MINE

Matthew 5:14-16 (ESV): *"You are the light of the world.*
A city set on a hill cannot be hidden. Nor do people
light a lamp and put it under a basket, but on a stand,
and it gives light to all in the house. In the same way,
let your light shine before others, so that they may see your
good works and give glory to your Father who is in heaven."

Imagine standing in a dark room. Then, all of a sudden, someone lights a candle. What happens? That small little flickering flame begins to illuminate the room. Before long, you can see around you, thanks to the light. This is the image that should come to mind when we think about being a light for Christ. We may see ourselves as small and insignificant, not having a lot of wealth or resources to offer others. The one thing we can do, though, is reflect Christ. In all that we say and do, we can allow the flame of the Holy Spirit to flicker in us. Before long, you will notice that the people around you are drawn to His light within you. Someone may stop by your desk to ask if they can share a personal burden with you. Someone may comment on how you always seem to "brighten the room" whenever you enter. Perhaps others will say, "There is just something about you." Whatever the response, the encounter is the same … Jesus. He is the light of the world and the light within you. Let Him shine brightly through you. No matter how small you may feel in the grand scheme of life, your little light can be a beacon for Christ.

Shine brightly for Christ today!

May 28
UNDER HIS WINGS

Psalm 91:4 (NIV): *"He will cover you with his feathers,
and under his wings you will find refuge;
his faithfulness will be your shield and rampart."*

Have you ever watched a mother hen with her brood of baby chicks? It is a wondrous sight. In times of fear or danger or when the chicks need rest, the mother hen will call to her babes and they will gather under her wings. There, the chicks are safe from weather and predators. No harm can come nigh them, because she uses her body to shield them. Likewise, God wants to cover His children with His wings. In times of stress, in times of fear, in times of loneliness, in times of weariness, we can run to our Father. We will find His arms open wide. He will lovingly gather us to Himself, and we are safe. Nothing and no one can harm us. He is our shield and fortress. God is a faithful parent who will use Himself to be a protective covering for His children. Aah … how comforting to know that we are safe and sound under His wings.

Abide in the shadow of the Almighty today!

May 29
WEAPON OF PEACE

2 Corinthians 10:4 (NIV): *"The weapons we fight with are not the weapons of the world. On the contrary, they have divine power to demolish strongholds."*

Over the history of the world, mankind has waged war against each other in the name of religion or a god, probably more so than any other reason. Today, the uprisings in Africa, in the Middle East, and in other places around the world are rooted in religious beliefs. In this country we still fight wars of prejudice, social injustice and rabid crime in certain areas. Paul is teaching us that the weapons we should fight with are the weapons of peace, love, humility and care. These are the divine powers that disarm; these are the weapons we need to bring to battle every day. Because when we armor ourselves with these powers and we have the Lord by our side, we are unconquerable; we can't be defeated. We have already surrendered to the Almighty; we already belong to his army; and we already belong to his omnipotent power.

As we face today and every day, be mindful of the gift of peace that we have been entrusted with, and let us spread it in our world; let us be the change in this world. We cannot control what others do or why they do it, we can only control what we do and how we do it; so let's put on the armor of peace, let's make a difference in this world, and let's do it for His glory.

Be a peacemaker today!

May 30
WHEN GOD SPEAKS

Genesis 1:3 (ESV): *"And God said,*
'Let there be light,' and there was light."

The word "universe" in the Greek is quite telling. "Uni" means single, and "verse" means sentence. Therefore, we live in a "single spoken sentence." The Lord God is the everlasting God. He is the Creator of all. He speaks, and the sound of His voice commands attention and a response. He spoke into nothingness, and all that is came into being. He speaks to the winds and the waves, and they are calmed (Luke 8:22-25). He speaks, and the sick are healed (John 4:50). At the command of His voice, the dead rise and live again (John 11:41-44). This same omnipotent One can speak peace over your situation. Nothing is too difficult for God (Jeremiah 32:17). Christ compels His children to ask, seek, and knock (Matthew 7:7-12), and He promises to hear our prayers and answer.

Nature knows the voice of God and obeys. Sin, sickness, and death know the voice of God and tremble. Do you know the voice of God? Allow Him to speak truth and life into your heart.

Listen closely…God is speaking to you today!

May 31
WORD OF HONOR

Matthew 5:37 (ESV): *"Let what you say be simply 'Yes' or 'No'; anything more than this comes from evil."*

In simpler days, a handshake could seal a deal. A promise made was a promise kept, and a person's integrity was founded on his word. Now, we write contracts and legally binding agreements. There is fine print that must be analyzed and dissected to make sure there are no hidden agendas. And when we really want to convince someone we are telling the truth, we swear on the Bible or on our momma's grave. Sad. As children of God, we should not participate in the world's game of telling half-truths. We should be men and women of whole truth. When we say "yes," then we do what we say. When we say "no," then we do not participate. It is when we say "well…maybe" that we find ourselves riding a fence that can lead to compromises in our standard of living and taint our testimonies for Christ. God does not want us to be double-minded or have a double standard for living. He wants us to be children of integrity. We are, after all, created in His image. Let us be true reflectors of our Father's character.

Speak words of truth today!

[fire yourself]
JUNE

June 1
A LITTLE GOES A LONG WAY

Mark 6:41 (ESV): *"And taking the five loaves
and the two fish he looked up to heaven and said a blessing
and broke the loaves and gave them to the disciples to set
before the people. And he divided the two fish among them all."*

God is the God of multiplication. He is the one who created everything from nothing. There is no doubt that He can take something small and do something great! What feels little in your life – finances, energy, love, hope, or faith? Give what you have to the Lord. He will take it, bless it, and return it back to you abundantly (Mark 6:41-42). It is a matter of trust. We can choose to cling to "our little," or we can give to our generous God who multiplies and completely satisfies!

Trust God to supply all of your needs today!

June 2
ABUNDANT WISDOM

James 1:5 (ESV): *"If any of you lacks wisdom, let him ask God, who gives generously to all without reproach, and it will be given him."*

Most people could probably quickly call to mind someone that they would consider to be wise. Perhaps this person always has the right advice or the right response in any situation. We look at these people and wonder, "How can they be so wise?" According to the Bible, wisdom is a gift that God generously bestows on those who ask Him for it. Need help knowing when to speak up or when to shut up? Ask God for wisdom. Desire help parenting an adolescent? Ask God for wisdom. Desperate to understand your spouse better? Ask God for wisdom. Wish you knew how to counsel a friend or coworker? Ask God for wisdom. Hungry for deeper insight into the Scriptures? Ask God for wisdom. Remember, our Heavenly Father delights in giving good things to His children!

Seek the mind of Christ today!

June 3
ARROWS

Psalm 127:4 (ESV): *"Like arrows in the hand of a warrior are the children of one's youth."*

In today's busy world, children are seen by some as burdensome or just another item on the never-ending "to do" list. According to God, though, children are a blessing. Christ even used a child to represent the kind of attitude and heart we should have when we approach God (Luke 18:16). Our little ones are meant to be treasured, to be loved unconditionally, and to be trained in the ways of God. So, one day when they are grown, these arrows can be taken from the protective quiver of mom and dad and shot out into the world to make a difference for the Kingdom of God.

Embrace your children today!

June 4

BE CAREFUL LITTLE EYES

Job 31:1 (ESV): *"I have made a covenant with my eyes...."*

There is a children's song that makes the profound statement, "Oh, be careful little eyes what you see...." It is important for us to remember that the eyes are the lamp of the body (Matthew 6:22). If your eyes focus on healthy things, the body will be full of light; but if they focus on harmful things, the body will be full of darkness (Matthew 6:22-23). A man in the Bible named Job went so far as to make a covenant with his eyes that he would not look lustfully upon a young woman. He did not want to open himself up to the opportunity to allow dark thoughts or impure desires to enter his mind and heart through his eyes. This was an intentional decision to guard himself and the sanctity of his marriage vows. It is too easy for the enemy to distract us with "a sneak peek" or "a quick glance." We need to make a covenant with our eyes that we will not focus on things that can compromise our personal integrity, our relationships, or our conscious before our Heavenly Father. Instead, we should be people who can appreciate true beauty in the Light!

See others through the eyes of Christ today!

June 5
BIG VALLEYS

1 Kings 19:3 (ESV): *"Then he was afraid, and he arose and ran for his life and came to Beersheba, which belongs to Judah, and left his servant there."*

The response of the prophet Elijah here in the book of 1 Kings, chapter 19, is almost puzzling. Why? Well, you have to go back and read the awesome acts of God on behalf of Elijah in chapter 18. God showed up in Elijah's time of need in dramatic fashion, and he was victorious over 450 prophets of the false god, Baal. Almost immediately after this mountaintop experience where Elijah felt invincible in God, however, the prophet found himself in a valley of fear and despair. Queen Jezebel had gotten word that Elijah defeated her prophets and she was out for his head! This man who had overpowered 450 men, without even breaking a sweat, was now afraid of a threat from one woman. Do the math … are you scratching your head, too? How can someone go from a mountaintop experience into such a big valley? Easy … it is the result of living in this flesh.

These eyes of flesh have a way of making circumstances look big…really big…bigger than God. But the truth is … they are not. This is why the Bible reminds us over and over that the just must look at all things through the eyes of faith (Habakkuk 2:4; Hebrews 10:38). We cannot focus on our problems; we must focus on our God. Likewise, we cannot lay down our shield of faith in moments of great victory, because our enemy is relentless. He is always preparing the next trap, the next temptation, and the next lie. Remember, the same God that we experience on the top of the mountain is the same God fighting for us in the valley. Regardless of your circumstances, lift your eyes of faith up to your LORD. He is your constant and faithful deliverer (Psalm 121:1-2)!

Praise God from the mountaintops and from the deep valleys today!

June 6
BORROWED FAITH

Matthew 25:8 (ESV): *"And the foolish said to the wise, 'Give us some of your oil, for our lamps are going out.'"*

There is a startling story told in Matthew 25:1-13. It is referred to as the Parable of the Ten Virgins. The Scriptures teach that ten virgins were looking forward to being in a wedding ceremony. None of the women knew the day nor the hour when the bridegroom would be coming for them, so it was vital for them to make the necessary preparations and be ready to leave at any moment. They each put on a nice dress, and they each carried a lamp so that everyone could look at them and see that they belonged in the bridal party. While the virgins waited, they became tired and fell asleep. During the night, however, a cry went out announcing, "The bridegroom is coming!" The virgins awoke, stirred themselves, fluffed their hair and their dresses, and quickly lit their lamps in preparation for the wedding. Tragically, only five of the virgins were wise and had put oil in their lamps. The other five virgins desperately asked, "Give us some of your oil!" Sadly, their foolish choice to not fully prepare caused them to miss out on the wedding.

On the outside, the ten virgins appeared to be the same. Each wore a nice dress, each carried a lamp in their hands, and each said they wanted to go to the wedding. There was one thing missing, though, for five of these women – the indwelling of the Holy Spirit. Jesus said there is only one way that we are going to go to heaven and be with God, and that is through Him (John 14:6). Salvation is not about us looking the part. We cannot clean ourselves up on the outside and think that God will accept us (1 Samuel 16:7). We must be filled with the oil of the Holy Spirit so that His light will shine in us. This happens as we accept Jesus as our personal Savior. We cannot borrow someone else's faith in Christ. Mom, dad, grandma, nor grandpa can have faith for us. We must be filled ourselves and believe in the only One who is the way to eternal life.

Be filled with the Holy Spirit today!

June 7
CAUGHT! ... NOW WHAT?

John 8:3-5 (ESV): *"The teachers of the law and the Pharisees brought in a woman caught in adultery. They made her stand before the group and said to Jesus, 'Teacher, this woman was caught in the act of adultery. In the Law Moses commanded us to stone such women. Now what do you say?'"*

Our accusers ... they are always watching, always eager to point out every little fault or sin. When we are doing well and going above and beyond, they are nowhere to be found. Slip up and say an ugly word or lose your cool, however, and there they are, with notepad in hand ready to record every dingy detail and with eyes casting an "I've got you now" stare. The Bible says that the devil is the accuser of the children of God; he takes great delight in going before the throne to tattle on us to God (Revelation 12:10). But for those of us in Christ, we have nothing to fear, because the Bible also says that we have an advocate with the Father, Jesus Christ our beloved Savior, who stands in our defense (1 John 2:1-2). In moments when we are caught in our unrighteousness, we should run to Christ. He loves; He forgives; He clothes us in His righteousness. In grace our Savior picks us up when we fall, and in love He empowers us to keep moving forward and to be victorious over sin.

In Christ, go and sin no more today!

June 8
CHOICES

Isaiah 30:21 (ESV): *"'And your ears shall hear a word behind you, saying, 'This is the way, walk in it,' when you turn to the right or when you turn to the left."*

Each day we make thousands of choices. The decision-making begins as soon as the alarm clock sounds. "Do I hit snooze, or do I get up?" We choose what to wear, whether or not to eat breakfast, and we choose how we will respond to others. At times it is easy to decide to smile or to step aside or to allow a car to pass. At other times, however, choosing to keep your mouth shut or choosing to respond with kindness is difficult.

Jesus was a great role model when it came to right choices. The Bible says that He never said an ugly word (1 Peter 2:22); He didn't retaliate out of anger (Isaiah 53:7); and He kept His cool even when wicked people were doing evil things to Him (Hebrews 12:3). When we feel overwhelmed by all of the choices in our day, we need to stop and seek the Holy Spirit for His guidance. When flesh doesn't have the strength to make the right decision, the Spirit can. When my mouth wants to add fuel to a fire, the Holy Spirit can speak peace and healing. When we choose to allow the mind of Christ to operate in us throughout our day, we will find that choosing right responses is not so difficult after all.

Choose to follow Christ today!

June 9
COUNT THE COST

Luke 14:28 (ESV): *"For which of you, desiring to build a tower, does not first sit down and count the cost, whether he has enough to complete it?"*

I have often thought that if Jesus ever tried to run for a public office, He should fire Himself as His own campaign manager. I do not know many people in such contests who make speeches like, "I have no home of my own (Matthew 8:20). If you follow me, you must forsake everything else that you consider important (Luke 14:33). In fact, the way that you love me must look like you hate everyone else (Luke 14:26). And, if you are with me, then you must deny yourself and take up a cross (Luke 9:23)." Yet, that is exactly what Jesus told those who approached Him about discipleship. It almost seems as though Christ was trying to talk them out of following Him! The truth is, though, that Christ wanted to be completely transparent (how refreshing!). He wanted these people, and He wants you and me, not to take lightly the decision to follow Him. The gate is narrow, and the way is hard (Matthew 7:13-14). We must consider the cost, because there will be things, or habits, or perhaps people that we hold dear that we must surrender to God in order to walk with Him. For most, the cost will seem too high, and they will choose to walk away. There will be a few, however, who will understand that when we put God first, He will fill our lives with good (Matthew 6:33).

Trust God with your life today!

June 10
CREATION PROCLAIMS GOD

Romans 1:19-20 (ESV): *"For what can be known about God is plain to them, because God has shown it to them. For his invisible attributes, namely his eternal power and divine nature, have been clearly perceived, ever since the creation of the world, in the things that have been made. So they are without excuse."*

Some people question the idea of a Divine Creator who made heaven and earth and mankind. However, the notion that somehow all of creation just came to be, apart from a Master Planner, is hard to understand. It is like taking a bag, filling it with springs and wheels and jewels, shaking it together, and when the contents are poured onto a table, expecting a watch to fall out of the bag. Ask any watchmaker, and he or she will tell you it takes an intelligent designer to create such an intricate timepiece. Likewise, it took a Master Designer to create such intricate masterpieces as earth and mankind. The Bible says that all of nature declares the glory of the Lord (Psalm 19:1). You and I were created to proclaim His glory too (Psalm 8). And, one day, the earth and all of her inhabitants will proclaim that Jesus is Lord. (Philippians 2:10).

Worship the one true God today!

June 11
EXALT GOD

John 3:30 (ESV): *"He must increase, but I must decrease."*

People have a tendency to categorize sinful behaviors. We will look at someone's actions and judge whether or not that was a "big sin" or a "little sin." What we need to understand, though, is that behaviors are not the real issue. The real issue is the attitude of the heart. A heart that is in rebellion towards God is what produces wrong behaviors (no matter the size!). Mankind declaring his independency from God is the nature of sin. Therefore, when we come to Christ, the first thing we surrender is our independent mindset. We take the focus off of self and place it firmly on God. The things we do, the things we think, and the things we say become about Him and are no longer all about self. We make much of God because He is God, and we now know that we are in desperate need of Him.

Let your life point others to Christ today!

June 12
FEAR LESS, TRUST MORE

Joshua 1:9 (ESV): *"Have I not commanded you?*
Be strong and courageous. Do not be frightened, and do not be
dismayed, for the Lord your God is with you wherever you go."

Poor Joshua ... he was used to following the lead of Moses, and he was a really good "second" man. But now that Moses was dead, God was taking the mantle of leadership and placing it directly on this young man's shoulders. He went from second to first in the blink of an eye. No warning. No preparation. But he did get a pep talk like no other! God reminded Joshua that there was no need to fear or worry, because He would never leave Joshua's side. What an amazing reminder from the Almighty! Don't we all need for God to grab us by our shirt collars once in a while and say, "It's not all on you, because the great I AM is and will always be with you." The truth is that any "work" that God calls you or I to belong to Him. Ultimately, He is responsible for its successful completion. What a relief to know that we do not have to be afraid of the things God calls us to or places in our paths! He is just looking for a pair of feet available for Him to walk in.

Don't allow fear to stop you from the call of God today!

June 13
FREEDOM

Galatians 5:1 (NIV): *"It is for freedom that Christ has set us free. Stand firm, then, and do not let yourselves be burdened again by a yoke of slavery."*

There is no greater measure of love than to lay down one's life for another. Jesus Christ laid down His life for you and me. He did this to show His love and to secure our eternal freedom. No longer are we chained to the slavery of sin. Because of Christ, we are free. Free to love, free to choose, free to live.

Freedom in Christ is yours today!

June 14
FRUIT INSPECTION

Matthew 12:33, 34 (ESV): *"Either make the tree good and its fruit good, or make the tree bad and its fruit bad, for the tree is known by its fruit...for out of the abundance of the heart the mouth speaks."*

If I asked, "Do you know someone who is a hot head?" You could probably think of a person you know who has a very short fuse. Or, if I asked, "Do you know someone who is kind?" Likewise, you could probably think of a person who is known for caring for others. The Bible teaches us this very practical truth, each of us is known by the "fruit" we bear in our lives ... our words, our attitudes, and our behaviors = our fruit. When we became a child of God, the seeds of His character were planted in our hearts. As believers, we are to represent Jesus Christ in all that we do and say. We are to bear His fruit in our lives; the good fruit from the Tree of Life (Galatians 5:22-23). If our words, attitudes, and behaviors are not Christ-like, it is time for a fruit inspection!

Bear good fruit for Christ today!

June 15
GO FISH

Luke 5:4-5 (ESV): *"And when he had finished speaking, he said to Simon, 'Put out into the deep and let down your nets for a catch.' And Simon answered, 'Master, we toiled all night and took nothing! But at your word I will let down the nets.'"*

The morning sun was shining bright. Two little boats were approaching shore ... the men onboard were tired; their nets were empty. The men had fished all night, but had caught no fish. As Jesus watched from the seashore, He called to them, "Go fish some more!" The idea of trying one more time seemed almost overwhelming. "Doesn't He know that we've already tried, and we've failed?" But there was something in Jesus' voice, or perhaps that look of knowing in His eyes, that compelled the weary fishermen to let down their nets one more time. The result? Their nets were so full of fish that they could barely contain the weight!

Are you tired? Weary of trying? Does it seem like no matter what you do things will never change? Let me encourage you today to listen to the voice of Jesus, and allow Him to lift your chin and refresh your spirit. Then, go fish! Get back out there and do all that you can do for the glory of God. What you cannot do ... Christ will handle in His own time. Who knows ... today may just be the day that your net is filled!

Be a fisher of men for Christ today!

June 16

GOD IS AT WORK IN ME

Psalm 138:8 (ESV): *"The Lord will fulfill his purpose for me; your steadfast love, O Lord, endures forever. Do not forsake the work of your hands."*

When God made you, He smiled. He looked at the work of His hands, and said, "He/she is good!" Sin has a destructive way, though, of tarnishing our lives and veiling the good that we can see. But here is some incredibly encouraging news … God will not forsake His work. He is a God of redemption who knows how to restore and how to make completely new. The problem for most of us is that we are always focused on how much work God still needs to do on us, instead of rejoicing in what He has already done. We look ahead at some distant and seemingly unattainable goal of perfection, instead of glancing over our shoulders to realize how far we have come. Today, I challenge you to rejoice over the work of God in your life! Now, rejoice is an inward emotion that requires an outward expression! It's that "whoop-whoop or body slam" kind of behavior when your team scores a goal. The Apostle Paul teaches us in Philippians 4:4 to go throughout our day with a "high five" mentality for what God is doing in our lives. Our Lord never slumbers nor sleeps (Psalm 121:3-4), and He will not quit on you (John 19:30). He will successfully and completely accomplish everything that He has purposed for you!

God is smiling on you today!

June 17
GOD IS THERE!

Psalm 139:7-8 (ESV): *"Where shall I go from your Spirit? Or where shall I flee from your presence? If I ascend to heaven, you are there! If I make my bed in Sheol, you are there!"*

When you are in a crowded shopping center, God is there. When you are alone in your room, God is there. When you are sitting at your desk at work or at school, God is there. When you are driving your car, God is there. When you are tending to your garden, God is there. When you are closing that big business deal, God is there. When you are on vacation with family and friends, God is there. When you are in the birthing room of a hospital, God is there. When you are standing by the grave of a loved one, God is there. When you are sleeping in the comfort of your bed, God is there. When you have no home to call your own, God is there. When you are singing at the top of your lungs, God is there. When you are weeping until all of your tears are spent, God is there. When you feel loved, special, on top of the world, God is there. When you feel lonely, afraid, like no one cares, even then … God is there.

Take comfort in knowing that the God who made you has promised to never leave or forsake you. In good times and in bad, in poor times and in rich, in sick times and in health, God is there!

Be encouraged … God is with you today!

June 18
GOD LOVES YOU

John 3:16 (ESV): *"For God so loved the world,*
that he gave his only Son, that whoever believes in him
should not perish but have eternal life."

Jesus flipped the religious community on its ear, when He came preaching that God wanted to have a relationship with mankind. He taught that God was our Father, and He even used the intimate, familiar term Abba when talking about God. This was in no way meant to diminish the authority and high exaltation of God; instead, it was meant to express the Almighty's great love for mankind. It is because of this love that the Father made a way for sinful men and women to come back into His presence. Jesus Christ is God's gift of love to you and to me. God is to be reverenced; He is to be worshipped and adored; He is to be exalted above all others, but He also gives all who believe in Him the right to be His children (John 1:12) and to become joint heirs with the Beloved Jesus (Romans 8:17).

Accept that God loves YOU today!

June 19
GOD OF TRUTH

Numbers 23:19 (NLT): *"God is not a man, so he does not lie. He is not human, so he does not change his mind. Has he ever spoken and failed to act? Has he ever promised and not carried it through?"*

Lies. Nothing breaks trust, credibility, or hearts like lies. When someone promises to love us, to provide for us, to be faithful to us, and then breaks that promise, we feel devastated. This will never happen with God, simply, because He cannot lie. God is the author of truth. It is His language; the only thing that comes out of His mouth is what is right, what is accurate, and what can be trusted. When God says He loves you, He does (John 3:16). When God says you are forgiven, you are (1 John 1:9). When God says that He does not think about your sins any longer, He doesn't (Isaiah 43:25). When God says He will provide for His children and meet all of our needs, He will (Philippians 4:19). When God says that you are holy, blameless, and righteous in Christ Jesus, you are (Colossians 1:22; Ephesians 1:4). When God says that NOTHING can remove you from His love, NOTHING can (Romans 8:35-39). And when God says that He will come again to take His children home to live with Him in peace, in joy, and in love for eternity, He will (John 14:3)!

The God of Truth claims you as His today!

June 20
GOT JOY?

Psalm 51:12 (ESV): *"Restore to me the joy of your salvation, and uphold me with a willing spirit."*

One thing that David is known for was his worship of God. The Psalms are filled with songs of thanksgiving and praise. David spent much of his life basking in the abundance of his relationship with the Heavenly Father, and the feeling was quite mutual. God referred to David as a man after His own heart (Acts 13:22). How then did David come to the place where he felt downcast, alone, and joyless? Psalm 51 was written after David had committed a great sin. He had committed adultery with another man's wife, had gotten her pregnant, then had the woman's husband killed to cover up his sin. At the beginning of that fateful day, David most likely had no idea that one "little sin" could spiral so far out of his control. He probably bought the same lie that you and I have bought from time to time: "Just once won't hurt, and nobody will ever find out." Yet, just once hurt everything, and thousands of years later people are still finding out!

The weight of unconfessed sin robs a person of the joy of salvation. Doubt that God can ever really forgive the most shameful deeds robs a person of the joy of salvation. Guilt from thoughts, words, and deeds robs a person of the joy of salvation. But God is a God of restoration (Joel 2:25). He can lift a heavy burden; He can chase off the darkness with His Light; and He can speak life back into a dying spirit. In David's most desperate time, he chose not to run from God, but to Him; and so should we. If you are experiencing joyless days, run to God. He will be your joy, your salvation, and your strength (Nehemiah 8:10).

Rejoice in the God of your salvation today!

June 21
HEALTHY ROOTS

Psalm 1:2-3 (ESV): *"but his delight is in the law of the Lord, and on his law he meditates day and night. He is like a tree planted by streams of water that yields its fruit in its season, and its leaf does not wither. In all that he does, he prospers."*

The healthiest trees are the ones with the deepest roots. Trees that are planted by streams of water tend to grow tall and strong. Why? Because they are connected to a life source that continuously feeds and nourishes them. When we choose to plant ourselves in the Word of God, we become like flourishing trees. The Fruit of the Spirit will be abundant in our lives. And even in times of spiritual storms, our roots are deep enough to hold us secure. Keeping our minds on God is the key to an abundant life.

Be rooted in Christ today!

June 22
HEAVEN AWAITS

John 14:2-3 (ESV): *"In my Father's house are many rooms. If it were not so, would I have told you that I go to prepare a place for you? And if I go and prepare a place for you, I will come again and will take you to myself, that where I am you may be also."*

In His last days on earth, Jesus began to share with His disciples the fact that He would not be with them in physical form much longer. The men were disheartened at the thought of Christ leaving. Jesus made them, and all believers in Him, a promise that day. He said, "I will come again!" Jesus came to earth to fulfill the plan of salvation. Then He returned to the right hand of the Father, where He awaits the great gathering day. One day, very soon, a trumpet will sound and those in Christ will arise to be with Him forever (1 Corinthians 15:52). Be of good courage, Beloved, this earth is not our final destination. Heaven awaits!

Allow your spirit to feel a little "homesick" for heaven today!

June 23

INNOCENT

Romans 8:1 (ESV): *"There is therefore now no condemnation for those who are in Christ Jesus."*

Satan takes great joy in pointing out our sins to us and to God. He loves to recount the wickedness of a thought or a deed, the wrong motivation of our hearts, pride, lies, or lust that provoke us during the day. The enemy will bait us, entrap us, break our leg, and then run to God and blame us for limping! The Bible says that he goes before the Almighty's throne to accuse us daily (Revelation 12:10), as if God will somehow see that satan is right. The enemy wants God to deem us worthless and turn His back on us. The real problem is not whether or not God will believe satan, but the question is whether or not you and I will believe the father of lies. Guilt is a powerful weapon that the devil uses against man, and he can keep us feeling low and unworthy, like the same old screw-up, if we do not fight back with truth. This is why Paul wrote Romans 8:1. He wants Believers to be reminded of who they forever are in Christ. Colossians 1:22 teaches that in Christ, we are holy (set apart for God), blameless (without fault or blemish), and above reproach (we cannot even be accused of wrong doing). When God looks at us, He sees Christ. When He looks at the devil, He sees a guilty offender without hope of pardon. Stand tall, Believer. The weight of your sin has been removed from your shoulders. Your debt has been cancelled at the Cross of Calvary (Colossians 2:14); you are declared innocent!

You are spotless in Jesus Christ today!

June 24
INTEGRITY

Job 1:1 (ESV): *"There was a man in the land of Uz whose name was Job, and that man was blameless and upright, one who feared God and turned away from evil."*

Integrity is consistency in character and one's steadfastness in upholding moral beliefs, regardless of who may or may not be watching. Think about that for a moment. How many times do we find ourselves conforming to the audience at hand? I may behave one way at work, another way at church, and even another way when I am with my friends. Understandably, some environments call for various levels of formality or casualness, but integrity speaks of a person's moral character. The fabric of who I am and who you are as a person should be consistent whether we are dressed to impress or dressed for the gym. Too often, though, we find ourselves compromising our integrity in order to be accepted, or at the very least, to not stand out. As Christians, though, it is our integrity of character that should make us stand out from the masses. There should be something about the way we do not conform that flickers like a little light in this world of darkness. People need to witness genuine boldness for Christ, not so we can be patted on the back "as a good guy or gal," but so others can see that Christ can help the weak to be strong (2 Corinthians 12:10) and those in fear to be brave (Isaiah 41:10). Our integrity speaks to the integrity of the one we claim to serve. Being honest and trustworthy and consistent in who we are and what we believe, actually encourages others to trust our Lord. Your life has the power to influence, either for good or for evil. Be a positive example for others to follow!

Respect God and others today!

June 25
MY REDEEMER LIVES

Job 19:25 (ESV): *"For I know that my Redeemer lives, and at the last he will stand upon the earth."*

The Scriptures teach that Job was a righteous man before God and his fellow man. He was also a very blessed man with family, friends, cattle, and riches. In a single day, however, Job lost all of his possessions… children, house, cattle…everything was taken away. In addition to his emotional pain, Job also became physically sick. Throughout his suffering, there were times when Job questioned God. "Where are you, Lord? Do you see me? Do you care?" But Job came to one conclusion despite his tragic circumstances; God was still God and He was ultimately in control.

We have all been in circumstances similar to Job, perhaps not as many grievances at once, but grievances, nevertheless. Things that make us cry out, "God, are you really up there?" God does not take pleasure in our pain. As a matter-of-fact, suffering comes upon the just and the unjust. It is a result of living in a world cursed from sin. God does, however, take pleasure when His children suffer well for His namesake. When we can find the courage to lift a voice of praise, regardless of what life is throwing our way; when we can declare that our God still reigns even when the ground seems to be caving under our feet; and when we can endure for just a little while longer because of the Hope before us, God receives glory. Whatever suffering you may be facing today, please know that God has not abandoned you. His heart breaks in your pain, but He rejoices in your unwavering faith in Him. And one day, Beloved, pain and suffering will be no more (Revelation 21:4).

Serve the Risen Savior today!

June 26
NO MORE BARRIERS

Mark 16:3 (ESV): *"And they were saying to one another, 'Who will roll away the stone for us from the entrance of the tomb?'"*

The women wanted to anoint the body of Jesus, but they were concerned about how they would get to Him. Men had rolled a large stone weighing about 1-1/2 tons to seal Christ in His tomb. When they arrived at the grave, though, the stone had been rolled away (Mark 16:4).

When Christ hung on the cross that fateful Friday, He cried out, "It is finished!" Then, He died. In that moment the veil of the temple was torn in two from top to bottom. This was the veil which had once divided man from God. The partition that said, "You can't come any closer" was removed once and for all. There were no more barriers; mankind had intimate access to God!

No more stones, no more veils, no more barriers. Nothing can separate us from the love of God (Romans 8:35-39). No man, no woman, and no demon can keep you and I from immediately approaching our Father. God invites us with open arms to come. Run to Him!

Come to Christ today!

June 27
NOW I SEE

John 9:25 (ESV): *"He answered, 'Whether he is a sinner I do not know. One thing I do know, that though I was blind, now I see.'"*

The Bible says there is power in the word of our testimony (Matthew 10:32; Revelation 12:11). Too often, though, we shy away from sharing Christ with others, because we think we don't know enough about the Bible, or we don't speak eloquently, or we fear someone may ask us a question about Christ that we don't know the answer to. So, in fear, we keep our mouths closed instead of proclaiming Him. I love the enthusiasm of this man in John chapter 9, though. He was born blind. One day Jesus came along and gave him sight! Imagine seeing the faces of your loved ones, seeing the sky and trees, seeing the world for the first time. He was filled with joy. He had been delivered from darkness, and there was no shutting him up! The religious leaders heard the news of this deliverance and asked the man how he received his sight. He told them Jesus had healed him. They rebuked the man and called Jesus a sinner. In that moment, the man did not try to impress or even convince the religious leaders to believe him. He simply spoke of what he knew to be true. "I was blind, now I see." What an incredible testimony! Can't we do the same? We have been transferred from the kingdom of darkness into the Kingdom of light. We were empty, but now we are filled; we were people of fear, but now we are people of hope; we were blind to our own sinfulness, but now we see the righteousness of God! If you have encountered Jesus Christ, share the Good News straight from your heart. Let your testimony serve to glorify God, to encourage yourself, and to instill hope in others.

Keep your eyes on Christ today!

June 28
OUR HOPE IS REAL

1 Corinthians 15:20 (ESV): *"But in fact Christ has been raised from the dead, the first fruits of those who have fallen asleep."*

The death of Jesus paid the penalty of our sins. The resurrection of Jesus secured our hope. If Christ had died and not resurrected, you and I would have no reason to believe in Him. He would be no different than any other human who talked a good talk, but in the end, could not fulfill His promises. But Jesus Christ was like no other man. He not only lived a life of perfection, but He died a death of victory by resurrecting Himself on the third day. In that triumphant moment, sin, sickness, and death were conquered and hope eternal was secured for the believer! Rejoice, Saints, because Jesus Christ, our blessed hope, is alive and real!

Christ wants to bless you today!

June 29

PEACE WITH GOD

Romans 5:1 (ESV): *"Therefore, since we have been justified by faith, we have peace with God through our Lord Jesus Christ."*

The Bible says that because of sin we were at enmity with God (Romans 8:7). We were hostile towards Him and His laws, and we were condemned in our sinful state. Oh, but when we accepted Jesus Christ as our Savior, that hostility was exchanged for life and peace (Romans 8:11). The word "justified" that the Apostle Paul uses in Romans 5:1 can be broken down into a simple phrase: "Just as if I'd never sinned!" How incredible to think that because of Jesus, we can stand before a holy God as perfect, blameless, righteous, and completely free from any residue of sin. Jesus became our peace offering to restore you and me back into a right relationship with God. Now, we have no need to fear God's wrath; instead, we can bask in His love. In Christ, we are on the same side!

Jesus loves you today!

June 30
PROCLAIM JESUS

Matthew 11:11 (ESV): *"Truly, I say to you, among those born of women there has arisen no one greater than John the Baptist...."*

Wow, what an accolade to get from the Son of God! Of all the people born up until that point in time, there was no man greater than John the Baptist. Does this mean that John was greater than Abraham or Moses? Yes. The prophet Samuel or wise King Solomon? Yes. How about Elijah or Elisha? Again, yes. What made John so special that he would be given the title of "Greater than" all others born thus far? Simple. John the Baptist was the first man to ever proclaim Jesus.

Do we proclaim Jesus, or do we stay silent? Do we spend our time sharing the good news of the Gospel? Are we concerned that those we pass by in the office or in the grocery store line may not know that there is a Savior who loves them and died for their sins? Do we let opportunities to witness pass us by for fear of the other person's response? True greatness is not about our family name, how much money we have in the bank, or what kind of car we drive. The one thing that raises up a person to the ranks of "great" in God's eyes is if we praise, extol, and lift high the name of Jesus (Psalm 145).

Tell someone about Jesus today!

[fire yourself]
JULY

July 1
SAINTS

2 Corinthians 5:17 (ESV): *"Therefore, if anyone is in Christ, he is a new creation. The old has passed away; behold, the new has come."*

When we ask Jesus to forgive us of our sins and we are grafted into the family of God, we are given a brand new identity and a brand new nature. Our identity is child of God, and our nature is Christ. Too often, I have heard believers refer to themselves as a "sinner saved by grace." While this is generally said with a humble heart, it incorrectly identifies them with someone who is dead and buried (Romans 6:6-11). A sinner is one who is devoted to sin, not freed from it. A saint, however, is one who has been washed in the blood of Jesus and is called His righteousness (2 Corinthians 5:21). Does this mean that we are perfect? Not yet! What it does mean, though, is that God sees what is eternally true about us, even while we are in the process of being sanctified day by day (Hebrews 10:14). So embrace the new you! Though you may look like the same old person on the outside, Christ now lives in you, and He calls you "saint" (1 Corinthians 1:2).

You have a new identity in Christ today!

July 2
SHHHH!

Psalm 46:10 (NIV): *"Be still, and know that I am God. I will be exalted among the nations, I will be exalted in the earth!"*

We are busy people! We are chatty people! Often, we start our day with what we call our "quiet time with God," and it is anything but quiet. We fill those 20 or 30 minutes with constant chatter about what we want God to do … who to bless, who to heal, what to fix, and how to fix it. Imagine God with His finger to His lips saying, "Shhhh! It's my turn to speak." If God has a plan and a purpose for our lives (Jeremiah 28:11), and He is the one who orders our steps throughout the day (Proverbs 16:9), shouldn't we start our day coming to Him with open ears and closed mouths? We need to invite the Lord to speak into our hearts and minds. His voice gives direction, comfort, and strength. God does invite us to bring the petitions of our hearts to Him, but it is far more important for us to hear what God has to say than for Him to hear what we have to say. Take time to be still before the Lord. It is never time wasted. When we do, we will find that He is all knowing and His ways are best.

Listen to the voice of God today!

July 3
SHOO IT AWAY!

Psalm 19:14 (ESV): *"Let the words of my mouth and the meditation of my heart be acceptable in your sight, O Lord, my rock and my redeemer."*

Did you know that every sinful act you and I commit begins in the mind? It's true. First, there is a thought, a tiny seed of an idea that is sown into our minds. Next, the longer that seed is allowed to stay, we begin to dwell on that thought and roots start to grow. Then, these roots penetrate our hearts and minds until they become firmly fixed in our belief system. Finally, once something gets into our belief system, we convince ourselves that it is valid or necessary and we act accordingly.

This is why the Bible reminds us over and over to guard our minds, because the mind is the wellspring of life (Proverbs 4:23), and it is the battlefield of sin (Ephesians 6:12). We are to renew our minds daily (Romans 12:2) and surrender every thought to the obedience of Christ (2 Corinthians 10:5). Be honest with yourself, when no one is telling you what to think – your boss isn't giving you a project; a teacher isn't giving you an assignment; your spouse isn't giving you a "honey do" list– and you are free to think your own thoughts, what kind of things do you choose to dwell on? Be careful! The enemy often cleverly disguises himself as "a harmless fantasy or daydream." A wise senior once told me, "You can't always help it if a bird flies over your head, but you don't have to let it build a nest there!" Just as we would shoo away a bird, we should shoo away negative and impure thoughts. May the things that we choose to think about and the words that we choose to say bring glory and honor to the Savior who chose to love us and give Himself for us.

Think about Jesus today!

July 4
SIGN SEEKERS

Mark 8:11-12 (ESV): *"The Pharisees came and began to argue with him, seeking from him a sign from heaven to test him. And he sighed deeply in his spirit and said, 'Why does this generation seek a sign? Truly, I say to you, no sign will be given to this generation.'"*

Jesus came proclaiming that He was the Son of God and that the Kingdom of God was at hand. The Pharisees wanted a demonstration of some sort for proof before they would believe. People have not changed much over the years. We often seek after a sign for direction or validation. That's why fortune cookies and magic eight balls have always been so popular! Even those of us who profess to walk in faith eagerly set our "fleeces" before the Lord and then wait for Him to prove that He really said what we think He spoke into our spirits. The problem is, though, that one sign is never enough (Judges 6:39). We need to realize that Christ has nothing left to prove. The Word declared a Messiah would come as a baby, die as a lamb, and rise as a King. Everything that was prophesied, Jesus Christ fulfilled. His "yes" is "yes" and His "no" is "no." Christ said blessed are those who do not need to "see" in order to believe (John 20:29). We need to learn to trust the Spirit of God in us. He knows how to make Himself clear to His children. God does not want to be mystical in our lives; He wants to be magnified in our lives by children who listen and obey…no other sign required!

Seek God today!

July 5
STRONG FOUNDATION

Matthew 7:25 (ESV): *"And the rain fell, and the floods came, and the winds blew and beat on the house, but it did not fall, because it had been founded on the rock."*

Ask any builder. A strong foundation is an absolute must if a house is to stand against the elements of nature. Likewise, we need to be established on the firm foundation of Jesus. He is the rock of salvation. When we are in Him, the winds may rage and the rains may fall, but we will stand victoriously.

Let Christ be your strong foundation today!

July 6
STRONGHOLDS

2 Corinthians 10:5 (ASV): *"casting down imaginations,
and every high thing that is exalted against the knowledge of God,
and bringing every thought into captivity to the obedience of Christ...."*

A stronghold is anything or anyone in our lives that tries to make itself bigger than God. Basically, it is a lie that we believe. Strongholds will keep us imprisoned in debt, addiction, fear, isolation, and guilt. Jesus Christ, however, is the answer to overcoming our strongholds, but we need to cooperate with Him. How? Every time the thought (our stronghold) comes to mind, we surrender it to Christ. "Here Lord, take this thought: Food is telling me I need it more than you ... Alcohol is saying that it can comfort me better than you ... My heart is telling me that I need a person in my life, because intimacy with you is not satisfying enough." Each time a thought comes to our minds and tries to convince us that "it" is the answer we need and not Christ, cast it down. Do not dwell on it. Do not consider it. Do not rationalize it. Do not even argue with it. Surrender it! We need to let Christ fight this battle for us. In Him, we are always victorious!

Christ will fight for you today!

July 7
THE NARROW GATE

Matthew 7:13-14 (ESV): *"Enter by the narrow gate.
For the gate is wide and the way is easy that leads to destruction,
and those who enter by it are many. For the gate is narrow and
the way is hard that leads to life, and those who find it are few."*

Take the path of least resistance … Just follow the crowd … Don't stand out; blend in with the crowd. These are the lines that satan feeds us. He makes "different" sound scary and isolating. Most people like to have a sense of fitting in or belonging, but exactly what are we choosing to fit in with? Christ told His disciples that following the crowd may be easy, but following Him will lead to eternal life. There are many who claim to follow Christ, but when it comes to total surrender of their lives to Him, there is no genuine commitment. Christ warned that a day will come when the true Believers will be separated from those who only talked a good talk but never actually walked with Him (Matthew 7:22-23). Take an honest look at your life and what you are choosing to fit in with. Do not be afraid to walk the narrow path today. You are not walking it alone. Christ goes before us, and He will never forsake us (Deuteronomy 31:8). He is leading the way to joy, to peace, to freedom, to home!

Choose God's way today!

July 8

THE SINLESS CHRIST

1 Peter 2:22 (ESV): *"He committed no sin, neither was deceit found in his mouth."*

Jesus asked his disciples a very profound question one day. He asked, "Who do men say that I am" (Matthew 16:13)? The responses varied. The disciples replied that some people thought he was John the Baptist, Elijah, or one of the prophets. If we asked men and women this same question today, we would most likely get a similar response: "He was a teacher or just a really good man." The truth is, though, either Christ was EXACTLY who He said He was … the perfect, sinless Son of God … or, He was a liar, a schemer, a trickster – anything BUT a good man. There is no middle ground.

After hearing what other people thought of Him, Jesus asked His disciples, "But who do you say that I am" (Matthew 16:15)? The Holy Spirit rushed upon Peter and he proclaimed, "You are the Christ, the Son of the living God!" Today, we must each answer this same question: Who do you say that Jesus is? May the power of the Holy Spirit open our eyes, like Peter, that we may see and know Jesus is the sinless One. He is the perfect Lamb who died to take away the sins of the world (John 3:16).

Proclaim Christ today!

July 9
THINK UPWARD

Colossians 3:2 (NIV): *"Set your minds on things above, not on earthly things."*

We are so busy living our lives and fulfilling our responsibilities on earth that we often fail to think about our home to come. The consequence? We feel stressed, overwhelmed, and stuck. For some, life becomes like a gerbil's wheel. We keep going around and around, but we never really get ahead. It is in thinking about heaven and our eternity with Christ, however, that we find the hope and joy and strength to keep moving forward in this world. Do not let the distractions of the day steal your attention away from Christ. Instead, we need to become intentional about our Christian walk. When our feet hit the floor in the mornings, we should set our minds on Christ. He should become the focus of all that we do during our day. In doing so, we begin to see purpose in the mundane and a joy in the end reward. Remember, life does have value and meaning when it is centered on Jesus.

Set your mind on Christ today!

July 10
THIRSTY SOUL

Psalm 42:1-2 (ESV): *"As the deer pants for streams of water, so my soul pants for you, my God. My soul thirsts for God, for the living God. When can I go and meet with God?"*

Water … there is nothing quite like it! When you are hot, tired, or parched, cool water satisfies the body's thirst; it refreshes and revives. The Psalmist painted a beautiful metaphor of how a deer, perhaps running through the woods from danger or a foe, is desperate, in need, panting for water – the source of his strength to go on. Likewise, our souls get weary, drained, desperate … it is the Living Water that we need. Jesus said, "…whoever drinks of the water that I will give him will never be thirsty again. The water that I will give him will become in him a spring of water welling up to eternal life" (John 4:14). Jesus Christ is the source and the answer to every need that we have. He will wash away our pains, our sorrows, and our fears. His love will fill us, refresh us, and revive us with life eternal. Jesus invites you to come and drink deeply from the fountain of living water today.

Jesus is your answer today!

July 11
TOUCH HIM

Luke 8:46 (ESV): *"But Jesus said, 'Someone touched me, for I perceive that power has gone out from me.'"*

The day was hot; the crowd was thick; but she pressed on with determination. This was her last hope. She had tried everything else – doctors, advice from friends, self-help remedies – but nothing could fix her need. She was desperate for healing. Today was the day she would reach out and touch Jesus. This woman had an issue of blood that left her body weak and frail, but a flicker of faith gave her strength to push through the masses to Christ. When she came in contact with the Great Physician, immediately she was made well.

This woman had no choice but to come to Jesus just as she was. Her deliverance was not based on her works but on her connection with Christ. Many people mistakenly believe they have to clean themselves up or get good enough to come to Christ, but He invites us to come as we are. Romans 5:8 tells us that Christ loves us so much that He died for us while we were sinners. Likewise, there are many people who surround Jesus and like to be in the crowd for social reasons, but they never really touch Him.

Reach out and touch Jesus today!

July 12

TUMBLING WALLS

Joshua 6:20 (ESV): *"So the people shouted, and the trumpets were blown. As soon as the people heard the sound of the trumpet, the people shouted a great shout, and the wall fell down flat, so that the people went up into the city, every man straight before him, and they captured the city."*

God had made a promise to Joshua, but a giant obstacle ... a wall, in fact ... stood in the way of Joshua receiving his promise. Instead of walking away from his promise or allowing feelings of hopelessness to settle over him, Joshua listened closely for instruction from the Lord. The word given to him seemed almost silly ... walk around that wall with a closed mouth and a ready heart. In faith, Joshua obeyed. On day seven, God gave Joshua a new command ... now shout with the voice of victory! The result? A tumbling wall! The power of God to breakdown obstacles in our lives is often thwarted by our dependency on our logic over authentic faith in Him. God works through the obedience and faith of His people. If it seems that you have insurmountable walls in your life standing between you and your promise, trust God and keep an expectant heart. And remember, a mighty shout of praise to the Lord ignites a mighty response from Him.

Walk in victory today!

July 13
UNREDEEMABLE

John 4:28-29 (ESV): *"So the woman left her water jar and went away into town and said to the people, 'Come, see a man who told me all that I ever did. Can this be the Christ?'"*

This story is a beautiful picture of how the "Son of Man came to seek and to save the lost" (Luke 19:10). John chapter 4 tells that on that fateful day Jesus had to pass through Samaria. If you know the history between the Jews and the Samaritans, however, you would understand that Jews did not ever pass through Samaria. They would rather turn a short journey into a long one just to circumvent going through what they considered a "dirty land." Jesus, however, had to go through Samaria, because He had a very important appointment to keep there. A woman, who'd had many husbands and much heartache, needed to encounter Him. So Jesus went, and He waited for her. A woman who most people would classify as retched and unredeemable had a face-to-face encounter with the Redeemer, and her life would never be the same!

Jesus loves you and me so much that He came looking for us (Matthew 18:11). The Apostle John reminds us that we only love God because He loved us first (1 John 4:19). We don't have to make ourselves clean enough or good enough to come to God. Christ comes looking for us, just as we are, and in His great mercy and love calls us to be His children (John 1:12).

Christ can make all things new today!

July 14
VESSEL OF HONOR

James 5:12 (ESV): *"But above all, my brothers,
do not swear, either by heaven or by earth or by any other oath,
but let your 'yes' be yes and your 'no' be no,
so that you may not fall under condemnation."*

Have you ever heard someone say, "I swear I mean it!" or, "I promise it's true!" Perhaps we've even made statements like this. Why do people feel the need to assert additional assurance when they want to convince someone that they are telling the truth? Well, I think it is because too often we do not tell the truth, the whole truth, and nothing but the truth. We pepper our conversations with half-truths, little lies, or simple exaggerations; and for the most part, we feel okay about doing this. It makes conversations more dramatic or entertaining. Sometimes, it drives a point we are trying to make. Subsequently, in moments when we want to make sure people believe what we are saying is right, our conscious compels us to add words like "promise" or "swear." The Bible says that we are to be vessels of honor and that we are meant for the Master's service (2 Timothy 2:21). Therefore, everything about our lives, even our conversations, should be without question or reproach. We should be such people of integrity that when we simply say "yes" or when we simply say "no," others know the response is true … enough said.

Live honorably before God and man today!

July 15
VICTORIOUS IN CHRIST

Galatians 2:20 (ESV): *"It is no longer I who live, but Christ who lives in me. And the life I now live in the flesh I live by faith in the Son of God, who loved me and gave Himself for me."*

Each day is a battle of faith … to believe God or to believe my circumstances. Once the battle of faith is settled, you come to a place of victory. You know you can face anything God gives you to go through; because whatever He gives you to go through, He will go through it operating as you. Remember the words of Paul, which remind us that it is now Christ living His life through you. The Son of God, who led the only perfect life in the flesh, will now do the same through your flesh and my flesh, if we surrender ourselves to Him. We are assured of winning when God is fighting our battles for us. What's our part then? Believe in the One whom God has sent to be our salvation and our victory (John 6:29).

Claim your victory in Christ today!

July 16
WHO & WHY

1 Peter 2:9-10 (ESV): *"But you are a chosen race, a royal priesthood, a holy nation, a people for his own possession, that you may proclaim the excellencies of him who called you out of darkness into his marvelous light. Once you were not a people, but now you are God's people; once you had not received mercy, but now you have received mercy."*

Some people go through life wondering who they are and why they were ever born. For those in Christ, there is no question of our "who" or of our "why." The Apostle Peter makes it very plain for us. Who we are is a chosen group with royal blood coursing through our veins, distinguished and called out. Why we are is to make much of the One who transferred us from darkness into light. We were once orphans, but because of Christ, we are adopted, heirs to an eternal kingdom. Once we were condemned and hopeless, but because of Christ, we are rich in mercy. There are no identity crises in the family of God. His children have a God-given identity and a God-given purpose. A sure foundation and a clear direction make navigating this temporary life on earth much easier and purpose-filled. If you are still wondering about your significance, turn to Christ. He will be what makes your life make sense.

You have an identity and a purpose in Christ today!

July 17
WHY DO YOU DOUBT?

Matthew 14:31 (NIV): *"Immediately Jesus reached out his hand and caught him. 'You of little faith,' he said, 'why did you doubt?'"*

The storm was raging. The boat was sinking. The men were afraid. And Jesus comes out of nowhere, in the midst of all this unsettledness and commotion, and asks the impossible. In faith or perhaps, just out of fear, Peter obeys and steps out of the sinking boat and onto the raging waves. For a moment, his eyes lock with Christ and his troubles seem inconsequential. Then, a splash of water against his face or the wind whistling in his ears distracted Peter and reminded him of his desperate situation. Instead of keeping his focus on Christ, Peter looked again to his circumstances, and he began to sink. Jesus immediately reached out and pulled Peter up; He did not allow His child to sink. The question was inevitable, though, "Why did you doubt?"

Why do we? Look over the course of your life. Hasn't Christ proven Himself to be faithful over and over again? Is there food on your table? Are there clothes on your back? Is there shelter over your head? Are your sins forgiven? Do you have an advocate with the Father? If He has kept His word in all of these things, why do we fear today's challenge? Nothing is too difficult for God (Jeremiah 32: 17, 27). Faith is acting like God is telling the truth. Trust Him with the circumstances of your day. God is faithful.

Place your faith in Christ today!

July 18
WONDERFUL WORKS

Psalm 139:14 (ESV): *"I praise you,*
for I am fearfully and wonderfully made.
Wonderful are your works; my soul knows it very well."

Did you know that the human brain makes up only 2% of the body's weight, but it consumes about 20-30% of the calories you take in on any given day? It contains 100 billion neurons and 100 trillion supporting cells. It also makes about 1,000,000,000,000,000 (1 quadrillion) connections among those cells. There are more connections being made in your brain than there are stars in the universe … Amazing! God was so careful and so thoughtful in planning every detail that makes you, you. From the intricacies of the body, to the things that make you laugh, the things that break your heart, the things that ignite you with passion, the things that bore you to tears – all of these come from the creative mind of an Almighty God. There is no one quite like you, and God wants you to know and embrace that. No matter your size, shape, age, or color, you are wonderfully made, and God loves you!

You are God's work of art…rejoice in your Creator today!

July 19
WORRY LESS, PRAY MORE

Isaiah 26:3 (ESV): *"You keep him in perfect peace whose mind is stayed on you, because he trusts in you."*

Worry promotes physical, emotional, relational, and spiritual stress, but it resolves absolutely nothing. Nevertheless, people are prone to worry. The Bible, however, has a guaranteed solution for overcoming our tendency to worry … prayer! When we pray, we cannot worry. Why? Because our focus is redirected from our problem to our God. When we pray, our mind is stayed on the Sovereign Lord who controls everything from the air we breathe to the number of our days. Keeping our mind constant on Christ results in perfect peace. There is an inner knowing that someway, somehow everything will be okay, because in the presence of God, all fears must flee.

Meditate on Christ today!

July 20
YES, LORD

Luke 1:38 (ESV): *"And Mary said, 'Behold,*
I am the servant of the Lord; let it be to me
according to your word.' And the angel departed from her."

The angel appeared to the young virgin woman to tell her that she would give birth to the Savior of the world. Imagine what must have been going through Mary's mind! At this time, she was espoused, or engaged, to be married to Joseph. Jewish law saw this commitment as just as binding as an actual marriage. A pregnancy, especially if Joseph was not the father, could not only mean the end of her reputation, but it potentially could mean the end of her life. Talk about a risky assignment! However, notice Mary's response to the angel. She simply said, "I will." She did not argue with the angel about what other people would think; she did not question what it would cost her personally; she did not offer an alternative plan; she was simply willing to be used. God is looking for willing vessels, people who will not argue, question, or try to change His plan for theirs. God is very busy, and He offers you and me the opportunity to join Him in His work. Will you say, "Yes, Lord"?

Be a willing vessel for God today!

July 21
A FAITHFUL SPOUSE

Malachi 2:13-15 (NIV): *"Another thing you do: You flood the Lord's altar with tears. You weep and wail because he no longer looks with favor on your offerings or accepts them with pleasure from your hands. You ask, 'Why?' It is because the Lord is the witness between you and the wife of your youth. You have been unfaithful to her, though she is your partner, the wife of your marriage covenant. Has not the one God made you? You belong to him in body and spirit. And what does the one God seek? Godly offspring. So be on your guard, and do not be unfaithful to the wife of your youth."*

How long has it been since you embraced your spouse and said, "I love you!" for no special reason and without provocation? How long has it been since your children have watched you romance your spouse with a special dinner, a bouquet of flowers, or a waltz around the house? The Bible teaches us that the marriage relationship is our best idea of how Christ loves us. We are not to ignore our spouses or to take them for granted. Busy lives are no excuse for lackluster marriages. The covenant you made with your wife or husband was to model for one another and for your children the love of Christ (Ephesians 5:25), remembering that Christ loves passionately, consistently, and eternally!

Recommit your marriage covenant with God and your spouse today!

July 22

A GLAD HEART

Proverbs 12:25 (ESV): *"Anxiety in a man's heart weighs it down, but a good word makes him glad."*

God intends for life to be enjoyed, not merely endured. While working hard is admirable, to assume that God's goal for our lives is material prosperity or success as the world defines it is a fatal mistake. Jesus said that He came to give us abundant life (John 10:10), but that abundance has more to do with people and relationships than material gains. We must remind ourselves that there is far more to life than just the few years we live on this planet. Our identity is in eternity, and our homeland is in heaven. So, the lives we live and the priorities we set should reflect this.

God is careful to warn us about the dangers of living for the here and now and adopting the values, priorities, and lifestyles of the world around us (James 4:4). The Bible reminds us that this world is not our home, so we don't need to make ourselves too cozy in it and indulge our egos at the expense of our souls (1 Peter 2:11)! When we realize that life on earth is just a temporary assignment, it should radically alter our values and priorities. The weight of "keeping up with the Joneses" and worrying about "stuff" can be lifted off our shoulders. In its place, we can share the good Word of the Gospel and be filled with the gladness of Christ.

Spread the cheer of the Lord today!

July 23

A HOLY REVERENCE

Nehemiah 8:5 (ESV): *"Ezra opened the book.*
All the people could see him because he was standing above them;
and as he opened it, the people all stood up."

Can you picture this scene … the crowd is thick, and people are chatting and greeting one another. Someone notices the man of God as he walks up to the podium. Without saying a word, he opens the Scriptures and an immediate hush falls over the place. In unison, the crowd stands to its feet and with undivided attention, and they reverently listen as God's Word is read.

Amazing! The Word of God prompted a holy hush. The Word of God evoked undivided attention. The Word of God became the unified focus of all. These people understood that God is to be reverenced. Do we reverence God? Too often in our fast paced world, we like to get our "God" the same way we get everything else—quick and easy. We don't like to be inconvenienced, and often, we don't like to have to think too hard. When we make it to our pew in church, the last thing we feel like doing is having to stand up again. Maybe it is time for a close inspection of our attitude towards the Almighty God. We need to remind ourselves of who He is and who we are. God loves you and me, but He is not to be taken lightly or treated as an accessory to our lives. God deserves our reverence and our undivided attention. When we honor God with first place in our lives, He will bring order to the other things in our lives (Matthew 6:33).

Reverence God today!

July 24
A TEACHABLE SPIRIT

Proverbs 13:1 (NLT): *"A wise child accepts a parent's discipline;*
a mocker refuses to listen to correction."

We are human, and as humans we can expect to make mistakes and fall short of perfection. However, the one thing that we should always maintain is a teachable spirit. It is through keeping an open mind and a humble heart that we learn and grow. Being able to admit that we are not always right and that we do not always know what is best, keeps our hearts as fertile soil for God to plant seeds of knowledge and wisdom. When we refuse discipline or instruction, though, because our proud hearts don't want to receive correction, we are unwise and unusable by God. Our daily prayer should be "teach me your ways, O Lord, that I may live according to your truth" (Psalm 86:11)!

Be open to the correction of the Lord today!

July 25

AN UNLIKELY CHOICE

1 Corinthians 1:27 (NIV): *"But God chose
the foolish things of the world to shame the wise;
God chose the weak things of the world to shame the strong."*

Repeat after me: "I am not God … His ways are not my ways … His thoughts are not my thoughts…And, He can do whatever He chooses to do!" There, now we can go through our day and leave the negative voices behind that would tell us we are not smart enough, or religious enough, or good enough to be used by God. The truth is that God loves to show off! He wants to display His mighty power through unlikely people. Look at Moses. God had to drag him out of hiding in a desert to become the deliverer of the children of Israel. Joshua, the man chosen to lead the army of God into battle against a fortified city, was shaking in his sandals as God had to encourage him over and over with, "It's going to be okay; I've got this one." And little David, the boy with sheep poo on his shoes and grass stains on his robe, was chosen by God to be the King of Israel. Were there better candidates for these lofty roles? Probably by man's standards, but in God's eyes, these unlikelies were precisely what He was looking for! When you feel weak, He is strong! When you feel unwise, He is a wellspring of knowledge. When you feel like you cannot, He can. When you think someone else could probably do the job better, you have just qualified yourself in God's eyes. He is not looking for what we can do for Him. God is looking for willing vessels who will allow Him to do whatever He wants through the power of the Holy Spirit working in them!

Be used by God today!

July 26
BE COOL

Proverbs 17:27 (NIV): *"Whoever restrains his words has knowledge, and he who has a cool spirit is a man of understanding."*

A short fuse causes fear. Abrupt anger causes anxiety. A bad temper raises stress levels. Hostile behavior does not resolve issues, and in fact, is a sign of self-focus and immature thinking. Patience, on the other hand, brings calmness. A soft response lowers stress and anxiety levels. A cool spirit says, "I love you, and I am a safe place for you to mess up."

Are you a safe place for others? Does your behavior always act lovingly towards others or only when things are going your way? The Bible teaches us that a person of wisdom will operate in the spirit of self-control and will consider the feelings of others, instead of the inconvenience of self. It is easy to love the lovely. It is easy to be kind to the kind. It is easy to be calm with those who always do things my way. So what? … Even sinners can exhibit good behavior in these cases (Luke 6:32). God calls us to do the supernatural and be cool, especially when the circumstances around us begin to heat up.

Surrender your temperament to God today!

July 27
BEAUTIFUL IN GOD'S SIGHT

Acts 7:20 (ESV): *"At this time Moses was born; and He was beautiful in God's sight."*

Ask any parent, and they will tell you that no child is as beautiful as their child! For those of us who have children, we know the feeling of a swelled heart, as we look into the face of our baby and think, "This child is perfect!" When Moses was born, God looked at that little baby and smiled. Why? Was Moses exceptionally more beautiful than other babies? Probably not. What was beautiful to God, though, was the plan He had for Moses' life, and the fact that Moses would be willing to fulfill that plan. God had destined Moses to be the deliverer of the children of Israel. He would be the one to lead God's children out of the many years spent in captivity. Would Moses be perfect? Oh, no! In fact he was a liar, hot-tempered, a murderer, a coward, and a top-notch excuse-maker. Beyond all of his many shortcomings and personality flaws, though, was a heart for God.

Beloved, you may have a list of negative traits a mile long, but who owns your heart? If it is surrendered to God, He can do amazing things in your life despite your flaws. When God looks at His children and finds those with a reckless abandonment from Him and His will, He simply smiles and says, "This child is perfect!"

A surrendered heart is beautiful to God. Give Him your heart today!

July 28
BILLBOARD FOR GOD

Hebrews 10:38 (ESV): *"but my righteous one shall live by faith, and if he shrinks back, my soul has no pleasure in him."*

Faith is a principle that the children of God must get comfortable with. God has told us in His Word that the righteous shall live by faith. Our faith, however, was never meant to serve as an insurance policy that we will never suffer or encounter hard times. We cannot always "believe" ourselves out of difficult circumstances. Instead, our faith is proven in the midst of difficult circumstances. It is in times of crises, when we are weak and powerless, that God can display His power and might. Our lives become a walking billboard for the glory of God.

When our days seem the darkest, God's light shines the brightest. Daniel learned that God was a lion tamer. Shadrach, Meshach, and Abednego discovered that God was a firewalker. Joshua learned that God was a demolition expert, and Paul and Silas found out that God was an earth shaker. If these people had never encountered troubles, they would have missed out on knowing firsthand the kind of God they served!

God wants you and me to trust Him in our times of trial. He will prove His faithfulness, and in turn, we will prove ours. Then we too can testify of a bill-paying, cancer-curing, marriage-restoring, pantry-filling, car-repairing, job-finding, child-saving, miracle-working God! Through faith we can live this life peacefully, as God takes pleasure in demonstrating His power in our lives.

God wants to display His power and love through you today!

July 29
BRAG ABOUT IT

1 Thessalonians 1:3 (NIV): *"We remember before our God and Father your work produced by faith, your labor prompted by love, and your endurance inspired by hope in our Lord Jesus Christ."*

It is easy to point out the mistakes and shortcomings of others. This is the stuff that juicy gossip is made of, and it's often the stuff that makes us feel a little better about our own messy lives. How long has it been, though, since you noticed someone acting godly and pointed that out to others? As children of God, we should rejoice when our brothers and sisters in Christ are behaving like Christ. It should fill our hearts with joy when we see our spouse or our children making wise choices or being long suffering towards others. We need to develop the habit of being a cheerleader for those who are honoring God with their lives. Verbally encourage and bless others. Let us be the kind of people who make good use of our words!

Encourage someone in the Lord today!

July 30
CHOOSE PEACE

John 14:1 (ESV): *"Let not your hearts be troubled.
Believe in God; believe also in me."*

"Let not" implies that we have the power either to do or not to do. I can let my son go in the yard, or I can choose not to let him go outside. The power of the choice belongs to me. Likewise, Christ is telling His disciples, "You have the power to choose not to be troubled by this news." What news? Christ was telling His disciples that His time on earth was concluding and that soon they would no longer be seeing Him as they were accustomed. Understandably, the disciples were distressed over this news. Christ, however, goes on to explain to them that He is only leaving in order to prepare their eternal home and that He will be back again for them. The one thing they must choose to do in His absence is BELIEVE HIM. In believing Him, their hearts will not be troubled.

What a great formula for a restful mind and a peace-filled heart. In the midst of our chaos, we can choose to let not our hearts be troubled. When we don't have all the answers to the problems in our lives, we can choose peace. When our emotions want to lead our minds into dark places, we can opt not to participate. How? By choosing instead to believe in God and the One He has sent, Jesus Christ. Believe what God says to be true, regardless of what your circumstances or man's wisdom try to convince you is true, and you will find solace in the midst of your storms.

Choose to trust God today!

July 31
CHRIST IS FOR YOU

Psalm 124:1 (ESV): *"If it had not been for the Lord who was on our side...."*

S ome days it just feels like it's you against the world. Nothing goes your way. The alarm clock does not go off on time. The coffee maker is on the fritz. The dog chewed a hole in your shoe. Your boss is standing over you with a critical eye. The guy in the next cubicle is secretly hoping today is the day you get the boot and he gets your chair. No support. No energy. No one to care. Oh, but wait ...there is One who is still rooting for you – Jesus! Christ is always for us. He never does anything to walk over us, push us down, or make us feel less. Christ wants to carry us, lift us up, and remind us that we can do all things through His power working in us (Philippians 4:13). Remember, no matter how difficult or chaotic life becomes, the Lord is always for you.

Jesus is for you today!

[fire yourself]
AUGUST

August 1
CHRIST PRAYED

Mark 1:35 (ESV): *"And rising very early in the morning, while it was still dark, he departed and went out to a desolate place, and there he prayed."*

Prayer with God is the most important conversation we will have all day. Prayer is our source of connection to our Father. It is our opportunity to commune with Him and to hear His voice speak directly into our spirits. The enemy knows the power that we receive when we pray. So, he will always come up with clever ways to distract us. He will even fill our minds with plenty of "good things" that we should do in order to neglect "the best thing" that we should do. Christ demonstrated the importance of prayer. He would get up in the earliest hours of the day to give God undistracted attention. The result? He lived a life of power, authority, and great victory. Were Jesus' circumstances perfect? By no means! But, His attitude and His heart were always perfectly in tune with the Father, because He took time to pray.

Make time to pray today!

August 2
CHRIST'S EXAMPLE

Philippians 2:1-2 (ESV): "*So if there is any encouragement in Christ, any comfort from love, any participation in the Spirit, any affection and sympathy, complete my joy by being of the same mind, having the same love, being in full accord and of one mind.*"

Jesus Christ was the only perfect person to ever walk the earth. He went through His life showing love, giving encouragement, and extending comfort to all He came in contact with. In doing so, Christ became our perfect example of how to live well with our fellow man. Do you want to know how to encourage someone? Look at Christ (John 16:33). Want to know how to comfort others? Look at Christ (John 19:25-27). Want to know how to truly love? Look at Christ (John 15:13). We are to be so filled with Christ that when others experience us, they feel as though they have just experienced Him!

Love others like Christ today!

August 3
CONSIDER THE SPARROW

Matthew 10:29 (NLT): *"What is the price of two sparrows—one copper coin? But not a single sparrow can fall to the ground without your Father knowing it."*

The sparrow … it's just a common little bird. There is nothing particularly unique about it that would make it standout from other birds. As a matter of fact, its value in Bible days was only about a penny. The sparrow is seemingly plain, ordinary, and not special. To God, though, every little sparrow matters. He watches and feeds each one, and when its time on earth is complete, He knows. If God takes such care to pay attention to a little bird, how much more does He care and pay attention to you and me? The Scriptures say that God formed us with His own hands (Genesis 2:7), breathed into us His own breath (Genesis 2:7), and created us in His own image (Genesis 1:27) – talk about special! There is nothing on earth more valuable to God than His children. His thoughts towards us are more than the sands on the seashore (Psalm 139:18). God knows what you are going through today, and He is with you (Zephaniah 3:17).

God sees you where you are today!

August 4
DECLARE HIM

Psalm 118:17 (KJV): *"I shall not die, but live, and declare the works of the LORD."*

There are times in this life when circumstances seem to overwhelm us, and we feel like we are going down for the final count. It is in those moments that the hand of God snatches us from the grip of despair, and He breathes new hope into our spirits. He lifts us up, and in turn, He wants us to speak up. Do not be silent when God comes to your rescue. Declare His mighty works to all who will listen. There are others who are going under the waves of despair, and they need to know there is a Savior who can rescue and revive them! We need to plant our feet on the Rock and determine that "I will not allow my faith to die in the midst of this circumstance. Instead, I will stand strong, despite the trial, and victoriously proclaim the goodness and faithfulness of God." This kind of faith makes our Father smile (Numbers 6:25).

Talk about God today!

August 5
DEPENDABLE

Psalm 119:160 (ESV): *"The sum of your word is truth, and every one of your righteous rules endures forever."*

There is no uncertainty with God. He is not ambiguous, and He does not change His mind according to how He feels from day to day. God is the same yesterday, today, and forevermore (Hebrews 13:8). God is not a liar (Numbers 23:19); He is the source of all truth (John 14:6). When God says something, it is absolutely right; therefore, He becomes the foundation for all that we know to be right and true and eternal.

When this life seems to become too overwhelming, God is your strong tower. When circumstances let you down, Christ will lift you up. When people make promises they do not or cannot keep, God is your promise keeper. Jehovah is the everlasting God. He is dependable, and you can count on Him!

You can depend on the Word of God today!

August 6
DISOBEDIENT HEARTS

Acts 7:39 (ESV): *"Our fathers refused to obey him, but thrust him aside, and in their hearts they turned to Egypt."*

This is such a sad verse. Luke recounts the exodus of the children of Israel, who were once slaves in Egypt but were rescued by God through Moses and on their way to the promised land. He writes this startling verse: "…in their hearts they turned to Egypt." God had performed miracle after miracle to make a way of escape for His people from their bondage and misery; He had provided food and drink; He made sure their shoes and clothes never wore out. Although the children of Israel were the beneficiaries of many blessings from the Lord, their hearts were still easily swayed away. They continuously thought back about their days in Egypt. Instead of remembering the evil done to them, they glamorized the memories of the pleasures that Egypt could offer.

Before we judge them too harshly, though, how many of us are guilty of the same thing? God delivers us from a habit, addiction, or bondage of some sort, and we allow our minds to drift and daydream and fantasize about the guilty pleasures. Before long, we may be playing the part of Christians and going through the motions, but our hearts are really turned back to Egypt. This is why the Scriptures warn us to guard our hearts (Proverbs 4:23) and to renew our minds (Romans 12:2). Our thought-life will cause our hearts to stray if we are not good managers of our minds. The enemy will always make promises that seem good, but he is a liar and his promises always end with our hearts broken.

Keep a pure heart before God today!

August 7

DIVINE APPOINTMENT

John 4: 3-4 (ESV): *"[Jesus] left Judea and departed again for Galilee. And he had to pass through Samaria."*

Jesus and His disciples are leaving Judea and heading for Galilee. At first glance, it might seem like the Scripture is indicating that the only way to get to Galilee would be to pass through Samaria. While that may have been the shorter route, it was also a very unlikely route for Jews to take. The Jews would do everything in their power to avoid Samaria, because they considered this an "unclean" land. Then why did Jesus say they had to go through Samaria, if it wasn't part of the route to get them to their ultimate destination? Simple. It was because in Jesus' mind, Samaria was the destination. He had a divine appointment with a little unknown woman at a well. This woman was insignificant in the minds of others, but to Christ, she was worth a special trip!

Day after day, this lonely woman would visit the well carrying her jar. Filling the bottle brought her temporary relief and comfort from the woes of her life. But it was short-lived, because soon that bottle would become empty again and so would she. This day, however, would be different for she was about to encounter Christ, the living water; the one who could completely satisfy her so that her soul would never be dry or barren again. After her personal encounter with Jesus Christ that day, this woman's life was never the same again. How do I know? Verse 28 reads, "So the woman left her water jar and went away into town…." Why did she leave her jar? She didn't need it anymore. She abandoned her futile self-effort and was filled with the fullness of Jesus Christ.

Are you feeling empty today? Tired of trying to satisfy yourself with things that only disappoint? How encouraging to know that Jesus wants to visit with you today. Believe in Him, and your soul will never be thirsty again (John 6:35).

Drink deeply from the fountain of living water today!

August 8
DIVINE ASSIGNMENTS

Exodus 3:10 (ESV): *"Come, I will send you to Pharaoh that you may bring my people, the children of Israel, out of Egypt."*

Moses had a long and somewhat checkered history with the Egyptians. The last time he was in their company, he killed one of the Egyptian taskmasters for mistreating an Israelite slave. For the next forty years, Moses hid out in the desert for fear his own life would be taken, and then God paid Moses a special visit to inform him that he had been specially selected for a divine assignment ... to go face his fears and demand the freedom of the children of Israel. Now, this would be no small assignment for any man, much less a coward like Moses. In fact, Moses tried to prove to God just how unusable he was for this job. He even offered God some helpful advice on who might be a better candidate! Doesn't that sound just like you and me ... we're always ready to help God improve upon His plans for our lives. God's plans are perfect, and He will not change His plans to suit man. Instead, He chooses to change the man to fit His plan. Moses' divine assignment from God seemed impossible, but our faithful Lord used this unlikely person to accomplish great things.

God has a divine assignment for each one of us. It will most likely be something that we are not qualified to do, at least not in our own strength or skill set. However, it is in our weakness that He is strong (2 Corinthians 12:10), and He will glorify Himself through our obedience to embrace our calling in faith (1 Peter 4:11).

Allow God's way to be your way today!

August 9
ETERNAL LIFE

John 17:3 (ESV): *"And this is eternal life, that they know you the only true God, and Jesus Christ whom you have sent."*

Because of God's great love for you and me, He sent His beloved and flawless Son, Jesus, to be the atonement for our sins (John 3:16). Jesus took on flesh and lived a perfect life. In doing so, He was worthy to die the perfect death, a death that would produce life. Does that sound like a foreign concept? It's not. Think about what happens to a kernel of wheat. It must be buried in order to produce many seeds, otherwise it will always remain a single seed (John 12:24). Likewise, the only Son of God died and was buried so that He could become the first of many sons and daughters (Romans 8:29). In Christ we have life. Not a temporary existence of flesh, but an eternal existence in the presence of God. Eternal Life is a gift from God to man. The only way to accept this gift, however, is to accept Jesus. If you have never asked for Christ to become your Savior, He is only a prayer away. And in the moment you receive Him into your heart, life springs forth in you.

You can have eternal life through Jesus Christ today!

August 10
GET UP

John 5:6 (ESV): *"When Jesus saw him lying there and knew that he had already been there for a long time, he said to him, 'Do you want to be healed?'"*

In Jerusalem there is a pool called Bethesda, which was believed to have healing powers. An angel would come and stir the waters, then the first person into the water would be healed from his infirmity. One day as Jesus passed by, He noticed a man who had made it his habit to be at this pool day in and day out for thirty-eight years! When Jesus saw the man and knew that he had been doing the same thing for so long with no result, He asked, "Do you want to be healed?" Now, one might think the man would immediately cry out, "YES! Can you help me?" But instead, he said with a resigned attitude, "I have no one to put me in the water" (John 5:7). Although the man was showing up, he had no real hope of getting up.

I have heard that the definition of insanity is doing the same thing over and over but expecting a different result. Jesus was about to put an end to this man's insanity by insisting that he do something different. Jesus said, "Get up" (John 5:8), and in his getting up, the man was healed (John 5:9).

How many of us are seeking answers to issues in our lives, but we are doing the same thing over and over trying to fix our problems? Maybe it is time to do something different. Do you want to be healed? Then don't lie there in your infirmity; get up! Get up the faith to trust Christ with your relationships, your job, your health, your finances, your addictions, your fears, your unforgiveness … whatever your circumstance or affliction. And in your getting up, trust God that your healing will come.

Jesus, the healer, is passing by today!

August 11
GOD IS MY HELP

Psalm 121:1-2 (ESV): *"I lift up my eyes to the hills. From where does my help come? My help comes from the Lord, who made heaven and earth."*

Church should not be a drudgery or an item we check off on our weekly "to do" list. Instead, we should look forward to worshipping in the House of God with eager expectation. It is the time that we can retreat from the busyness of the world and spend time in the presence of our Father. We bring our offerings of praise and thanksgiving to Him, and we are fed from His Word. The House of God is our refuge, where we are encouraged and fortified. We get filled up so we can return to a dark world and shine with the love of Christ. Do not neglect corporate worship with your fellow believers (Hebrews 10:25). Christ loves the church, and He wants us to love one another.

God is your help today!

August 12
GOD SMILES

Numbers 6:24-25 (ESV): *"The Lord bless you and keep you; the Lord make his face to shine upon you and be gracious to you;"*

Did you know that God smiles when He watches His children? It's true! Just like any parent who smiles when she looks out of the window and sees her child playing, laughing, and enjoying playmates, God smiles when He sees His children enjoying life and relationships that He has provided. God is a perfect Father. He does not withhold good from His children. Instead, He delights in us and beams over us. What a blessing to know that God is pleased with you and me, simply because when He looks at us, He sees Jesus (2 Corinthians 5:21).

Bask in the love of God today!

August 13
GOD'S DAY

Psalm 118:24 (ESV): *"This is the day the Lord has made; let us rejoice and be glad in it."*

The Book of Genesis gives the account of God's creation. After He made the heavens and the earth, the sun and the moon, the birds of the air, the beasts of the field, the fish in the sea, the man and the woman, He looked at His work and said, "It is good!" Creation did not stop at the Garden of Eden, though, every day the Master Creator is busy shaping and forming and bringing new things into being. Today is a new thing that God has made. Since everything that God makes is good, we can rightly conclude that this day is good. And, as children who benefit from their Father's work, we can rejoice and be glad for this day that He has made for us. Do not let frustrations steal your joy. Do not let fears rob your jubilation. Do not let unmet goals silence your song. None of these things change the fact that because of God, we can rejoice today!

Rejoice in the handiwork of God today!

August 14
GOD'S SUPPLY

Philippians 4:19 (ESV): *"And my God will supply every need of yours according to his riches in glory in Christ Jesus."*

Our Heavenly Father is the owner of all things (Psalm 50:10). There is nothing that He lacks or is in need of. We, on the other hand, are needy people! Fortunately for us, God is more than able to supply ALL of our needs. Notice the verse above, though, where it says that God supplies our needs through Christ Jesus. This is a very important principle for us to embrace. God never offers us something apart from Himself, because HE is what we need. Whether our needs are physical, relational, financial, emotional, mental, or spiritual, God offers Himself through Christ Jesus, and He is more than enough. When we are filled up with Christ, we lack no good thing. God reminds us that there is nothing that goes unnoticed by Him (Psalm 139:1-6). He does not want us to worry about our needs, because He is our provision (Matthew 6:25-34)!

Jesus will meet your needs today!

August 15
GOOD SENSE

Proverbs 16:22 (ESV): *"Good sense is a fountain of life to him who has it, but the instruction of fools is folly."*

Have you ever stopped to ask for directions, only to quickly realize the person you are asking is more clueless than you are?! It is foolish to take advice from someone who does not know what he or she is talking about. This is one reason why Christians should be very cautious of whom they seek advice from. To consult a nonbeliever about spiritual truths will always result in folly. On the other hand, we can seek wisdom from the Holy Spirit. God's Word says the Holy Spirit will guide us on paths of truth and never lead us astray (John 16:13). To take the sure way just makes good sense!

Have the good sense to follow Christ today!

August 16
GRACE

1 John 1:9 (ESV): *"If we confess our sins, he is faithful and just to forgive us our sins and to cleanse us from all unrighteousness."*

Your sin does not surprise God. Maybe that surprises you. But there has never been a time when you caught God off guard with your sins. He has never said, "Whoa, I didn't see that one coming. I'm not sure I can forgive this one right away. I just need to let it soak in for a few minutes." No, the truth is from the moment you were saved and God took responsibility for you as His child, He not only knew every sin that you had ever committed, but He was also completely aware of every sin that you would commit. This is why we have been given grace through Christ Jesus, our Savior (Romans 5:17) and our Advocate (1 John 2:1). It is this beautiful gift of grace that gives us confidence in God. Remember how we used to want to hide our sins? We were fearful that someone would see the "real us." Thanks to grace, instead of hiding, we can run right into the open arms of our God and cry, "Abba, Father!" In Christ our sins have been nailed to a cross, and the debt is cancelled forevermore (Colossians 2:14)! Jesus is our security and our righteousness.

The God of grace loves you today!

August 17
HIS JOY

John 15:11 (NIV): *"I have told you this so that my joy may be in you and that your joy may be complete."*

Joy is not an emotion but a state of being. It is not dependent on circumstances or on people; instead, it is a stand-alone condition that anchors the soul. The Bible calls the joy of the Lord our strength (Nehemiah 8:10). In fact, that is the source of Jesus' strength as He faced the Cross of Calvary (Hebrews 12:2). How incredible is it that Jesus imparts to you and me the ability to persevere through difficult situations with the exact same source of strength He used to endure His most difficult situation … joy! We do not have a High Priest who is unable to relate to our trials and heartaches (Hebrews 4:15). Christ knows each one of us personally and intimately. He knows the circumstance each of us is dealing with right now, and He offers us His joy. Jesus never offers you and me anything apart from Himself, because whatever the situation, HE is what we need.

Be filled with the joy of the Lord today!

August 18
HOT COALS

Romans 12:20 (NIV): *"On the contrary: "If your enemy is hungry, feed him; if he is thirsty, give him something to drink. In doing this, you will heap burning coals on his head."*

Have you ever found yourself ranting and raving spewing out your anger on another person, just to have them answer you back in a soft voice or with a kind smile? Nothing silences an angry outburst faster than a peaceful response. Likewise, the Bible teaches us that we are not to go around seeking our own vengeance. Instead, we trust that God will be our vindicator (Isaiah 54:17). We are to cooperate with the work of God by acting Christ-like in ALL that we do; including our responses to people who behave wrongly towards us. The result? Our attackers will begin to feel the heated pressure of conviction in their hearts and minds, as the Holy Spirit goes to work on them. Kindness burns away the dross of evil intention, and an encounter that someone meant for our harm can become something used for God's glory (Genesis 50:20).

Show the unmerited love of Christ to others today!

August 19
I AM SAYS I AM

John 1:12-13 (ESV): *"But to all who did receive him, who believed in his name, he gave the right to become children of God, who were born, not of blood nor of the will of the flesh nor of the will of man, but of God."*

Too many people who claim to have a personal relationship with Jesus Christ still struggle with an identity crisis. Guilt and shame from sins (past or present), performance-based thinking ("I try to be good enough for God"), and a low sense of self-worth ("I don't deserve any better than this") keep the children of God living like orphans, instead of the adored, royal heirs that we are. The Bible is clear that when we are in Christ, we are without blemish and free from accusation (Colossians 1:22). This transformation is not a work that you and I have accomplished in ourselves, but a work that Christ perfectly completed on the Cross of Calvary (Ephesians 2:9). The face in the mirror may try to remind you of who you were, but remember that what "I AM" says about you is true. And, I am who I AM says I am forevermore (2 Corinthians 5:17; Romans 8:1; 1 Peter 2:9)!

Trust what God says is true about you today!

August 20
I COULD BE WRONG...

Proverbs 17:10 (ESV): *"A rebuke goes deeper into a man of understanding than a hundred blows into a fool."*

We like to think that we are right. Our views, our opinions, our advice ... right, right, right. And most of us, if we are honest, do not like to be corrected. The truth is, though, there are many times when we are wrong. Pride can keep us from confessing those wrongs. Some of us have probably even sacrificed the health of a relationship just to defend our "wrong" position. This is not how love behaves. The Apostle Paul was inspired by the Holy Spirit to write a beautiful definition of love in 1 Corinthians 13:4-7. In this passage, he explains that love keeps no records of wrong; instead, it rejoices in the truth. Let us act lovingly toward others and be willing to admit and correct our errors. In doing so, we defeat our enemy and glorify our Father.

Trust the correction of the Lord today!

August 21
LIGHTEN UP

Proverbs 14:30 (ESV): *"A tranquil heart gives life to the flesh, but envy makes the bones rot."*

Wise King Solomon gives us a wonderful rule to live by in this Proverb. He is basically saying, "Lighten up!" Too often, we go through life with a heavy heart, because we are so focused on things that have no eternal value. Fears, anxieties, jealousies, and pride all weigh us down. If we are going to enjoy the abundant life that Christ promised was available to us (John 10:10), we have got to remember two VERY important things: 1) Don't sweat the small stuff; 2) From God's viewpoint, it's all small stuff!

Remember when you were a child. Do you recall how you use to look up to your father and think, "Wow, he's so big!" or "Dad is so strong!" He could throw you into the air and catch you. As you squealed with delight, you never even considered the fact that he might drop you. Well, we have a Heavenly Father who is so big and so strong. We need to place complete trust in the One who can still catch us, no matter what. Isaiah 41:10 gives us this assurance, "Fear not, for I am with you; be not dismayed for I am your God; I will strengthen you, I will help you, I will uphold you with my righteous right hand." Delight in your Father who loves you and cares for you, and you will experience a lighter heart and a merrier spirit.

Place your confidence in Father God today!

August 22
LIVE INTENTIONALLY

Luke 9:23 (ESV): *"And he said to all,*
'If anyone would come after me, let him deny himself
and take up his cross daily and follow me.'"

The Christian life is not passive; it is intentional. We cannot say a simple prayer and then sit back and complacently wait for Christ to return to take us to heaven. We cannot expect that not much about our lives will change now that we claim the name of Jesus Christ. As a matter of fact, just the opposite is true. It does not matter "how good" of a life we may have lead apart from Christ, our walk with Him will be dramatically different. The way we think, believe, and interact with others will be remarkably different from the non-Christian. Every day we get up and make a conscious choice to deny "me" and follow "Him." His ways are not my ways. His thoughts are not my thoughts. His choice to forgive is not my choice to forgive. His decision to be merciful is not my decision to be merciful. His will to love is not my will to love. Christ is looking for disciples who will intentionally live a life that is reflective of Him.

Live on purpose for Christ today!

August 23
MISSION IMPOSSIBLE

1 Samuel 1:10-11 (NIV): *"In her deep anguish Hannah prayed to the Lord, weeping bitterly. And she made a vow, saying, 'Lord Almighty, if you will only look on your servant's misery and remember me, and not forget your servant but give her a son, then I will give him to the Lord for all the days of his life, and no razor will ever be used on his head.'"*

The corruption of the children of Israel had spread into the temple of God. The priest Eli had set up a throne for himself while his sons, Phineas and Hophni, treated God's house like a no-tell motel. Evil was rampant, and this broke the heart of Hannah, a woman who truly loved God. Additionally, Hannah was barren. She longed for a child, and she longed order in the House of God. To her, the desires of her heart seemed impossible, and she wept before the Lord. Fortunately, with God NOTHING is impossible (Luke 1:37). God heard the prayers of His daughter and implemented a solution that no one ever saw coming! He gave Hannah the son she desired and used that very child to bring order to His House. Hannah gave birth to Samuel, and at the age of three, she took Samuel to the temple to serve God. When Samuel became an adult, he was the very prophet who anointed David, a man with a heart for God, to be King of Israel.

Wow! Talk about a Mighty God! What breaks your heart today? What desire seems impossible, but your deep longing for it moves you to tears? Why not do what Hannah did? Be transparent with God. Share with Him your heart. Trust God with the impossible, and watch as He beautifully fulfills His will for your life.

Place your faith in God today!

August 24
NOT TOO HOT...
NOT TOO COLD

Revelation 3:15-16 (NIV): *"I know your deeds,
that you are neither cold nor hot. I wish you were either one
or the other! So, because you are lukewarm—
neither hot nor cold—I am about to spit you out of my mouth."*

Lukewarm water...what is it good for? Bathing? Nope, not hot enough. Swimming? No thanks. Drinking? Yuck! Likewise, God says that living a lukewarm life for Him is pretty much good for nothing. Yet, that is the "safe option" that many Christians choose. They do not want to be seen as over-the-top or fanatical about Christ, yet they also do not want to miss out on the blessings that come from claiming Him. So, they find a safe spot right on the fence where they can blend in with the crowds and go through life without causing much of a stir one way or another. To these individuals, God simply says, "You make my stomach churn!" Stand for something! Do not be complacent in this walk for your Lord. He is not hesitant to come to our defense and fight our war against sin (Exodus 14:14). He is not slack in His love or His forgiveness towards us (2 Peter 3:8-9). And God does not keep silent about who belongs to Him (Luke 15:7). God wants children who are not ashamed of Him. If your love for Christ has grown cold, allow the Holy Spirit to reignite a fire in you. Spend time in prayer and with His Word today. Fall in love all over again with the One who loves you to death (John 3:16)!

Let your light for God burn brightly today!

August 25
OBEDIENT CHILDREN

Ephesians 6:1 (ESV): *"Children, obey your parents in the Lord, for this is right."*

As a child, this is one of the very first Scriptures that my parents taught me. It was a good reminder that God expected me to listen and obey my mom and dad. These were the people that He chose to rule over me, to teach me, and to guide me. As long as I was in their care, I should do what they said, as long as it did not conflict with what was pleasing to the Lord.

This verse, however, is not limited to small children being obedient to earthly parents. It is also an admonition that, we, the children of God—no matter how old we are— should obey our Heavenly Father. He knows what is best for us. He wants to teach us and guide us. He also wants to bless us. God, however, will not bless our disobedience, because He will never reinforce our wrong behavior with His rewards. Remember, God's ways are not our ways, but His ways are always right! We can show God we trust Him by obeying Him.

Obey Father God today!

August 26

PERFECT UNITY

John 14:20 (ESV): *"In that day you will know that I am in my Father, and you in me, and I in you."*

God is a God of unity. Part of His plan for redeeming mankind includes our being unified with Him. How is that possible? It is through the power of the Holy Spirit. God places His very own Spirit inside of you and me when we come to a saving knowledge of Jesus Christ. In that moment, we are connected to the Father and the Son through the Spirit. This is how we can have the mind of Christ (1 Corinthians 2:16), the love of the Father (1 John 2:15), and the power of the Holy Spirit (Acts 1:8). We are meant to be in a perfect relationship with God. Thankfully, He is the One who acts on our behalf to make this impossible task possible (mark 10:27)!

Believe in Christ today!

August 27
POSITIVE INFLUENCE

Proverbs 14:1 (NIV): *"The wise woman builds her house, but with her own hands the foolish one tears hers down."*

We are always influencing others, whether for good or for bad. This is true even when we are not intentionally trying to persuade others. People are watching our lives. They see the way we react in times of stress or sorrow. They listen to the words we use in moments of anger or disappointment. They notice the places we go and the people we associate with. The way we live our lives is always molding someone else. You might ask, "Well, is that really my problem?" The emphatic answer is YES. God holds His children accountable for our words and our actions (Luke 12:48; Matthew 12:36). We are working to build the Kingdom of God. If we are careless, however, we can cause others to stumble or even doubt a loving God. The result? We foolishly tear down instead of building up. We need to create the habit of praying Psalm 19:14: "Let the words of my mouth and the meditation of my heart be acceptable in your sight, O LORD, my rock and my redeemer." Let's intentionally live our lives to positively influence others for Christ!

Let your life point someone to Christ today!

August 28

RECIPE FOR LESS STRESS

Philippians 4:6 (ESV): *"do not be anxious about anything,*
but in everything by prayer and supplication with thanksgiving
let your requests be made known to God.
And the peace of God, which surpasses all understanding,
will guard your hearts and your minds in Christ Jesus."

Worried? Anxious? Feeling uneasy? Then give God praise! When troubles try to present themselves to be bigger than God, it only makes sense to remind ourselves of how BIG our God really is. It is hard to stay upset and anxious when we shift our thinking from the size of our problems to the size of our God. The recipe for less stress is simple. It only has two ingredients … a God-focused mind and a heart full of praise! Hills of fear melt like wax in the presence of our Lord (Psalm 97:5).

Surrender your worries to Christ today!

August 29
SEAT OF HONOR

Psalm 23:5 (ESV): *"You prepare a table before me in the presence of my enemies; you anoint my head with oil; my cup overflows."*

Large family dinners all tend to have one thing in common…a lack of seats at the big table. It is inevitable that someone will be booted to the kiddie table. Typically, it is the "adult" that all of the other adults still view as wet behind the ears! Sometimes people will make you feel disrespected, small, or insignificant. This is not always intentional. Maybe they don't share your vision; instead, they see you as a "dreamer." Maybe they don't understand your calling; instead, they think you've passed up a great opportunity to settle for pastoring that little church or working for a mission. Maybe they just don't relate to your love relationship with Christ; instead, they see you as a bit fanatical and over the top. The negative remarks or lack of support can sometimes feel like an attack against what you want to do for Christ. Remember this, you are not looking for man's approval or his applause. Instead, dream your dreams; fulfill your calling; love your God…and one day, your God will give you a seat of honor at the big table with Him!

Christ wants to bless you today!

August 30
SPRING CLEANING

Psalm 139:23-24 (ESV): *"Search me, oh God, and know my heart!
Try me and know my thoughts! And, see if there be
any grievous way in me, and lead me in the way everlasting!"*

How many of us clean our houses every day? I mean really clean—vacuum, scrub bathrooms and dust boards, wash windows and blinds ... probably not many of us! Most of us straighten up and pick up so that our homes have the appearance of being clean. Then, one day your child brings you a fuzzy M&M and asks if it's okay to eat it. To your horror, you learn he found it in the couch! That's it ... It's time to do some serious spring cleaning. So, we get out the vacuum, pull the cushions off the couch, and discover all the clutter and dust bunnies that were allowed to collect and grow. All the while, we thought our houses were okay and looking pretty good.

This is the same thing that happens in our spiritual houses. We get caught up in the busyness of our lives. We work long hours. Our children have homework and extracurricular activities. We go to bed late and get up early. Little by little, we miss a day of devotions here and our quiet time with God there. Before we know it, we've got cobwebs and dust bunnies growing inside of us that we are completely unaware of. The Psalmist David said, "Search me oh God, and know my heart!" What a brave prayer! We should all follow his example, and invite God to do a little spring-cleaning in our hearts!

God wants to spend time with you today!

August 31
TAKE A STAND

Joshua 24:15 (NIV): *"But if serving the Lord seems undesirable to you, then choose for yourselves this day whom you will serve, whether the gods your ancestors served beyond the Euphrates, or the gods of the Amorites, in whose land you are living. But as for me and my household, we will serve the Lord."*

We live in a society that frowns on people who take a stand for values that go against the norm of the day. It is easier to keep our values and beliefs to ourselves than to go against the grain. Jesus calls for His followers to be bold and courageous, knowing that He is always with us when we stand for His truth (Joshua 1:9). The enemy wants us to quake in our boots every time he says, "Boo!" or anytime we have to pick a definitive side of right or wrong. Do not be afraid! The Lord is our strength and our courage. In Him we are safe. We honor Him by taking a stand for Him. God says that He has called us to be lights on a hill so that a dark world can see Him in us. Do not hide your light; and do not be intimidated by a defeated foe. Stand tall for Christ. He is worthy of our allegiance.

Choose to serve Jesus today!

[fire yourself]

SEPTEMBER

September 1
THE HOUSE OF GOD

Psalm 122:1 (ESV): *"I was glad when they said to me, 'Let us go to the house of the Lord.'"*

Church should not be a drudgery or an item we check off on our weekly "to do" list. Instead, we should look forward to worshipping in the House of God with eager expectation. It is the time that we can retreat from the busyness of the world, and spend time in the presence of our Father. We bring our offerings of praise and thanksgiving to Him, and we are fed from His Word. The House of God is our refuge where we are encouraged and fortified. We get filled up, so we can return to a dark world and shine with the love of Christ. Do not neglect corporate worship with your fellow believers (Hebrews 10:25). Christ loves the Church and He wants us to love one another.

Make a commitment to get involved with a church body today!

September 2
THE PATH OF GOD

Psalm 119:35 (ESV): *"Lead me in the path of your commandments, for I delight in it."*

The path of God is wise, purposeful, and victorious. His commandments are sure, steadfast, and right. When we fall in love with Jesus Christ, His ways are not burdensome to us. In fact, we delight in following the voice of our Savior. For it is in doing things according to His will that we find perfect satisfaction and genuine delight in this life. We were created for God (Ephesians 2:10). Apart from Him, this life will never make sense.

Follow the path of God today!

September 3

THE STRONG ARM OF GOD

Isaiah 52:10 (ESV): *"The Lord has bared his holy arm before the eyes of all the nations, and all the ends of the earth shall see the salvation of our God."*

Our God is a mighty God. There is no fear in Him. Who can possibly compare? What could ever hope to stand against Him? When troubles come our way, we need to run to God, our strong tower and deliverer (Psalm 18:2). He will fight for us (Exodus 14:14). When God rolls up His sleeve and flexes His muscle, our enemies will flee! We waste precious time and energy trying to tackle battles on our own. Instead, we need to learn to call out to our Father and trust Him for our salvation.

Trust in the strength of God today!

September 4
THE WAY

John 14:6 (ESV): *"Jesus said to him, "I am the way, and the truth, and the life. No one comes to the Father except through me."*

Some have said that Christians who believe that there is only one way to access God are narrow-minded. Well, I have to agree. However, this is a "family trait," because our Father is narrow-minded as well. He is the One who decided that the only way mankind could come to Him would be through the righteousness of His perfect Son, Jesus Christ. He is the One who said that the broad way is the path that many will choose to follow, but it leads to destruction (Matthew 7:13). Too many people want to approach God on their terms. Sadly, pride will be their downfall. If we are to approach a holy God, we will do it humbly, and we will do it His way … the only way, through Jesus Christ.

Jesus is the way today!

September 5
TRIUMPHANT PROCESSION

2 Corinthians 2:14 (ESV): *"But thanks be to God, who in Christ always leads us in triumphal procession, and through us spreads the fragrance of the knowledge of him everywhere."*

In the Bible days, the victor of a war would often lead his prisoners of war in a parade of sorts through the streets of the town. The captives were now under the servitude of the victor. Christ is the champion in our battle against God. What? We were in a fight against God? Yes! The Bible says that before we came to Christ, we were the enemies of God (Romans 5:10). Thankfully, He is victorious over our battle with sin. He has won our hearts and our loyalty. Now, He leads us in triumphal procession, and we pledge our service to Him. As others watch our lives and see what kind of master Christ is, it is like an inviting fragrance that fills the environment around us. Others come to know the sweetness of our Lord by the way we follow Him.

Serve the Lord with gladness today!

September 6
WHAT'S IN A NAME?

Romans 1:7 (ESV): *"To all those in Rome who are loved by God and called to be saints. Grace to you and peace from God our Father and the Lord Jesus Christ."*

Names are important to us. Ask any parent, and they all have a story of how they finally chose "the" name for their child or children. It is not a decision to be made lightly, because this name will be with a person as part of his or her identity always. In the Bible, names had particular significance. Often, a name would reveal the person's character or be a foreshadowing of a particular calling. This was the case in the life of Jacob. The second born twin, Jacob was always on the lookout for ways to promote himself. He schemed and manipulated most of his early life to get the things that he felt he deserved. One night he had an encounter with God, and it changed his life forever (Genesis 32:22-32). To acknowledge the new man, God changed Jacob's name, which meant "leg-puller," to Israel, which meant "persevered with God" (Genesis 32:28). Never again would this man be identified as a schemer, but now and forevermore, he will be known as one who walks with God … pretty cool!

What is so encouraging about this story is that this is exactly what God does for those of us who have an encounter with Him and accept His gift of salvation! God changes our name and our identity. Once we were called enemy (Romans 5:10); now we are called friend (John 15:15). Once we were called orphan (Colossians 1:21); now we are called child (John 1:12). Once we were called sinner (Romans 3:23); now we are called saint (Romans 1:7). Embrace your new name. It is the identity that Christ declares about you to be true!

Accept who God says you are today!

September 7
WHO CAN COMPARE?

Job 38:4 (ESV): *"Where were you when I laid the foundation of the earth? Tell me if you have understanding."*

Genesis 1:1 teaches us that "In the beginning, GOD…." He was the only One there at the time of creation, so He is the only valid witness to creation. Mankind makes frail attempts to disprove God. He tries to logically conclude how all things came to be apart from a Divine Creator. Ideas such as a random explosion happened, and the world and all of its inhabitants just evolved magically over time. This is the equivalent of telling a watch maker he is unnecessary, because we can put some springs and cogs in a bag, shake it up, and a watch will just pop out. Sounds ridiculous, doesn't it? Yet, somehow our intellects want to say this is what happened with creation. The truth is no one or nothing can compare to God. Out of His mind and mouth came the world. From His hands He sculpted mankind. By His breath, life was given. It is by His power that all that is … is! We like to imagine ourselves as independent and self-sufficient. But without God, we cease to exist. He is the author and sustainer of all life. You are not a random happenstance; you are an intentional design from the beautiful mind of God. And, He has a plan for you!

God is your truth today!

September 8
WINNER!

Romans 8:37 (ESV): *"No, in all these things we are more than conquerors through him who loved us."*

We win! Because of Christ, no matter what our plight, no matter what our fight, we win! When Jesus Christ died on the cross, was buried, and resurrected Himself, He became the victor over death, disease, the curse of sin, and the gates of hell. There are no foes left for Him to conquer. When we are in Christ, we inherit His position of champion! No foe can overcome us; no devil can defeat us. This life is filled with small battles that sometimes cause us to fear. But we need to remind ourselves of the eternal truth of who we are – "More than conquerors through him who loved us."

We are victorious in Christ today!

September 9
A COMPASSIONATE FATHER

Luke 15:20 (NIV): *"So he got up and went to his father. But while he was still a long way off, his father saw him and was filled with compassion for him; he ran to his son, threw his arms around him and kissed him."*

It is hard to describe the love a parent feels for his child, even during times when the child is pulling away from the parent's love. How happy it makes a father's heart, though, when a wayward son or daughter returns home. The strongest human affection is but a fraction of how God feels for us. His love for us is immense, even when we are away from His care. He patiently pursues us and draws us back to Himself. When we come to our senses and return to Him, Father God is waiting with open arms. His compassionate heart overflows with joy that a child has come home.

God's mercies are new today!

September 10
A FATHER'S INFLUENCE

Ephesians 6:4 (ESV): *"Fathers, do not provoke your children to anger, but bring them up in the discipline and instruction of the Lord."*

Anger…When inflamed and out of control, this emotion will kill off any other tender emotions. It hardens the heart and starves the soul. It is miserable and empty, and it seeks to make others feel the same. Paul gave a warning early on in the Book of Ephesians (4:31) for people to deal with the bitterness hidden in their hearts. Paul knew, especially with fathers, that undefeated anger would be transmitted to their children. Excessive yelling, short attention spans, harsh discipline, sarcasm, and lack of interest are all behaviors that are bred in a bitter heart and provoke a child's heart to become bitter as well. A father has such a powerful influence over his children. How then can he use this influence for good and not for harm? The answer is found in Christ. He must learn to forgive as Christ forgave; he must learn to love as Christ loves. In doing so, not only will his heart be freed from its angry prison, but he also will guard his children from entering through those same prison doors.

Dad, teach your children about Christ today!

September 11
ACCESS TO THE FATHER

Ephesians 3:12 (NLT): *"Because of Christ and our faith in him, we can now come boldly and confidently into God's presence."*

In the Old Testament, only the priests were allowed to go into the Holy of Holies where the presence of God abided. They approached His alter with ceremonial reverence to offer the sacrifice for the sins of the people. The experience was fearful at best. Thanks to Jesus, however, we no longer have to go through a ceremonial process to get to God. We no longer need a priest to go to God on our behalf. Thanks to the finished work of Jesus on the Cross of Calvary, we can now enter into the presence of God freely and without trepidation. He is our Father and He welcomes us into His holy presence.

Come to God today!

September 12
ADOPTED

Ephesians 1:5 (NLT): *"God decided in advance to adopt us into his own family by bringing us to himself through Jesus Christ. This is what he wanted to do, and it gave him great pleasure."*

You might want to reread the verse above…slowly. Did you get that? You were chosen by God. He decided that He wanted you to be a part of His family. In fact, it gave God great pleasure to bring you to Himself, write His name on your heart, and call you "child." People may overlook you, or mistreat you, or forsake you. But God chooses you, loves you, and keeps you eternally.

God calls you "child" today!

September 13
ALIVE FOREVERMORE!

Romans 6:9 (ESV): *"We know that Christ,
being raised from the dead, will never die again;
death no longer has dominion over him."*

When Jesus resurrected Himself from the dead, He became the Victor over sin, sickness, and death. There is no foe that He has not defeated. Jesus Christ reigns supreme! When we are in Christ, we too are victorious over the curse of sin. Temptations may pester us, but they can no longer master us. There is no longer fear in sickness, because it is a temporary state, or in death, because it has lost its grip. Thanks to Jesus Christ, we will live forevermore!

You can have eternal life in Christ Jesus today!

September 14
AT THE BOTTOM OF THE SEA

Micah 7:19 (ESV): *"He will again have compassion on us;*
he will tread our iniquities underfoot.
You will cast all our sins into the depths of the sea."

Have you asked Jesus Christ to come into your heart? If so, then your sins have been forgiven. Not only have they been forgiven, they have been cast into the depths of the sea never to be remembered. God intentionally chooses not to focus on the old man and the old ways (Isaiah 43:25). Instead, He is perfectly satisfied with the new man who is now clothed in the righteousness of Jesus Christ (Romans 5:1). So, the next time the enemy tries to accuse you of past sins, tell him to go jump in the sea!

God will forgive your sins today!

September 15
AUDIENCE OF ONE

1 Thessalonians 2:4 (NIV): *"On the contrary, we speak as those approved by God to be entrusted with the gospel. We are not trying to please people but God, who tests our hearts."*

Too often we try to please people. We want others to like us and accept us, so we will go out of our way to win their favor. Perhaps we just seek to avoid confrontation at all cost, so we compromise or conform in order to keep someone else satisfied. Christ wants to free us from slavery to man's opinions. The only approval that truly benefits us comes from God. So, how do we get God's approval? We accept Jesus Christ as our Savior. When we are in Christ, we are clothed in His righteousness, and God is perfectly pleased with Jesus. We don't have to work hard to be really, really good. We don't have to go faster, be smarter, look prettier, or weigh less; we just need to be in Christ. That, Beloved, is the truth, and it will set you free from the trap of people pleasing (John 8:32)!

Live for an audience of One today!

September 16
BALANCING LOVE & JUSTICE

John 3:36 (ESV): *"Whoever believes in the Son has eternal life; whoever does not obey the Son shall not see life, but the wrath of God remains on him."*

It is easy to have an unbalanced perspective of God. Some people see Him as a strict disciplinarian. They imagine God with a ruler that He is constantly holding up to us, and we are always falling short. Therefore, we must try harder, work longer, and do more to win God's approval. Then, there are those who only see God as softhearted and eager to dole out His love on whomever will allow Him. We are free to live any way we want, because God will always forgive us no matter what. Both of these views are out of balance. The Bible teaches us that God is a righteous judge (Psalm 7:11), as well as a God of love (1 John 4:8). It is in understanding His holiness and His judgment of sin that we can fully appreciate and embrace the love and mercy He extends to mankind. There will come a day when God will judge all sin that has not been covered by the blood of Jesus. In the meantime, because of God's great love, we can receive forgiveness of sins and be justified forevermore (Romans 5:1). We do not have to do better or work harder to earn God's approval, because when we are in Christ, God accepts us completely (Colossians 1:19-22)!

Abide in Christ today!

September 17
BORN AGAIN

John 3:5-6 (NIV): *"Jesus answered, "Very truly I tell you, no one can enter the kingdom of God unless they are born of water and the Spirit. Flesh gives birth to flesh, but the Spirit gives birth to spirit."*

Nicodemus came to Jesus with a genuine question. He wanted to know what he must do to inherit eternal life. Nicodemus was a Pharisee who was respected, intelligent, and knowledgeable about the Law. He had lived an upstanding, moral life and was obedient to all of the religious doctrines. Jesus informed him that although living morally is right, that in itself is not the answer. The only way to receive eternal life is to be born of the Spirit. Good behavior may make you and me nice people to be around, but God is looking for holy people. This can only happen through the work of the Holy Spirit moving into the soul of a person and remaking our nature, radically changing our hearts and minds (2 Corinthians 5:17). Performing well for God does not replace a relationship with God. We will never be good enough in our own works, but we are ALWAYS good enough through the finished work of Christ. Invite Jesus into your heart and be born again!

Call on Jesus today!

September 18

BRIDGE OVER TROUBLED WATERS

Matthew 14:28-29 (NIV): *"Lord, if it's you,' Peter replied, 'tell me to come to you on the water.' 'Come,' he said. Then Peter got down out of the boat, walked on the water and came toward Jesus."*

The disciples were in their fishing boat, out in the middle of the sea on that stormy night. The winds were fierce, the waves were angry, and the men were tired. They did all that they could to keep their boat from going under, but fear for their lives had overtaken them. Their circumstances screamed, "Give up! You've lost! It's hopeless now!" Then, through the blackness of night, a light hovered above the waters. At first, the men thought it was a ghost! But then they heard that familiar, calming voice of Christ. Peter called out, "Lord, if it's you, tell me to come." Jesus said, "Come to me." With eyes steadfast on Jesus, Peter did the impossible. He stepped out of the boat and onto the troubled waters. The circumstances had not changed. The storm was still raging, but Peter's focus had changed. Instead of listening and looking to the physical, he was listening and looking to the spiritual. Jesus had become the bridge over his circumstances.

Is your mind troubled? Does fear fill your heart? Then do what Peter did … change your focus. Stop listening and looking to the natural, and focus on the supernatural. God is not limited by the laws of nature, and He is not afraid of your circumstances. Christ will show up when you cry out, and He will be the bridge over your troubled waters. Your circumstances may not change immediately, but your outlook will. We are never alone. NEVER look away from Christ. Fix your gaze upon Him, and He will lead you safely home.

Focus on Christ instead of your circumstances today!

September 19

CALL IT FOR WHAT IT IS

Matthew 16:23 (ESV): *"But he turned and said to Peter, 'Get behind me, Satan! You are a hindrance to me. For you are not setting your mind on the things of God, but on the things of man.'"*

Jesus came to the earth for one reason and one reason only ... to die for the sins of mankind. For three years, Peter walked with Jesus and ministered side by side with Him. Christ shared with Peter and the other disciples that He was the promised Messiah, and He was the way back into the presence of the Father. But Peter still did not fully understand the mission of the Savior. One day Jesus began to unfold the details concerning His death and resurrection to the disciples, and Peter ran to Jesus's side and told Him that he would never allow such terrible things to happen. Peter, in his pride or naivety, was prepared to defend his friend; he was going to save Jesus.

Peter did not realize how the enemy was trying to use him to discourage Jesus from fulfilling God's plan of salvation. Christ, on the other hand, saw through the devil's scheme, and called him out on it. Notice, in the verse above, Jesus does not fuss at or attack Peter. Instead, He calls the situation for what it is – a scheme of the enemy. What grace Christ showed to Peter! Shouldn't we do likewise for the ones that we love? If you are married, you and your spouse are on the same side. The enemy may try to discourage you through an unaware mate, but call it for what it is ... a hindrance from satan. When our spouse hurts our feelings or offends us, instead of turning on that person, shouldn't we turn on the real culprit – satan? We need to remember who is for us and who is against us. Don't fight against your spouse, instead fight with him or her against your common enemy. A house divided against itself cannot stand (Mark 3:25), but there is strength in unity (Ecclesiastes 4:12)!

Look at your circumstances through the eyes of Christ today!

September 20

COURAGE

Joshua 1:7 (ESV): *"Only be strong and very courageous, being careful to do according to all the law that Moses my servant commanded you. Do not turn from it to the right hand or to the left, that you may have good success wherever you go."*

Fear can paralyze us. It can keep us from experiencing the fullness of life that Christ intended for us. This is why God encourages us to be strong and courageous. We can move ahead trusting that God goes before us (Deuteronomy 31:8), and He guards us from behind (Isaiah 52:12). Fear is just an illusion from the enemy of our soul that tries to present itself as more powerful than God. We need to remember, though, that there is nothing that will come against us that is too mighty for our God. In His presence all darkness must flee. What, then, is there for us to fear? In Christ, we are more than conquerors (Romans 8:37)!

God can give you a courageous heart today!

September 21
DO YOU LOVE ME?

John 21:16 (NIV): *"Again Jesus said, 'Simon son of John, do you love me?' He answered, 'Yes, Lord, you know that I love you.' Jesus said, 'Take care of my sheep.'"*

When we consider all that Christ has done for us, our hearts should be eager to serve Him. Genuine gratitude should motivate us to ask the question, "What can I do for you, Lord?" While we cannot do anything to earn Christ's love or His gift of salvation, we can demonstrate our love and gratitude for Him by "feeding His sheep." We should actively tell others the good news of the Gospel. People need to know that there is a Savior who loves them and wants to reconcile them back into the family of God. We are the Body of Christ, and He wants to love others through us. If we love Him, we will love others (Matthew 22:36-40).

Allow Christ to love others through you today!

September 22
FACT OR FRAUD?

Luke 12:34 (NLT): *"Wherever your treasure is, there the desires of your heart will also be."*

Bling, shiny things, fast cars, fast food, Powerball lottery, smart electronics, reality television, Gangnam-Style dancing, diet fads, and "if it feels good, do it" attitudes ... welcome to the culture of the 21st century! There are so many distractions in this world. Things that cry out for our attention and want to steal away our hearts from God and family. The devil cleverly disguises himself behind the pleasures of this world and methodically lures us to himself. This is why the Apostle Peter warns us to be sober-minded and alert (1 Peter 5:8). He says, "Pay attention!" The enemy of your soul is an expert at presenting himself as something good, but he is a fraud (John 8:44).

The fact is we need to be careful what we give our attention to, because the heart will quickly follow. Jesus said that we will know with whom our allegiance really lies by the things that we fill our days with. So, how do we break free from the culture trap? We break free by giving our time and attention to Christ. Spend time with Him. Read His Word. Meditate on His goodness. Devote yourself to things that truly matter, like your spouse, children, parents, and loved ones. Fill your heart with the things of God, and there won't be room for the trappings of this world!

Believe the fact that God is for you today!

September 23
FORMER THINGS

1 Corinthians 6:11 (NLT): *"Some of you were once like that. But you were cleansed; you were made holy; you were made right with God by calling on the name of the Lord Jesus Christ and by the Spirit of our God."*

"I used to…." Beginning a statement with this phrase indicates that at one time you participated in something, but you do not anymore. This is the idea behind the talk Paul is giving to the church in Corinth. There is some confusion about who they are now. Even though they have accepted Christ as their Savior, many of them are still behaving and thinking like the old man enslaved to sin. Paul wants to remind them of their new identity in Christ and encourage them to walk out what God already says is true about them.

We need this same reminder today. How often do we look in the mirror and see that same old face? You know the one … the screw up, the "whoops, I did it again" face, the one with all of the baggage. And because we see that face, we think we are still that person. God, however, sees us much differently. He sees the former person as crucified with Christ (Galatians 2:20); and a totally new person has been resurrected to life (2 Corinthians 5:17). This person is holy, blameless, and righteous because of Christ. Now, we just need to accept the fact that we are in the process of becoming who God already says we are forever in Him (Hebrews 10:14)!

Live by what God says is true about you today!

September 24
GENUINE REPENTANCE

Luke 5:32 (NIV): *"I have not come to call the righteous, but sinners to repentance."*

My dad was a soldier in the United States Marine Corps in his younger days. Later in life, he became a minister. I remember him explaining the word "repent" to me by using the illustration of a marching platoon. He said that when a unit of soldiers would march in one direction, the drill sergeant would give a one-word command, and the entire company of soldiers would immediately turn and march in the opposite direction. The word? Repent! Too often, we mistake the word repent to simply mean "I'm sorry." But the word really means to turn and go in another direction. When we repent of our sins, we turn away from them. While we were in sin, we were walking away from Christ. When we repent, we turn and walk towards Him. It is good to be sorry for wrongdoing, but it is better to repent!

Walk towards the LORD today!

September 25
GOD HATES SIN

Nahum 1:2 (NIV): *"The LORD is a jealous and avenging God; the LORD takes vengeance and is filled with wrath. The LORD takes vengeance on his foes and vents his wrath against his enemies."*

God hates sin! There is no way to soften or sugarcoat this fact. He is long-suffering with sinners, but He is filled with wrath against sin. Why does He feel so strongly? Simple. It is because of sin that there is a gap between God and mankind. It is because of sin that there is pain, suffering, sickness, and death. It is because of sin that many people will remain separated from the love of God for all of eternity… God hates that! But God loves you, and He loves me. It is because of His great love for mankind that He has given His beloved Son Jesus to be our redemption (John 3:16). In Christ, we are adopted into the family of God, and we become the beneficiaries of His eternal life.

God loves you today!

September 26
GOD WILL PROVIDE

Genesis 22:13 (ESV): *"And Abraham lifted up his eyes
and looked, and behold, behind him was a ram, caught in a thicket
by his horns. And Abraham went and took the ram
and offered it up as a burnt offering instead of his son."*

There was a time in the life of Abraham when God tested his love. God wanted to see if Abraham trusted Him with everything in his life. God told Abraham to give back the son that God had given to him. Once you get passed the shock of God's request, hold on to your seat because Abraham's response will really knock you over! Genesis 22:3, 5 -says, "So Abraham rose early in the morning, saddled his donkey, and took two of his young men with him and his son Isaac. And he cut the wood for the burnt offering and arose and went to the place of which God had told him…Then Abraham said to his young men, 'Stay here with the donkey; I and the boy will go over there and worship and come again to you.'" WHAT??!! Don't miss this—Abraham did not question God; Abraham did not delay in fulfilling God's command; Abraham did not even look at his obedience as a sacrifice. Abraham considered the opportunity to give his most prized possession to God an act of worship! He also believed that God would give back to him anything that he gave to God (notice, he said we will worship and come again to you). Amazing!

Do not withhold anything from God. You can trust Him with every part of your heart and life. God will never ask you to give Him more than He will give back to you. As a matter of fact, all that we have is from His hand. He is our provider. God will give us courage when He calls us to act courageously. God will provide us with finances when He asks us to give abundantly. God will fill us with love when He calls us to love unconditionally. And, God will establish our faith when He calls us to trust Him.

God can meet your needs today!

September 27
GOD WITH US

Matthew 1:22-23 (ESV): *"All this took place to fulfill what the Lord had spoken by the prophet: 'Behold, the virgin shall conceive and bear a son, and they shall call his name Immanuel' (which means, God with us)."*

God created mankind, because He wanted to be in a relationship with us (1 Corinthians 1:9). He did not create us then distance Himself to watch us randomly perform on the stage of life. Instead, the gap that formed between God and man came as a result of mankind's decision to disobey. Even in our disobedience, though, God desired fellowship with us. So, He made a way to reconcile our un-holiness with His holiness. How? Through Immanuel (John 3:16), God created us (Genesis 1:27); He came to us (Matthew 1:23); He redeemed us (Colossians 2:14); and God has always been and forever will be with us (Deuteronomy 31:6).

God is with you today!

September 28
HAVE FAITH IN GOD

Mark 11:22 (ESV): *"And Jesus answered them,
'Have faith in God.'"*

People often pray for faith, this ability to believe in the unseen. The truth is, though, that we each have a measure of this ability already in us. When I walk into a dark room, I do not see light. I have faith, however, that when I turn on the light switch, light will appear. I do not always understand the physics behind gravity, but I trust when I jump into the air that I will come down again. The ability to believe is in us. The question is where do we choose to place that faith? In what or in whom will I believe? If I place my faith in money, it will soon be spent. If I place my faith in self, I may fail. If I place my faith in people, they may let me down. If I place my faith in God, He will not falter or fail. God is an all-powerful, all-knowing, all-loving, and ever-present God. He is the only place where we can deposit our faith and get a secure and abundant return!

Have faith in God today!

September 29
HOMESICK

Hebrews 13:14 (NLT): *"For this world is not our permanent home; we are looking forward to a home yet to come."*

My son is a freshman in college. After an especially rough week on campus, he came home for a weekend visit. The look of joy on his face when he walked through the door is hard to put into words. The first thing he did was hug his father and me. He was home!

Just imagine … one day we will walk through the gates of Heaven. The joy we feel will seem inexpressible. The first thing we will do is embrace our Father. We will finally be home!

Meditate on the joys of Heaven today!

September 30
I'M STILL STANDING

Hebrews 11:7 (NIV): *"By faith Noah, when warned about things not yet seen, in holy fear built an ark to save his family. By his faith he condemned the world and became heir of the righteousness that is in keeping with faith."*

In the days of Noah, people were wicked and godlessness was rampant. In a world gone wild, Noah still chose to walk with God. He led his family in the ways of the Lord, and God was pleased with him. One day the Lord told Noah to build a great ark, because He was going to flood the earth. He gave Noah specific instructions to follow, and Noah did. For many years, Noah obediently worked on a boat with no body of water in sight. For years Noah warned his neighbors about the rains to come when no one had ever seen rain before. The people watched Noah and his family and thought they were the ones who needed help. The day came for Noah and his family to enter the ark. God closed the door, and rained down His righteous judgment over the earth. The only people left standing were Noah and his family.

Sometimes it feels like the whole world is against us, and all we are trying to do is live a life that is pleasing to the Lord. Know this; you are not alone. People may try to discourage you, hurt you, or tear you down, but be of good courage! When you take a stand for God, He will stand with you!

God will stand with you today!

[fire yourself]
OCTOBER

October 1
IF ME...THEN ANYONE!

1 Timothy 1:16 (NIV): *"But for that very reason I was shown mercy so that in me, the worst of sinners, Christ Jesus might display his immense patience as an example for those who would believe in him and receive eternal life."*

Long before Paul became an Apostle of Jesus Christ, He was Saul, the Christian's worst nightmare. He dedicated his life to torturing followers of Jesus. Even while he was committing evil acts, God was patient with him. God had a plan for Saul's life, and in love, He pursued this sinner. As a result of God's patience, Saul repented of his sins and became the Apostle Paul, a disciple of Jesus Christ ... Amazing! Now, Paul wants you and me to know that God showed mercy on him and was patient with him to serve as an example. If God can forgive and love him, as evil as he was, God will love and forgive each one of us. When we stop and think of God's great patience with us, like Paul, we too can share the good news with others, "If me...then anyone!"

It is true ... God loves you today!

October 2
IMAGO DEI

*Colossians 3:9-10 (NIV): "Do not lie to each other,
since you have taken off your old self with its practices
and have put on the new self, which is being renewed
in knowledge in the image of its Creator."*

Salvation is not merely a one-time prayer that we say to relieve our consciences or spare ourselves from punishment. Instead, it is a progressive act of change – taking off the old self, with its thoughts, actions, and attitudes, and putting on the new self, with the thoughts, actions, and attitudes of Christ. Galatians 2:20 teaches us that the old man is crucified when we ask Christ to be our Lord. The Holy Spirit moves in, and He begins to clean up the carnage that the old man left behind. He gradually replaces the old with the new. Day by day, we are patiently being restored to the image of our Father, becoming exact imprints of His likeness (Ephesians 4:24). The persevering work of the Spirit produces godly children – not by our works of trying really hard to be really good, but as a natural outgrowth of the Spirit being cultivated in our hearts and minds (Ephesians 2:9).

Trust the work of God in your life today!

October 3
JEALOUSY

Genesis 30:1 (ESV): *"When Rachel saw that she bore Jacob no children, she envied her sister. She said to Jacob, 'Give me children, or I shall die!'"*

When Jacob first laid eyes on Rachel, he fell head over heels in love with this woman. He pledged to work seven years for her father Laban as a dowry payment for her hand in marriage. After seven long years, the wedding day finally came. The veiled bride marched down the aisle, vows of commitment were exchanged, and then the couple went off to the honeymoon tent! When Jacob lifted his bride's veil, he was shocked that instead of Rachel, he had married her older sister, Leah. Jacob confronted Laban who agreed to give him Rachel also for seven more years of labor.

Poor Leah. She was the older, less attractive sister. The sister forced to participate in a devilish scheme, just to get her married off. She must have felt humiliated! Her younger sister, Rachel, was the beautiful one, the loved and chosen one. Leah was the tag-along. However, God blessed Leah with many children, including her son Judah – the lineage from which Jesus would be born. Rachel became extremely jealous. She could not allow Leah to steal attention or glory from her. In her envious rage, she accused Jacob of purposely not also giving her children.

That's what jealousy does ... it causes us to behave in ridiculous and hurtful ways. We are so focused on what we think we are missing out on that we do not consider the injury we are causing in the wake of our emotional tantrums. The Bible says that envy makes the bones rot (Proverbs 14:30). It is our ultimate declaration that "God is not good!" How could He be good, if we think He is withholding something good from us? The truth is, though, we can trust God with the desires of our heart. And in wisdom and love, He will satisfy our every longing with Himself, even if He does not give us everything we think we want.

Let gratitude for God's love replace any jealousy in your heart today!

October 4
LOVE YOUR ENEMIES

Luke 6:29-31 (NASB): *"Whoever hits you on the cheek,
offer him the other also; and whoever takes away your coat,
do not withhold your shirt from him either. Give to everyone who
asks of you, and whoever takes away what is yours, do not demand
it back. Treat others the same way you want them to treat you."*

It is easy to be kind to those who are kind to us. It is easy to love those who love us, but it is nearly impossible to turn the other cheek! When someone hurts us or wrongs us in some way, the natural instinct is to retaliate. Jesus, however, challenges us to do the supernatural. He asks us to be kind to those who are not kind, and to love those who are not lovely. When someone wrongs us, instead of returning that wrong, we are to extend forgiveness. Walking away from abusers, setting healthy boundaries, and positive confrontation are all appropriate responses in the face of wrong actions. It is the attitude of our hearts towards our enemies, though, that demonstrates the love of Christ. Because God forgives us, we can forgive others. If you are wounded today, trust God with your pain and pray for your enemy.

Let God's love shine through you today!

October 5

MYSTERY REVEALED

Colossians 1:26-27 (ESV): *"the mystery hidden for ages and generations but now revealed to his saints. To them God chose to make known how great among the Gentiles are the riches of the glory of this mystery, which is Christ in you, the hope of glory."*

The promised Messiah had been foretold for many generations. The Old Testament prophets wrote of Him, patriarchs taught their children to look for Him, and wicked men dreaded Him. When Christ was born, few noticed Him. Jesus lived the perfect life and died for the sins of mankind. He then rose from the dead and ascended to the right hand of the Father. Now the mystery of this promised Savior is revealed not only to the Jews but to the Gentiles as well … Christ has come to live in us and to live this life for us! What we are powerless to accomplish on our own, Christ will do on our behalf. How will you and I ever meet the standards of perfection before a Holy God? Christ in us!

Christ wants to live in you today!

October 6
OUR ADVOCATE

Romans 8:34 (NLT): *"Who then will condemn us? No one—for Christ Jesus died for us and was raised to life for us, and he is sitting in the place of honor at God's right hand, pleading for us."*

Jesus Christ lived a perfect life on our behalf. He then paid the penalty for our sins by dying on a cross. And He resurrected Himself from the dead so that you and I could experience new life. Right now, He is sitting at the right hand of God interceding on our behalf. Who then can condemn us? No one! Who can stand up to the Son of God and accuse us? No one! Who can march up to the throne and remind God of our sins? No one! The work of Christ secures our position in Christ. He has redeemed us; He keeps us; and He calls us His own forevermore!

Jesus Christ is fighting for you today!

October 7
OVERCOMING TEMPTATIONS

1 Corinthians 10:13 (NLT): *"The temptations in your life are no different from what others experience. And God is faithful. He will not allow the temptation to be more than you can stand. When you are tempted, he will show you a way out so that you can endure."*

Temptations are a tool the enemy uses to come against the children of God. He will bombard our minds with thoughts and images to try to lure us into sinful actions. When we are in Christ, however, sin may pester us, but it no longer has power over us. The Holy Spirit is our strength. He is our voice to say, "No!" He is our legs to walk away. He is our eyes to look away. The Spirit of God, who defeated the power of sin on the cross, can overcome temptations that rise up against you.

Remember this … just because you are tempted, does not mean that you have sinned. Sin comes when we dwell on the temptation and then act on it. Temptations, however, do not have to turn into sin when we allow the Holy Spirit to guard our hearts (Proverbs 4:23) and minds (2 Corinthians 10:5).

The Holy Spirit is your power source today!

October 8
PERSONAL SAVIOR

Job 19:25 (ESV): *"For I know that my Redeemer lives, and at the last He will stand upon the earth."*

People do not need another set of rules to follow. They are not interested in a list of religious do's and dont's. What people need is an authentic relationship with a personal Savior. Jesus offers a "come as you are" invitation to a "never be the same" encounter with Him. He gives; He loves; and He keeps. Christ is our Redeemer.

Get personal with Christ today!

October 9

RECOGNIZING ANSWERED PRAYERS

Jonah 2:1-2 (NIV): *"From inside the fish Jonah prayed
to the Lord his God. He said: 'In my distress I called to the Lord,
and he answered me. From deep in the realm of the dead
I called for help, and you listened to my cry.'"*

The Lord told Jonah to go and preach to the people in Nineveh.
Jonah, however, did not want the people of Nineveh to have an
opportunity to repent of their sins. In his opinion, they were wicked and
deserved the wrath of God. Therefore, Jonah chose to disobey God, and
he ran in the opposite direction. In his rebellion, he found himself in
the middle of a dire predicament – drowning in the middle of a raging
sea. Jonah cried out for God to save him, and a great fish came up from
the deep and swallowed him. Now some may think that Jonah's situation just went from bad to worse, but from God's perspective, Jonah's
prayer was answered; everything was under control; and all was good.
While in the belly of the fish, Jonah had the opportunity to repent of
his disobedience and was given another chance to preach in Nineveh.

Have you ever prayed a prayer only to watch your situation take seemingly downward twists and turns? God works like that sometimes. His
ways are not our ways, and His thoughts are not our thoughts (Isaiah
55:8). God, however, always answers our prayers. We need to recognize
that the way He answers may not always line up with what we would
like, but it is always for our best!

God will answer your prayers today!

October 10

RESPECT

Romans 13:1 (ESV): *"Let every person be subject to the governing authorities. For there is no authority except from God, and those that exist have been instituted by God."*

Years ago there was a song with the lyrics, "R-E-S-P-E-C-T, find out what it means to me!" People may like the idea of respect, but from God's perspective, it is not just a nice idea—it is a command. He tells us in His Word that we are to submit ourselves under the leadership of those in authority. Why does God care whether I listen to people in positions of authority, such as my parents, my boss, my minister, or a police officer? Because if you and I refuse to be subject to visible authorities, we will never submit to an invisible God. We also need to keep in mind that God is the one who raises up kings and who also removes them from their thrones (Psalm 75:7), which means that positions of authority and the people who fill them have been instituted by Him. We may not always like our authority figures or even fully trust them at times, but we can trust God. Our allegiance is ultimately to Him. Therefore, our thoughts, words, and behaviors should reflect a right attitude. We honor God by showing respect to those who govern. Let us cultivate a habit of praying for those in leadership over us. There is a great responsibility placed on their shoulders, for which they are ultimately accountable to God.

Honor God by treating the authority in your life with respect today!

October 11
RICH IN CHRIST

Ephesians 1: 13-14 (ESV): *"In him you also,*
when you heard the word of truth, the gospel of your salvation,
and believed in him, were sealed with the promised
Holy Spirit, who is the guarantee of our inheritance until
we acquire possession of it, to the praise of his glory."

The Apostle Paul starts out his letter to the church in Ephesus with some really good news … they are the beneficiaries of every spiritual blessing in the heavenly places in Christ (Ephesians 1:3). There is absolutely nothing they lack. God lavished His love and His resources upon them through Jesus Christ. Then to top it all off, God gave His Holy Spirit as a guarantee of their (and every believer's) eternal inheritance. A lottery ticket or sweepstakes cannot even begin to compare to the wealth of God's children! Paul goes on to make several requests of God on behalf of this church. What is so interesting about Paul's prayer, though, is that he never asks God to give the people in Ephesus something more. Instead, he simply asks for God to reveal to them what they already have.

We need to know that when we are in Christ, we have everything we need to live this life abundantly and victoriously. We don't need Christ "plus" a good job; or Christ "plus" a good spouse; or Christ "plus" perfect health. We just need Christ. If this truth is not sealed in your heart today, then pray over yourself what Paul prayed for his church, "Lord, open the eyes of my heart; enlighten me to your truths and my reality, that I may know the hope you have called me to and the riches that have been given to me" (Ephesians 1:18).

You have riches untold in Christ today!

October 12
SEASONS

Ecclesiastes 3:1 (NLT): *"There is a time for everything, and a season for every activity under the heavens...."*

Spring gives birth to new life ... flowers bloom, trees bud, and the earth is green. Summer comes and the days lengthen. People spend as much time as they can enjoying the beauty of the outdoors. Fall arrives with cooler temperature and changing leaves. Nature paints a colorful display of warm oranges, yellows, and reds. Then comes winter. The days shorten, temperatures grow cold, plants curl up and retreat underground, and we long for spring to come again.

Much like the changing seasons of nature, we go through cycles in our life. There are times of joy and times of sorrow; times of laughter and times of crying; times of working and times of playing; times of birth and times of death. The seasons remind us that everything has a beginning and an end. Maybe you have been struggling through a long winter of the soul. Difficulty has surrounded you, and pain has been a constant companion. The good news is the difficult time you are going through right now is but a season, a distinct period of time that will not last forever. The Bible teaches us that "Three things will last forever — faith, hope, and love — and the greatest of these is love" (1 Corinthians 13:13).

If it seems like you have been struggling through a never-ending winter, keep looking ahead because the Son is coming (Revelation 22:12-14)! He will deliver us from the curse of sin on this world. There will be no more sickness, no more sin, no more death, no more pain, no more loneliness, no more fear, and no more seasons of change. When Christ comes, we will abide forever in the loving presence of the Son.

Christ is coming soon – believe on Him today!

October 13
SOLITUDE

Luke 5:16 (NIV): *"But Jesus often withdrew to lonely places and prayed."*

Prayer was a priority for Jesus. The Scriptures reveal how Jesus would often withdraw to spend time alone with His Father (Mark 1:35). He found strength in God (Mark 14:32). He found direction in God (John 5:19), and Jesus found joy in God (Hebrews 12:2). Moments of solitude in the presence of the Father can do the same for us. Do you need strength? Are you seeking direction? Is your soul longing for deep-seeded joy? Then withdraw from the busyness of life; put aside the distractions that rule your mind; and find a quiet place to sit with God. He will restore your soul (Psalm 23:3).

Spend time alone with Christ today!

October 14
THAT'S NOT FUNNY

Proverbs 12:18 (ESV): *"There is one whose rash words are like sword thrusts, but the tongue of the wise brings healing."*

Many people will try to pass sarcasm off as humor. It is not. Humor is fun, light-hearted, and makes people feel good. Sarcasm, on the other hand, is harsh, destructive, and makes people feel belittled. It is a weapon used by the cowardly to covertly wound another person. The cowardly, you ask? Yes, the cowardly. These people want to hide their own jealousies and insecurities behind clever words in the hopes of drawing positive attention to themselves and negative attention to their target. God is not pleased when we behave like this. He wants us to be kind and affectionate towards one another (Ephesians 4:32). The Scriptures teach us that the power of life and death resides in the tongue (Proverbs 18:21), and we will be accountable for every word we speak (Matthew 12:36). Let us learn to be life infusers! Let us speak words of encouragement and blessings over others and share genuine humor that uplifts and ignites pure laughter. May the words of our mouth bless others and honor God (Psalm 19:14), because unkind words are just not funny.

Encourage someone today!

October 15

THE ARMY OF THE LORD

2 Kings 6:16 (NLT): *"Don't be afraid,' the prophet answered.
'Those who are with us are more than those who are with them.'"*

The Arameans were at war with the children of Israel. Each time they set up a plan to attack, however, the Lord would reveal the plan to Elisha and he would go and warn the king of Israel. The king of Aram began to suspect that he had a traitor in his troops. His men told him they were not traitors, but a certain prophet of God named Elisha was the one telling Israel all of their battle plans. The king of Aram sent his soldiers to capture the prophet. On that day, Elisha's servant looked out of the window and saw that their house was surrounded by the Aramean army. He was afraid. Elisha calmed his servant and asked God to open the eyes of the young man, and God did. When the servant looked out of the window again, he saw that the Aramean army was surrounded by an army of angels on horses and flaming chariots!

The Bible tells us that God commands His angels to watch over His children (Psalm 91:11). The enemy will try to send his minions to capture us, but we have nothing to fear. We are never left to defend ourselves. Our God, who is always watching over us, has His mighty Army in place to fight for us. The next time you find yourself afraid, remind yourself that you are surrounded by the Army of the Lord (Psalm 139:5)!

God will give His angels charge over you today!

October 16

THE HOLY SPIRIT
WILL PRAY FOR US

Romans 8:26 (ESV): *"Likewise the Spirit helps us in our weakness. For we do not know what to pray for as we ought, but the Spirit himself intercedes for us with groanings too deep for words."*

There are times we have heavy hearts and tear-filled eyes but wordless prayers. We do not know how to express what is on the inside of us; we do not know what we should ask for or what steps to take next. It is in these moments that the Holy Spirit of God, which indwells the children of God and who knows the will of Father God, does something incredible … He prays for us. And He knows exactly what to say and to ask, because He is perfectly in tune with the mind of the Father. How reassuring to know that God will not only pursue us, redeem us, and keep us, but He will also pray for us. Truly, this Christian life is completely in His hands (Ephesians 2:8-9)!

The Holy Spirit will intercede on your behalf today!

October 17
THE JOY OF ASSURANCE

1 John 5:13 (ESV): *"I write these things to you
who believe in the name of the Son of God that you may
know that you have eternal life."*

God does not want us to be fearful about our salvation from one day to the next. He wants us to have full confidence that the work Christ has done on our behalf is sufficient. There is nothing that you and I can add to what Christ has already perfectly done. Salvation is God's work, a grace-filled gift that we accept. Jesus takes the responsibility for our lives and gives us the credit for His life. Then, God seals us until the day of redemption by placing His very Spirit on the inside of us (Ephesians 1:11-4). The Holy Spirit is our blessed assurance that we are in Christ, and He is in us. Do not let the enemy steal your joy or peace of mind. There will be days of failure. These times do not take our Sovereign God by surprise. They are moments of teaching, correcting, sifting, molding, and shaping. Trust that He who began this good work in you will be faithful to carry it on to completion, until the day of Christ Jesus (Philippians 1:6)!

Have confidence in Christ today!

October 18
THE LONGEST DAY

Judges 10:12-14 (ESV): *"On the day the Lord gave the Amorites over to Israel, Joshua said to the Lord in the presence of Israel: 'Sun, stand still over Gibeon, and you, moon, over the Valley of Aijalon.' So the sun stood still, and the moon stopped, till the nation avenged itself on its enemies, as it is written in the Book of Jashar. The sun stopped in the middle of the sky and delayed going down about a full day. There has never been a day like it before or since, a day when the Lord listened to a human being. Surely the Lord was fighting for Israel!"*

Joshua and his men were fighting against the Amorite kings. God had already told Joshua not to be afraid, because the victory would be his. As Joshua and his men moved in for war, God threw the armies of the Amorites into confusion, and Joshua's men easily overtook them. Then, the Amorites began to flee, so Joshua and his men went in pursuit after them. The daylight hours were quickly dwindling away, so Joshua asked God for the impossible. "Please make the sun stand still!" And, God did. The sun stopped and was delayed going down by a full day – giving the children of Israel enough time to finish fighting the battle and walk away in complete victory!

What burden are you trying to bear alone? What problem do you wrestle with that you are convinced is too big for your God? Are you afraid to ask God for the impossible? We serve a God who is capable of moving heaven and earth on behalf of His children. The prayers that we pray reveal our faith in the might of our God. He is so much bigger than we allow Him to be in our lives! We need to know that we serve a God who will fight for us, and He can do what no one else can do. Trust God.

Nothing is impossible with God today!

October 19

THE LORD WILL MAKE A WAY

Exodus 14:13-14 (NIV): *"Moses answered the people,
'Do not be afraid. Stand firm and you will see
the deliverance the Lord will bring you today.
The Egyptians you see today you will never see again.
The Lord will fight for you; you need only to be still.'"*

A sea in front of them and a fierce army behind them, the children of Israel didn't need anyone to tell them they were in big trouble! What they did need, though, was someone to fight for them … Enter God! No matter how big our problems or how bleak our circumstances, our God can make a way when there seems to be no way, no answer, and no hope. He specializes in demolishing any strongholds or illusions the enemy tries to present as too difficult for God. When you feel like your back is against the wall – be still – because your Mighty Redeemer will fight for you!

Trust Christ Jesus to fight for you today!

October 20

THE PATIENCE OF GOD

Romans 2:4(NIV): *"Or do you show contempt for the riches of his kindness, forbearance and patience, not realizing that God's kindness is intended to lead you to repentance?"*

Turn on the nightly news, any channel or network, and it is all the same … pain, suffering, wrong doing. Evil seems to be running amuck! It is easy to question why God would allow such chaos in the world. We need to remember, though, that nothing goes unnoticed by our Sovereign God. He is patient with mankind and extends grace so that hearts have an opportunity to repent. It is not God's desire that any should perish and be separated from Him for eternity (2 Peter 3:9), so He is patient. For the innocent and injured, do not fret. God is a just God. He will judge all deeds at the appropriate time (Acts 17:31). Until then, He is merciful, and we who have benefited from this unmerited favor are very, very grateful that He is a patient God.

Be thankful for the heart of God today!

October 21
WEDDING DAY

Revelation 19:6-8 (ESV): *"Then I heard what seemed to be the voice of a great multitude, like the roar of many waters and like the sound of mighty peals of thunder, crying out, 'Hallelujah!*

For the Lord our God the Almighty reigns. Let us rejoice and exult and give him the glory, for the marriage of the Lamb has come, and his Bride has made herself ready....'"

A man and woman fall in love. They want to spend the rest of their lives together, so they decide to get married. A date is circled on the calendar and preparations begin. Soon, the day arrives. There is great celebration as the bride walks down the aisle to be joined with her groom forever.

Beloved, a matrimony like none other is coming. The date is circled on the heavenly calendar. Jesus Christ is making preparations to take His bride to be joined with Him for all eternity (John 14:2-3). The earth will rejoice; nature will resound; and all of Heaven will exult the long anticipated marriage of the Lamb. This is one wedding you do not want to miss! Surrender your heart to Christ today, and you can live happily ever after with Him.

Rejoice in the promises of God today!

October 22
TRUSTING GOD WITH LESS

1 Kings 17:12-13 (NIV): *"'As surely as the Lord your God lives,'*
she replied, 'I don't have any bread—only a handful of flour
in a jar and a little olive oil in a jug. I am gathering a few sticks
to take home and make a meal for myself and my son,
that we may eat it—and die.' Elijah said to her, 'Don't be afraid.
Go home and do as you have said. But first make a small loaf
of bread for me from what you have and bring it to me,
and then make something for yourself and your son.'"

All of us have probably fantasized at one time or another about what it would be like to win the lottery or a sweepstakes. And if you are anything like me, in that fantasy, you become the most generous person on the face of the earth! We would take care of our families, give to charities, or bless the church. There would be nothing selfish about our good fortune and gain. The more we have, the more we would willingly share or give away. That does sound like a fantasy! We should take a look at the way we are living our lives now. Are we generous with the little that we do have? You see, if we don't trust God with the $1 that is in our pocket, we would not trust Him if we had $1000 more. That is the true measure of faith…trusting God with less. The widow in the Bible verse above only had a tiny amount of flour and oil to make a small loaf of bread to feed her son and herself one last time. She obeyed the prophet of God, though, and gave what she had to feed him first. In doing so, we learn that she and her son never ran out of flour or oil (1 Kings 17:14-16). Remember, God is a God of multiplication! When we offer Him all that we have, no matter how small, He will take it, bless it, and multiply it. In doing so, we, and others are blessed, and God is glorified.

Trust God with all that you have today!

October 23

UNDER GRACE

Psalm 55:22 (NIV): *"Cast your cares on the LORD and he will sustain you; he will never let the righteous be shaken."*

As children of God, our Heavenly Father takes complete responsibility for our care and meeting our needs. Our responsibility is to keep our eyes on Him. Too often, though, we are guilty of looking at our circumstances or considering our limited resources; then we are filled with fear and worry because we are not able to resolve our situations. God is not limited by our lack. He is the one who made everything out of nothing! He created all things; He owns all things; and He controls all things. Surely, our God can meet your needs and my needs. Remember, we who are "under grace" are never trapped "under the circumstances!"

Jehovah is a "can do" God today!

October 24
UNDER THE SUN

Ecclesiastes 1:14 (ESV): *"I have seen everything that is done under the sun, and behold, all is vanity and a striving after wind."*

Solomon was the wisest and wealthiest man that ever lived. Yet, all of his wisdom and riches could not satisfy his longing for something more. Unsure of what that something was, he made it his sole purpose to try anything and everything that world could offer. His final conclusion was that everything under the sun is vanity. It is like trying to catch the illusive wind. Notice that every place he searched and everything and everyone he pursued was under the sun. The pleasures of this earth, apart from God, will never satisfy our deepest longing, because He is our soul's greatest need. God created man to crave Him. When you discover that people, places, and things are not enough, stop searching under the sun, and look up to the Son! You will find, like Solomon, that the ultimate fulfillment and purpose of your life is to be in a relationship with God (Ecclesiastes 12:13).

Give God His rightful place in your life today!

October 25
UNFULFILLED POTENTIAL

Judges 13: 24 (ESV): *"And the woman bore a son and called his name Samson. And the young man grew, and the Lord blessed him."*

The birth announcement of Samson was heralded by an angel of the Lord. He would be a child of promise, uniquely created to fulfill great plans by God. Samson had an incredible gift of strength. God wanted to use Samson to defeat the Philistines, who had dominated the children of Israel for the last forty years. Samson, however, grew into a man that struggled with complete surrender to God. As we read his story in the Book of Judges, we find that he was a man who had a willing spirit to serve God, but his flesh was weak. He was ruled by his emotions instead of by the Spirit. Lust, anger, and lack of emotional control caused Samson to live an almost life instead of an awesome life.

Samson sounds a lot like many Christians today. God has amazing plans for our lives. He wires us with all kinds of potential: skills, talents, and abilities. Without the control of the Holy Spirit, though, we cannot operate in our full potential. We find ourselves up and down in our spiritual walk; always waffling between faith and failure. And although the Spirit moves on us from time to time, we never give Him complete control. Do you want to live an almost life or an awesome life? If an awesome life is your choice, surrender yourself to the Holy Spirit today. He is the One who knows the mind of God and the path that has been laid out for each of our lives; then watch as He glorifies the Father through you!

Dedicate your life to Christ today!

October 26
WAITING WITHOUT WORRYING

Genesis 22:5 (NASB): *"Be anxious for nothing,*
but in everything by prayer and supplication with thanksgiving
let your requests be made known to God.
And the peace of God, which surpasses all comprehension,
will guard your hearts and your minds in Christ Jesus."

We live in an age of "instant" – coffee, microwaves, and communication. We don't like to wait. As a matter of fact, whenever we do have to wait, it often leads to worrying. Christ invites us to make our requests and concerns known to Him, and then instructs us to wait peacefully for His response. We must remember that God's timing is always perfect. Faith says, "I trust you, Lord." This means we trust His "how" and His "when." So, what are we supposed to do in the meantime? Give thanks to God for the answer that is on the way!

God's timing is perfect today!

October 27
WISDOM

Ecclesiastes 10:12 (NIV): *"Words from a wise man's mouth are gracious, but a fool is consumed by his own lips."*

Words from the mouths of the wise bring life and healing, while a fool's words destroy. How can we learn to speak wisely? God has given us His Holy Word so that we can know truth. It is in understanding truth that we become wise men and women of God—people who make good choices, who give helpful counsel, and who speak encouragement into the downcast. Spend time in God's Word, and He will graciously impart His wisdom into your life (James 1:5)!

The Holy Spirit is your wisdom today!

October 28
WORSHIP

Psalm 40:3 (NIV): *"He put a new song in my mouth, a hymn of praise to our God. Many will see and fear the Lord and put their trust in him."*

The Bible teaches us to praise God. Whether our circumstances are good or bad, God is always worthy of our praise just because of who He is. When God answers a prayer or uplifts our hearts in some way, though, we should open up our mouths and tell what God has done. It is through the testimony of our lives that other people come to know God. They experience Him through us. God wants to display His glory to the world, and He chooses to use vessels like you and me. We become walking billboards for the power, love, and forgiveness of Jehovah God. He gives us a song to sing about Him and for Him, so let us honor the Lord with our hymns of praise!

Worship the LORD today!

October 29
A TWIG OF HOPE

Genesis 8:11 (ESV): *"And the dove came back to him in the evening, and behold, in her mouth was a freshly plucked olive leaf. So Noah knew that the waters had subsided from the earth."*

Noah and his family had been on that ark for what seemed like an eternity! Forty days and forty nights of flooding rain and waters had rocked their world. Then, the waiting came. Waiting for the waters to recede and the land to appear. Day after day, night after night, feeding animal after animal … the routine must have seemed endless! Have you ever had days like that? When waiting for an answer, for a healing, for a change seems endless? Keep looking up! Noah did, and one day a little dove brought him a twig of hope. One hundred ten days after the rain stopped, the ark landed on Mt. Ararat. God kept His promise to Noah, and God will keep His promises to you. Wait patiently on Him. Cling to your twigs of hope. God is working even when you cannot see!

You have a hope in Christ today!

October 30

ABOVE ALL THINGS

Revelation 21:6 (ESV): *"And he said to me,*
"It is done! I am the Alpha and the Omega,
the beginning and the end. To the thirsty I will give
from the spring of the water of life without payment."

Jehovah God is above all things. He is the beginning of all things. He is the sustainer of all things. He is the ending of all things. God has set His throne in the heavens, and He rules over all things (Psalm 103:19). As children of the Most High God, knowing that our God is sovereign should fill us with joy, courage, and gratitude. The Almighty God loves you and me today. He is not too busy, and He is not too weary to care for us (Isaiah 40:28-31). If we are going to give our allegiance to a god, shouldn't it be the One True God (John 17:3)?

Serve the LORD of Lords today!

October 31

ABSOLUTELY NOTHING

Romans 8:38-39 (ESV): *"For I am sure that neither death nor life, nor angels nor rulers, nor things present nor things to come, nor powers, nor height nor depth, nor anything else in all creation, will be able to separate us from the love of God in Christ Jesus our Lord."*

Jesus loves you. There is nothing you can do to change that fact. You cannot be too bad; you cannot sin too much; and you cannot ignore Him enough to make Him love you less. Likewise, you cannot be too good; you cannot work too hard; and you cannot be too nice to make Him love you more. Jesus's love for you is not dependent upon anything that you do or do not do. He loves you, because He chooses to do so. Because of this fact, there is nothing that can remove you from the love of Christ. Once you belong to Him, you are safe in the palms of His hands (Isaiah 49:16). Who or what could possibly snatch you away from the all-present, all-knowing, all-powerful God of the universe? Absolutely nothing!

Jesus loves you today!

[fire yourself]

NOVEMBER

November 1
ADDICTED TO PEACE

Psalm 34:14 (ESV): *"Turn away from evil and do good; seek peace and pursue it."*

Peace is a choice. Every day we decide whether or not we are going to rest in the Father's care or whether we're going to manage the day and its circumstances on our own (John 14:1). When we decide to take control, it doesn't take long before life begins to feel out of control. Conflicts aggravate us, people disappoint us, and thoughts discourage us. When we choose to rest in God, though, His peace seals us, because our attention is steadfast on Him. The peace of God, once experienced, is something that you will want to experience again and again. There is only One source for it, and there is only One way to remain in it – God. He is the Author and Sustainer of our heart's rest.

Choose the peace of God today!

November 2
ALIVE AGAIN!

Ezekiel 37:1-3 (ESV): *"The hand of the Lord was upon me,
and he brought me out in the Spirit of the Lord
and set me down in the middle of the valley; it was full of bones.
And he led me around among them, and behold,
there were very many on the surface of the valley, and behold,
they were very dry. And he said to me, 'Son of man,
can these bones live?' And I answered, 'O Lord God, you know.'"*

We go through "dry seasons" in this life. During these times, we think that God is a million miles away. Our souls feel thirsty and parched. Our hearts struggle to beat. Perhaps we struggle with an addiction or sinful habit. We are joyless, lifeless, and our bones are dry. But there is a Hope in Jesus Christ! He can speak over our soul, quench our thirst, and breathe new life into our spirit. Can these dry bones live again? In Christ, all things are possible! When the Life Giver breathes on us, we can come alive again (Ezekiel 37:5)!

Christ can breathe new life in you today!

November 3
ANCHORED

Hebrews 6:19 (ESV): *"We have this as a sure and steadfast anchor of the soul, a hope that enters into the inner place behind the curtain...."*

We do not have to be tossed about by winds of emotions and waves of circumstances. We can remain sure and steadfast, no matter how we feel or what we face, when we are anchored to Jesus. He is our redeemer and our hope. Christ goes before us to prepare our way. In Him we hold fast to truth. Regardless of what human logic says, regardless of what popular opinion says, regardless of what our feelings say, we can live by faith tied to the anchor of truth!

Let Christ be your anchor today!

November 4
BE A BOOSTER

Ephesians 4:29 (ESV): *"Let no corrupting talk come out of your mouths, but only such as is good for building up, as fits the occasion, that it may give grace to those who hear."*

People are fragile. Words can easily wound and deflate spirits. This is why the Bible teaches us that we will be accountable for every word that comes out of our mouths (Matthew 12:36). Therefore, we should speak wisely. Instead of tearing down with sarcasm, gossip, or negativity, let's be a booster! A booster is one who uplifts and has a positive effect on another. Building up others is a spiritual gift that rightfully reflects the Father's character (Romans 12:4-8). So, let's be encouragers and honor God with our speech.

Encourage someone today!

November 5
BUT, IT'S NOT MY FAULT

Matthew 5:23-24 (ESV): *"So if you are offering your gift at the altar and there remember that your brother has something against you, leave your gift there before the altar and go. First be reconciled to your brother, and then come and offer your gift."*

We've all been on the frigid side of a cold shoulder … burrrr! It is so easy to become standoffish when we know that someone is mad at us or is intentionally avoiding us. God, however, does not accept this type of response from His children. He instructs us to be the peacemakers, even if we do not believe we have done anything wrong. The burden of extending love and peace falls on the strong ones, not the weak ones. We, who have been empowered with the Holy Spirit and are called to be reflectors of His light, are responsible for reconciliation. Keep in mind, we are not held accountable for the other person's receptiveness to our peace offering. Nevertheless, we are expected to extend it anyway. Sometimes this includes using the words, "I'm sorry." Yes, even if we do not think we are in the wrong. We should be "sorry" for the division, because we know God's will for His people is unity. So, choose to be a peacemaker! In Christ, we can do all things through Him who gives us strength (Philippians 4:13).

Christ can empower you to be a peacemaker today!

November 6
CHILD-LIKE FAITH

Luke 18:16 (ESV): *"But Jesus called them to him, saying,
'Let the children come to me, and do not hinder them,
for to such belongs the kingdom of God.'"*

Jesus is not impressed with our skills, abilities, and independent points of view. He is looking for men and women with the tender hearts and pure faith of children. Just as little ones acknowledge their dependency on mom and dad, Christ wants us to acknowledge our desperate need for Him. The Scriptures teach us that apart from Him, we can do nothing (John 15:5). The very air that we breathe comes from the generosity of our Creator and Sustainer. God is our Source. We need Him every day, and He loves us enough to be there for us each and every day.

Trust the heart of God today!

November 7
CHRIST IS FIRST

Colossians 1:15 (ESV): *"He is the image
of the invisible God, the firstborn of all creation."*

Jesus ... there is none like Him. Everyone and everything is second to Him. Christ is "preeminent." This word means, "first place." Christ is first. He is above all. Everything was created by Him and for Him. He is before all things, and in Him all things are held together. He is the head of the church. He is the perfect One. He is the Beloved Son of the Father. He is the source of life. In Him the fullness of God dwells. He is the first of many sons.

The question for you and me is ..."Is Christ first in my life?" He cannot be second; He will not be second. And we need Him to be first, to take the lead. When we give Christ His rightful place in our lives, He will bring everything else we need to us.

Give Jesus His rightful place in your life today!

November 8
CITIZENSHIP

Philippians 3:20 (ESV): *"speaking to one another with psalms, hymns, and songs from the Spirit. Sing and make music from your heart to the Lord...."*

According to the U.S. Citizenship and Immigration Services, the United States welcomes approximately 680,000 new citizens through naturalization ceremonies each year. America is the promise land for many immigrants who are looking for a better world. As great as America is, though, she pales in comparison to the world that awaits those who are sealed by the Holy Spirit of God (Ephesians 4:30). Jesus said that He has prepared a place for us, with many rooms, where we can live eternally without sickness, pain, sorrow, or sin (John 14:2-3). The world with all of its riches and beauties could never outshine the glories of Heaven. For those who have surrendered their hearts to Christ, you have been given citizenship into this eternal land. The welcoming ceremony to celebrate your homecoming is on the horizon (Revelation 22:12)! Until then, make it your mission to tell others who are looking for a better world about the Promised Land of God (Matthew 28:19).

You can become a citizen of Heaven today!

November 9

CLOSED MOUTHS
& OPEN EARS

James 1:19 (ESV): *"…let every person be quick to hear, slow to speak, slow to anger…."*

Listening is an underused skill. Too often, instead of giving someone our full attention in a conversation, we are already planning our brilliant response. We care more about that person hearing what we want to say, instead of respectfully listening to his or her words. This often leads to miscommunications, hurt feelings, and unnecessary arguments. The Bible says instead of always being the one to have your opinion heard, be quiet! Listen intently. Then, if appropriate, respond with an attitude of love and humility. Conversations should not be about out talking or out proving one another. They should be to exchange thoughts, feelings, ideas, and information. Cultivating good listening skills is a way to genuinely love other people. The next time someone engages you in a conversation, look him or her in the eyes, close your mouth, and open your ears. You might be surprised what you can learn from the words of another. At the very least, that person will walk away feeling like he or she matters to you!

Listen to the voice of God today!

November 10
DO I TAKE SIN SERIOUSLY?

Genesis 19:14 (NIV): *"So Lot went out and spoke to his
sons-in-law, who were pledged to marry his daughters.
He said, 'Hurry and get out of this place, because the LORD is about
to destroy the city!' But his sons-in-law thought he was joking."*

Sodom and Gomorrah were wicked cities. Because of the vileness in the land and the rebellious hearts of the people, God decided that He would destroy the towns. Lot and his family were the only righteous people to be found, so God warned Lot to take his family and leave. Lot tried to warn the young men betrothed to his daughters and begged them to come along. The men thought Lot was crazy and would not go with him. The result? They perished in the burning sulfur that God rained down on the cities.

The men died, because they failed to believe in the salvation that was offered to them. How sad! How about us? Do we take sin seriously? Do we see the dangers of hanging around people who are actively rebelling against God? Do we think that God's anger towards sin is a joke, or do we fail to see the necessity of salvation? God sent His Son Jesus to save mankind from His coming wrath against sin. Remember Sodom and Gomorrah. Take sin seriously. Accept God's gift of salvation today!

Christ is your hope today!

November 11
FOCUS ON YOUR FAMILY

Psalm 127:3-5 (ESV): *"Behold, children are a heritage from the Lord, the fruit of the womb a reward. Like arrows in the hand of a warrior are the children of one's youth. Blessed is the man who fills his quiver with them! He shall not be put to shame when he speaks with his enemies in the gate."*

No one can fill us with joy or drive us to the brink of frustration quite like family! This group of fragile and faulty people have been assigned to us by God to love on and to walk through life with … do not neglect this divine calling! There is no higher duty, no greater task we can do for God any more important than ministering to the ones He has entrusted to our care. Therefore, spouses, love one another. Parents, invest your time as well as your resources in your children. Children, obey your moms and dads. Families, love unconditionally and forgive freely. Your home should be a grace-filled sanctuary that mends its members from the battle wounds of life. It should be the one place where we can find peace, joy, and love no matter what the rest of the day looked like. Family should be on the same side of this spiritual battle we are all on. The enemy will try to make it look like the fight is between us. It is not. It is against us. Therefore, we must unite together and hold fast to truth. The people that God has chosen for us may at times cause us grief, but they are our greatest blessing! We demonstrate our genuine love for God by genuinely loving them.

Praise God for your family today!

November 12
FOR ALL WHO BELIEVE

Romans 3:21-22 (ESV): *"But now the righteousness of God has been manifested apart from the law, although the Law and the Prophets bear witness to it – the righteousness of God through faith in Jesus Christ, for all who believe. For there is no distinction...."*

There is a standard that each one of us must meet in order to stand before a Holy God. The standard is Himself, the righteousness of God. In the Old Testament, the standard for living a moral life was written down as the Law, the Ten Commandments. The Law pointed out our sins and pointed us to a Holy God. In the New Testament, though, the standard of the Law, the very righteousness of God, manifested itself in Jesus Christ. Not only did Christ die the death to pay the penalty of sin, He lived the perfect standard of God that you and I fall so far short of meeting. Then He said that for all who believe in Him, He would cover us with His righteousness. In the righteousness of Christ, we meet God's standard. We are able to come into the presence of a Holy God without fear. We are accepted. It does not matter what color our skin is, which gender we are, who are parents or grandparents are, how much money we make – there is no distinction. We all sin. All are in need of a Savior. And all who believe will receive!

Believe on Jesus Christ today!

November 13
FOREVER

Ecclesiastes 3:11 (ESV):
"...he has put eternity into man's heart...."

We were made to long for God. There is an insatiable appetite deep in our souls that only He can satisfy. The trouble is we try to appease a craving for eternity with a temporary fix. We are so accustomed to this temporal world that we fail to focus on what lies ahead. It is hard for us to imagine that there can be more to living than what we are currently experiencing. Many of us may even fear that somehow we will be losing something by leaving this world and going to Heaven. The truth is, though, that earth, even with all of it beauties and pleasures, could never hope to compare with the eternity that God has planned for His children. The Scriptures tell us that "Eye hath not seen, nor ear heard, neither have entered into the heart of man the things which God hath prepared for them that love Him" (1 Corinthians 2:9). The God who made this world is making a new world, a forever world. And He wants you and me to live in it eternally with Him.

Focus on the joys of Heaven today!

November 14
FREEDOM IN CHRIST

John 8:32 (ESV): *"and you will know the truth,
and the truth will set you free."*

Christianity is the only religion where the follower is commanded to rest instead of perform, because our Lord has completed the work of redemption. Too many of us Christians, though, still walk around bound in chains of performance, trying to be good enough for God. We need to understand that we are not set free by what we do or how we behave. We are set free by believing in the finished work of the Cross! That is the Good News of the Gospel – Christ did for us what we cannot do for ourselves. By accepting this truth, we are delivered from the chains of sin, self, and performance. We are free indeed!

Enjoy the freedom found in Christ today!

November 15

FRIENDSHIP WITH JESUS

John 15:15 (ESV): *"No longer do I call you servants, for the servant does not know what his master is doing; but I have called you friends, for all that I have heard from my Father I have made known to you."*

Friendship is a wonderful gift. By sharing yourself with a kindred spirit, joys are doubled; troubles are shared; and laughter is so much heartier when shared with a friend. There is no such thing as calling too late or needing too much. Friends are available at all times. This is the kind of relationship that Jesus wants to have with you and me. He wants to increase our joy and bear our sorrow. He wants to fill our hearts with laughter and listen intently whenever we call. Jesus said that He is a friend who will never leave us (Hebrews 13:5); always love us (John 3:16); and be closer than our nearest relative (Proverbs 18:24). Friendship with Jesus … what a wonderful gift!

You have a friend in Christ today!

November 16
GOD IS DEPENDABLE

James 1:17 (ESV): *"Every good gift and every perfect gift is from above, coming down from the Father of lights with whom there is no variation or shadow due to change."*

God is not human. There is nothing about His ways that can be reduced to man's ways. Stocks will rise and fall, but God is consistent (Malachi 3:6). People will love you one day and divorce you the next, but God's love is unceasing (Romans 8:38-39). Bodies grow weak and frail, but God never grows tired or weary (Isaiah 40:28-31). The day turns to night; and God is the Eternal Light that never darkens and is never shadowed (James 1:17). He is always honest, always powerful, always forgiving, always loving, and always dependable. We can trust in God, because He is faithful. It is intrinsic to His character; thus, He can never be unfaithful! We will even fail ourselves, but God will not. Place your life in the hands of a trustworthy God. He will always keep you!

You can count on the unchanging God today!

November 17

GOD IS MY HELP

Isaiah 41:10 (ESV): *"fear not, for I am with you;*
be not dismayed, for I am your God; I will strengthen you,
I will help you, I will uphold you with my righteous right hand."

God will never abandon His children. There will never come a time when God will leave you or me to fight our battles alone, bear our burdens alone, or solve our crises alone. In fact, God tells us to not even think about that. We are not to be anxious or dismayed, because He promises to strengthen us in times of weakness, help us in times of need, and uphold us in times of trouble. Our God is our very present help! Fear not.

God has you in His care today!

November 18

GOD WON'T FORGET ME

Isaiah 49:15-16 (ESV): *"Can a woman forget
her nursing child, that she should have no compassion
on the son of her womb? Even these may forget,
yet I will not forget you. Behold, I have engraved you on
the palms of my hands; your walls are continually before me."*

Sometimes we wonder, "God, do you love me? Do you really know my name and care about what is going on in my life?" In response to that, He lovingly stretches out His hands and says, "Yes!" God forever proved His love for us, when He stretched out His body on a cross and died for our sins. Then, He relentlessly pursues us to draw us to Himself. For His own sake, God saves us and claims us as His (Isaiah 43:25). We are forever before the Lord. His thoughts of us outnumber the sands on the seashore (Psalm 139:17-18). He has inscribed us on the palms of His hands; permanently grafted into His body. God will not and cannot forget His own! We are loved.

You are carved in the Body of Christ today!

November 19
GOD'S DREAMS

Genesis 37:20 (NASB): *"Now then, come and let us kill him and throw him into one of the pits; and we will say, 'A wild beast devoured him.' Then let us see what will become of his dreams!"*

Joseph was a dreamer. God had begun giving this young man glimpses into the future. Although Joseph did not fully understand the God's plan for his life, he knew that it included him ruling over his own family. Needless to say, his older brothers did not like the idea of Joseph ruling over them. They put a wicked plan into action to try to silence the dreamer. What they didn't realize, though, was it wasn't Joseph's dream they were trying to steal. ..It was God's. The Scriptures remind us that "Many are the plans in the mind of a man, but it is the purpose of the Lord that will stand" (Proverbs 19:21).

Joseph encountered many hard and confusing years before God fulfilled the dream of leadership that He had given Joseph as a boy. Through the midst of his trials, it probably never crossed Joseph's mind that this was God's process to prepare him to rule. But God had a plan that was perfect, and He needed Joseph to become the man who would be able to carry out such a plan. The same is true in our lives. God has a specific intention for each one of us. Often, the preparation for our divine assignments include hardship – a molding and shaping process – so that we will be the kind of people God can use. Be assured, though, that absolutely no man, woman, child, or devil can ever thwart God's plans for our lives. God holds our destiny, and His timing is perfect.

God has BIG dreams for your life today!

November 20
HABITS

1 Corinthians 6:12 (ESV): *"All things are lawful for me," but not all things are helpful. "All things are lawful for me," but I will not be enslaved by anything."*

Got habits? And everyone said, "Amen!" From biting fingernails, to speeding (just a little!), to embellishing a story when we tell it … we can all identify some custom, pattern, or addiction in our life that attaches itself to us. Perhaps that way has been with us so long that it has actually become a part of our identity – we are known as the speeder or the liar. One day Jesus walked into the temple, and He began to read aloud from the scroll of the prophet Isaiah. He read, "He has sent me to proclaim freedom for the prisoners … to set the oppressed free" (Luke 4:18). Then, He looked around the room and said, "Today, this scripture is fulfilled in your hearing" (Luke 4:21). Christ has come to free us from bondage, from oppression, from anything that attaches itself to us and weighs us down. In and of itself, the action or object of a habit may not be that bad. When the action or object begins to control and dictate our lives, however, we are enslaved. If you are struggling with a habit today, Christ can set you free. He is your freedom. You do not have to go through the rest of your life with the same quirks, mannerisms, or chains that have followed you thus far. In Christ, we are more than conquerors! Surrender your habit to Him, and let your identity be sealed in Jesus alone.

Make a habit of spending time with Jesus today!

November 21
HE KEEPS ME

Jude 1:24 (ESV): *"Now to him who is able to keep you from stumbling and to present you blameless before the presence of his glory with great joy...."*

Jesus is not only our redeemer, He is our keeper. When we are not able to control our lusts, Christ can. When we are not able to control our anger, Christ can. When we are not able to make ourselves walk uprightly, Christ can. When we are not able to make ourselves holy, Christ can. Jesus saved us to Himself, for Himself; and He will keep us from stumbling. Then on that day when we stand before God the Father, He will see us as blameless and perfect because of Christ alone.

Jesus is all you need today!

November 22
HE'S IN THE BOAT

Mark 4:38-40 (ESV): *"But he was in the stern, asleep on the cushion. And they woke him and said to him, 'Teacher, do you not care that we are perishing?' And he awoke and rebuked the wind and said to the sea, 'Peace! Be still!' And the wind ceased, and there was a great calm. He said to them, 'Why are you so afraid? Have you still no faith?'"*

Jesus was tired. He laid down to rest in the bottom of the boat, as the disciples set sail across the glassy lake. Suddenly, a great storm arose. The boat was violently tossed to and fro and even began to take on water. The disciples became very afraid, as they battled to keep their boat from sinking. All of a sudden, someone noticed that Jesus was not in panic mode with them. He was not bailing water or battening down the hatches! So, they woke Him up. Jesus wiped the sleep from His eyes, commanded nature to behave, and then looked at His men puzzled. The question was simple but piercing ... Do you still not believe in me?

The disciples were in a frightening situation, but they were never alone. The disciples tried to save themselves, but salvation was in the boat with them. The disciples woke Jesus but only to question His love for them; they could have woken Him because they believed in His power to deliver. Ugh ... these poor men! We can relate to them and feel their pain, can't we? We want to believe, and we want so desperately to not be afraid ... but time and time again, we find ourselves trying to bail ourselves out. The only time we call on Jesus is in panic mode. Christ promises that He is in the boat with us. It cannot sink. We are safe with Him, no matter if our circumstances try to convince us otherwise. When we call on Christ, He will deliver. Let us call out in faith, because we know He will deliver – and not in fear, because we doubt His love.

Jesus is your peace-speaker today!

November 23
HEAVEN CELEBRATES YOU

Luke 15:10 (ESV): *"Just so, I tell you, there is joy before the angels of God over one sinner who repents."*

You matter. It's true! You may feel small or insignificant. There may be times when other people ignore you, or divorce you, or dismiss you. But you still matter! There is a God in heaven who took great care in designing you, intentionally creating you to be in a relationship with Him. And, on the day that you opened your heart to receive His love, Heaven rejoiced! We're not talking about a little smile or a polite clap but an all-out explosion of cheers and praises! Music played, angels danced, and Heaven stopped to celebrate you ... the one who Jesus loves. A banner now hangs in glory with your name that says, "Welcome to the family of God!" (Luke 10:20).

Jesus loves you today!

November 24
I GIVE YOU MY ALL

Luke 21:1-4 (NIV): *"As Jesus looked up, he saw the rich putting their gifts into the temple treasury. He also saw a poor widow put in two very small copper coins. 'Truly I tell you,' he said, 'this poor widow has put in more than all the others. All these people gave their gifts out of their wealth; but she out of her poverty put in all she had to live on.'"*

Jesus and His disciples stood in the temple as the people came by to give their offerings. Many people gave large gifts, but only one gave an extravagant gift ... a little widow woman. This woman joyfully dropped two copper coins in the plate, and Jesus' heart was stirred with excitement. "Look! Did you see that? Wow, what a gift!" His disciples tried to figure out who Jesus was talking about. They would have never guessed Christ would be ecstatic over two cents. What thrilled Jesus, however, was not the money; it was the trust in Him that the money represented. This woman was poor, yet she gave all that she had, because she trusted God more than monetary resources. Will we follow her example and trust God with all that we are? Or, will we choose to hold back parts of ourselves? God gave us His all; we can trust Him with our all!

Give Jesus all of you today!

November 25

I JUST WANT TO BE HAPPY

Proverbs 10:28 (ESV): *"The hope of the righteous brings joy, but the expectation of the wicked will perish."*

The elusive goal of happiness … How often have we thought, "I just want to be happy." The truth is, though, happiness is a fleeting feeling. It is an emotional high that comes, and it goes. What we should desire is joy. This is a deep-seeded state of being that anchors our hearts and minds regardless of the fickle emotions of the day. Solomon wrote that the hope of the righteous is what seals joy in our spirits. What is that hope? Jesus Christ! Because of Christ, we are filled with the hope of eternal life spent with Him and free from sin, sickness, sorrow, and death. No circumstance in our day can shake this hope. Solomon went on to say that the expectation of the wicked would perish. Why? Because everything apart from Christ will fade away. It is temporary and will not last. Christ is the only true source of contentment and fulfillment. Seek Christ today and be filled with His joy!

Rejoice in the Lord today!

November 26
I SHALL NOT BE SHAKEN

Psalm 62:1-2 (ESV): *"For God alone my soul waits in silence; from him comes my salvation. He only is my rock and my salvation, my fortress; I shall not be greatly shaken."*

There are times in life when troubles and trials prevail. Our normal instinct may be to worry or fear. The Psalmist, though, offers a better way to manage times like these … wait on God. He is our salvation, our rock, and a fortress that cannot be penetrated by the evils of this world. In Him we are deeply rooted. We will not be shaken when the storms of life blow our way. We are secure in our Father's love.

God is your sure foundation today!

November 27

I'M NOT QUALIFIED

Joshua 1:2,5 (ESV): *"…Now therefore arise, go over this Jordan, you and all this people, into the land that I am giving to them, to the people of Israel…No man shall be able to stand before you all the days of your life. Just as I was with Moses, so I will be with you. I will not leave you or forsake you.'"*

God's servant, Moses, has just died. God calls out Joshua as the one to become the new leader of the children of Israel. He will be the one to take the people into the Promised Land. Wow, a promotion! Joshua must have been thrilled! Not exactly … the poor man was filled with anxiety and fear. His own inadequacies overwhelmed him and left him quaking in his flip-flops. Did God abandon Joshua and move on to a more qualified candidate for this prestigious job? Not at all. Instead, God encouraged Joshua the same way He encourages you and me today. God reminded Joshua that He would never leave him nor forsake him (Joshua 1:6-9). Joshua did not need to be qualified for the task at hand. He only needed to be willing to courageously move forward with bold faith in the God who could do what he could not. When God gives you a divine assignment, it is not because of your ability, it is because of your availability! Do not be intimidated by your own limitations; instead, dare to be available and watch God do the impossible through you!

God will equip you today!

November 28
I'M NOT RELIGIOUS

Ephesians 2:8-9 (ESV): *"For by grace you have been saved through faith. And this is not your own doing; it is the gift of God, not a result of works, so that no one may boast."*

Religion says: "I obey to be accepted." In Christ, we say: "I am accepted. Therefore, I obey."

Religion says: "I do to earn the favor of God." In Christ, we say: "Through the work of Christ done on my behalf, I have favor with the Father."

Religion says: "If I fail to live up to the standard, I fall from grace." In Christ, we say: "If I fail to live up to the standard, I run to grace."

God is not looking for religious people. He is seeking men and women who understand that we need Christ. In Christ, we are accepted; we find favor; we receive grace; and we are adopted by Father God!

In Christ we are secure today!

November 29
IN CHRIST ALONE

Romans 3:23-25 (ESV): *"for all have sinned and fall short of the glory of God, and are justified by his grace as a gift through the redemption that is in Christ Jesus, whom God put forward as a propitiation by his blood, to be received by faith...."*

Where is your hope placed today? Is it in your good job, your nice family, your good name, or your perfect church attendance? Do you hope that one day, when you stand before God, He will be delighted by all of your goodness and welcome you into His Heaven? If your hope is in your efforts, I must tell you that your hope is misplaced.

We have all sinned and fallen short of the righteous standards of a holy God. Consequently, sin cannot enter into the presence of God. In fact, sin will be punished by death and eternal separation from Him. Mankind's goodness is like filthy rags in the sight of God (Isaiah 64:6). There is only One who has lived the standard of perfection that God requires – Jesus Christ. The Bible says that Christ is the "propitiation" of our sins. Propitiation means, "to satisfy." Christ satisfied the wrath of God against the sin of mankind by living the perfect life and dying a substitutionary death on our behalf. In Christ alone we are saved. In Christ alone we are perfected. In Christ alone we have hope. In Christ alone we will live eternally!

Place your hope in Christ alone today!

November 30
IN MY RIGHT MIND

Luke 8:35 (ESV): *"Then people went out to see what had happened, and they came to Jesus and found the man from whom the demons had gone, sitting at the feet of Jesus, clothed and in his right mind, and they were afraid."*

He was a social outcast, the town freak. The man ran naked through the graveyards and lived among the corpses. The townspeople lived in fear of him and warned their children to steer clear of him. Many tried to capture him, but no chains could hold him. He was possessed by a legion of demons. The man was literally out of his mind. Then, Jesus came by. Immediately, the man, who spent his days running from the living, ran to the Author of Life and bowed before Him. Jesus had compassion on the man and commanded the evil spirits to leave him. The next time the townspeople saw the man, he was sitting at the feet of Jesus clothed and in his right mind. The demons were powerful, but they were no match for Jesus.

Sin makes us feel inappropriately, think irrationally, and behave erratically. Christ, however, can stabilize our emotions, calm our racing minds, and change our behavior. In Christ, we regain a sense of purpose and wellbeing. We operate in our right mind, because we have the mind of Christ operating in us!

God will give you the mind of Christ today!

[fire yourself]
DECEMBER

December 1
IS GOD REALLY GOOD?

Psalm 136:1 (ESV): *"Give thanks to the LORD,*
for he is good, for his steadfast love endures forever."

If God is good, then why do bad things happen? Have you ever asked this question? I think at some point in our lives most of us have wondered about this. We hear tragic stories, and we experience unfair circumstances and wonder, "Why God?" The truth is that we do live in a sin- cursed world; as a result bad things happen, but God is still good. It is because of His loving kindness that He helps us to persevere through hard times. Christ told us that in this world we would experience troubles, but we should remain encouraged, because He has overcome the world (John 16:33). He never leaves us alone or hopeless. God's goodness ensures that this evil existence is temporary. There will come a day, however, when God will cleanse the earth of all unrighteousness. Until then, He is patient for the sake of those who have not yet surrendered their hearts to Him—because in God's eyes, all unrepentant sin is evil (2 Peter 3:9). Knowing this, we should give thanks to God for His goodness towards all mankind.

Give thanks to God for His steadfast love and goodness today!

December 2
JUSTIFIED

Romans 3:23-24 (ESV): *"for all have sinned
and fall short of the glory of God, and are justified by his grace
as a gift through the redemption that is in Christ Jesus...."*

There has never been a single person born, apart from Jesus Christ, who is sin free. We have all sinned. The Bible says, if we deny this fact, we are only deceiving ourselves (1 John 1:8). The problem with this truth is that God's standard is holiness and perfection. If we are stained by sin, how then can we be holy and perfect? Enter Jesus! His death on the cross performed the supernatural work of justification for all who believe in Him. Being justified means perfected, just as if I'd never sinned! In Christ we can stand before a holy God and be received by Him, because we are flawless. Amazing! Though past sins may haunt us and present sins taunt us, the justification of Christ triumphs over that sin. We are perfect in Christ!

Believer, you are the righteousness of Christ today!

December 3

LIVING UNTROUBLED
AND UNAFRAID

John 14:27 (KJV): *"Peace I leave with you,*
my peace I give unto you: not as the world giveth, give I unto you.
Let not your heart be troubled, neither let it be afraid."

Jesus told His disciples that He was giving them peace, and not just any kind of peace – but His peace. What is the difference between the peace of the world and the peace of God? The world's peace is only found in temporal things – money, jobs, houses, vehicles, and people. All of these things can break or fail or pass away. The peace of God, however, is found in Himself, and He cannot break or fail or pass away. Because of the security we have in a God who will never leave us nor forsake us (Deuteronomy 31:8); a God who created all things and owns all things (Colossians 1:16); and a God who was and who is and who always will be (Revelation 1:8), we can choose to live untroubled and unafraid!

Choose to have a peaceful heart because of Christ today!

December 4
LOVE GOD AND OTHERS

Matthew 22:37-40 (ESV): *"And he said to him, 'You shall love the Lord your God with all your heart and with all your soul and with all your mind. This is the great and first commandment. And a second is like it: You shall love your neighbor as yourself. On these two commandments depend all the Law and the Prophets.'"*

God gave Moses the Ten Commandments carved into stone tablets with His very own finger. These laws were to be the moral guidelines for mankind to live by. On the surface, they seem simple enough to obey: honor God, honor mom and dad, don't lie, don't kill, don't steal … not too much to ask of a sophisticated society. All the Law did, however, was point out how far from "good" man really is. Enter Jesus … because we failed to do what the Law required, Jesus came and perfectly satisfied all of its demands. Now, He offers to live in each one of us. We may fall short of the standard of God, but through Christ we can learn to love God and others perfectly.

Let the love of God fill you today!

December 5
MAKES ME WANT TO DANCE!

2 Samuel 6:14 (ESV): *"And David danced before the LORD with all his might...."*

Happy doesn't describe the feeling. Excited is a little closer. The moment was more like an overwhelming joy that bubbled up from deep inside of King David and spilled out of him in dance. The man could not help himself; the joy of the Lord had overcome him! The Ark of the Covenant, the very presence of the Lord, was being restored to its rightful place in Israel, and a glorious celebration was the only proper response. Not everyone shared David's need to cut a rug; namely his wife, Michal. She rebuked him for such a disorderly display and accused him of trying to draw attention to himself. David, however, was unapologetic for his righteous fervor.

There will be times when our hearts overflow with the joy of the Lord. We may even feel like dancing in honor of Him. Not everyone will share in or understand such acts of praise. Even so, if your heart wants to dance for your King, then dance! Your relationship with God is personal. Your praise is intended for Him alone. You worship before an audience of One. So, go ahead, and get your praise on!

Praise God with a dance of joy today!

December 6
MORNING PEOPLE

Psalm 30:5 (ESV): *"... Weeping may tarry for the night, but joy comes with the morning."*

What is it about the dark that seems to magnify problems? We lay our heads down to sleep at night, and our thoughts begin to race; images of worst-case scenarios play on the big screen of our minds, problems seem unsolvable, and fears become insurmountable. Then something miraculous happens ... the morning sun begins to shine and our anxiety fades with the darkness. Jesus said, "I am the Light of the world; he who follows Me will not walk in the darkness, but will have the Light of life" (John 8:12). We are children of the day, people who rejoice with the promise of morning (1 Thessalonians 5:5). Hard times and sad times may try to draw us into dark places, but we do not have to remain there. We can open the windows of our soul to the Son and welcome in His light. In Christ we can sing, for our Joy has come!

Let the Son shine on you today!

December 7
NO REARVIEW MIRRORS

Genesis 19:26 (KJV): *"But [Lot's] wife looked back from behind him, and she became a pillar of salt."*

A car is equipped with side and rearview mirrors. These are designed for defensive driving. A quick glance to the left, to the right, and behind can help a driver see if there are any dangers encroaching upon him. The rearview mirror, however, was never meant to be the driver's mainline of focus. If a driver spends all of his time looking behind, he will never successfully move ahead. In fact, it can be totally destructive!

The same principle is true on our spiritual journey. While we make take a quick glimpse of remembrance for what God has delivered us from, the last thing we want to do is to dwell in the past. The more we look over our shoulder, the more susceptible we are to the lies of the enemy that somehow we are leaving behind something good. We need to fix our gaze upon the joys that God in Christ has placed before us (Hebrews 12:2). In doing so, we will successfully move forward and upward!

Fix your eyes on Jesus today!

December 8
NO TRESPASSING!

Proverbs 4:14 (ESV): *"Do not enter the path of the wicked, and do not walk in the way of the evil."*

No Trespassing! Keep Out! Do Not Enter! Danger! These are warning signs with clear-cut messages. These signs set a concrete boundary that should not be crossed or compromised. Why? Because dangerous consequences lie ahead. The Scriptures give us many warning signs about opening ourselves up to sin. Wise King Solomon instructed us not to trespass into territory that we do not belong. If we are to overcome temptations and a lead a victorious lifestyle, then we need to stay away from people, places, or things that ignite that battle between the flesh and the spirit in us. The Apostle Paul simply said, "RUN!" (1 Corinthians 6:18). Sin is a powerful siren that will lure and entice us away from the ways of God. The results are detrimental to us mentally, emotionally, spiritually, relationally, and physically. Do not be deceived. Sin has pleasure but only for a short season. Its ultimate destination is destruction and death. Stay off its path!

Walk with God today!

December 9
NOT I BUT CHRIST

Galatians 3:2-3 (ESV): *"Let me ask you only this:*
Did you receive the Spirit by works of the law or by hearing
with faith? Are you so foolish? Having begun
by the Spirit, are you now being perfected by the flesh?"

Jesus Christ died on a cross to save us from our sins (John 3:16). We gratefully accept the work of our Savior and His gift of eternal life. But as we live our day-to-day lives, we go into "self-maintenance" mode, as though it is on us to keep ourselves saved. We try really hard to be really good; Before you know it, we're burnt out on Christianity. We find that perfecting "self" is just too hard. The Apostle Paul in his letter to the church in Galatia asked them the question, "Why? ... Why do you think that salvation from the Spirit now requires the work of the flesh to perfect it?" If Paul were around today, he would ask us the same question. The truth is we cannot save ourselves, and we cannot keep ourselves saved. It is the work of God (Ephesians 2:8-9). He began it, and He will complete it (Philippians 1:6). We are kept by the grace of God, while He is accurately reproducing His character in us (Ephesians 4:22)!

You are kept by Christ alone today!

December 10
PRAY BELIEVING

Acts 12:5 (ESV): *"So Peter was kept in prison, but earnest prayer for him was made to God by the church."*

Herod had just had James killed, and now Peter was arrested. Herod's intention was to kill Peter when the time of Passover had ended. While Peter was in prison, his church family began to pray earnestly to God for his deliverance. The night before Herod was to bring Peter before the blood-thirsty mob for execution, God sent an angel to set Peter free. At first the dazed disciple thought he was dreaming! Then he quickly made his escape to the home of Mary, the mother of John Mark. On the inside of the home, people were praying. On the outside of the house, stood their answer… knocking. A servant girl named Rhoda went to the door. When she heard the voice of Peter, she ran back to tell the others. The church people told Rhoda she must be mistaken! Peter knocked even harder and was eventually let into the house. God answered their prayers!

This was a glorious miracle indeed, but notice the unbelief that tried to creep in among these believers. A prayer was prayed. An answer was given. Unbelief, however, tried to deny the answer. Fortunately for Peter, the door was eventually opened. How does this compare to our prayer life? When we pray, do we really believe that God is listening? Do we keep the door of our hearts locked denying the answer God sends, or are we praying expectantly with ears attentive to His knocking? Let us pray believing, because we serve a God who hears and answers our prayers (Mark 11:24)!

God still answers prayers today!

December 11
PURR-FECT FAITH

Daniel 6:16 (NIV): *"So the king gave the order, and they brought Daniel and threw him into the lions' den. The king said to Daniel, 'May your God, whom you serve continually, rescue you!'"*

Daniel had been taken into captivity in Babylon. During this time, however, he had won favor in the eyes of the Babylonian King, Darius, because he was seen to be a man of great faith and integrity. God had also blessed Daniel with wisdom and the ability to interpret dreams. His giftedness was recognized by the king, and he planned to put Daniel in charge of all the other satraps in the kingdom. This did not go over well with the other satraps. They put an evil scheme in place to try to get rid of Daniel. Appealing to the king's ego, the satraps created a decree that no man should bow down to any other in worship except for the king for thirty days; pleased by this, Darius signed the decree into law. The penalty for breaking the law was the lion's den.

Daniel was a man of prayer. Three times a day, he opened the windows of his room and cried aloud to God. He did not fear man's law, and he continued to bow down to worship God only. The satraps caught Daniel in the act of prayer to God and reported him to Darius. Grieved, the kind had Daniel thrown in the lion's den. The next morning, the king rushed to see if Daniel survived the night. To his amazement, Daniel was alive and the lions were as calm as house cats. Darius had Daniel pulled up from the den and had the other satraps thrown in. The Bible says the lions crushed their bones before the men ever hit the den floor. A new decree went out – worship God!

Do not fear man. Trust God. His strength is made perfect in our times of weakness (2 Corinthians 12:9). Our faith in God will never leave us hopeless (Zephaniah 3:17). In Him we are always victorious (1 Corinthians 15:57)!

Have faith in God today!

December 12

REDEEMED

Romans 3:23-24 (ESV): *"for all have sinned and fall short of the glory of God, and are justified by his grace as a gift through the redemption that is in Christ Jesus...."*

In the Bible days, there were three classes of people: slaves, men who had always been free, and people who used to be slaves but who were set free. This last group of people used to be under a taskmaster, forced to labor for another, not knowing the blessing of coming and going on their own will. Until one day, for whatever reason, someone has compassion on them and paid a price to redeem them. This act of redemption declared the slave to be a free man.

This is what Jesus Christ did on the cross for you and for me. We were slaves to sin. It was our taskmaster. Whenever sin yanked our chains, we responded. Jesus Christ came on our behalf to redeem us. The price? His life. He gave His life so that you and I could walk in freedom. No longer are we under the power of sin. Oh, it may still pester us, but it can never again master us, thanks to our Redeemer, Jesus Christ!

In Christ, you are redeemed today!

December 13
REMIND YOURSELF

Psalm 42:5 (KJV): *"Why art thou cast down, O my soul? And why art thou disquieted in me? Hope thou in God: for I shall yet praise him for the help of his countenance."*

It is so easy for our souls to become downcast. We focus on circumstances and limited resources. The thought of being without terrifies us, and we find ourselves retreating into the dark caves of our minds. It is in moments like this that we need to shake ourselves and stir the Holy Spirit inside of us. We need to remind ourselves of the truth that our God is mighty and faithful and that our hope is not in this temporal world but in our eternal Lord.

The Psalmist reminds us to praise God for the help of His presence in our lives. And God is always present. I learned in my marketing days that you have to repeat the same message three times in order for it to stick with your audience ... God is an ever-present help in the time of trouble. God is an ever-present help in the time of trouble. GOD IS AN EVER-PRESENT HELP IN THE TIME OF TROUBLE! There, now that should stick!

Encourage yourself in the Lord today!

December 14
RESURRECTION POWER

Philippians 3:10 (ESV): *"that I may know him
and the power of his resurrection...."*

Jesus Christ came to earth wrapped in the flesh of a baby boy. At the age of thirty, He began His crusades of teaching people about the Kingdom of God. Three years later, He surrendered Himself to be crucified. Jesus died for the sins of mankind in order to satisfy God's wrath against sin. His story does not end there, though. Three days after being laid in a borrowed tomb, Jesus resurrected from the grave! And in His rising, Jesus became our victor over the curse of sin, death, and hell. The resurrection of Jesus Christ is the power of God on displa.; It's God bearing His arm to satan and the curse of sin. Because Jesus lives, we, who were once dead in the trespasses of our sins (Ephesians 2:1), will live also. There is no fear in sickness and no sting in death. Because Jesus is alive, our victory is secure!

Jesus Christ is alive today!

December 15
RUN!

1 Corinthians 6:18 (NLT): *"Run from sexual sin! No other sin*
so clearly affects the body as this one does.
For sexual immorality is a sin against your own body."

RUN! The warning is clear. Don't waste any time, and don't slowly distance yourself. Get away from sexual sin now! Many people close their ears when the conversation turns to sexual purity. We feel that we have the right to do whatever we want to with our own bodies. Even more, why would God create us to be sexual beings, if He is just going to deny us from the experience? We need to remember that God is good, and everything that He does is good. He created the gift of sex for a husband and wife to unite and for their mutual pleasure. Like any good parent, however, our Father sets boundaries on our lives for our protection. Good things, when misused, can become very destructive. The enemy knows this better than anyone, so he intentionally baits us into thinking that God is prudish and must not really be good to be so restrictive on us (sounds like an immature teenager's mindset against mom & dad!). Sex, when misused, can become destructive to our health, minds, self-esteem, our ability to trust, and to our relationships with God and others. When used rightly in the context of marriage, though, a healthy sexual relationship not only blesses you and your spouse, but it also brings honor to our God.

Trust Jesus with all of your needs today!

December 16
SELFISH

Philippians 2:3-4 (ESV): *"Do nothing from rivalry or conceit, but in humility count others more significant than yourselves. Let each of you look not only to his own interests, but also to the interests of others."*

What is the most poisonous fish in the world and it is local to you and me? A sel-fish! It's a bad joke, I know. It does, however, make a valid point. People are selfish and that is toxic. There is only one cure for this condition … the cross! We have got to die to self and allow the Spirit of God to live His life through us (Galatians 2:20). He can empower us to see as He sees, speak as He speaks, and love as He loves. The miracle of Christ in us is that everyone benefits! Others receive love, forgiveness, and validation. And we receive the blessings that always follow obedience to God (Deuteronomy 28:1-13). Focus on Christ instead of self, and He will delight in you!

Jesus wants to love others through you today!

December 17
SIN IS AGAINST GOD

Genesis 39:8-10 (ESV): *"But he refused and said to his master's wife, 'Behold, because of me my master has no concern about anything in the house, and he has put everything that he has in my charge. He is not greater in this house than I am, nor has he kept back anything from me except you, because you are his wife. How then can I do this great wickedness and sin against God?'"*

Joseph was a servant in the house of Potiphar. Because of his good character and hard work, Joseph had earned the trust of his master. Potiphar gave him free reign throughout the house and allowed him to oversee many important tasks. One day Potiphar's wife tried to seduce Joseph. He resisted her advances and ran from the temptation. Why? Was he afraid that Potiphar would throw him in jail? Was he afraid of ruining Mrs. Potiphar's good name? Was he afraid of losing his job? No, no, and no. His first concern was how such an act would affect his God. We must be like Joseph and understand that sin, first and foremost, affects the heart of God. Other people may feel the consequences of our actions, but ultimately we have opposed the God who loves us and gave Himself for us. Because of God's great love for us, let us resist the pull of sin and take the way of escape that He will always provide (1 Corinthians 10:13).

The Holy Spirit will be your strength today!

December 18
SONGS OF THE HEART

Ephesians 5:19 (NIV): *"speaking to one another with psalms, hymns, and songs from the Spirit. Sing and make music from your heart to the Lord...."*

What is on the inside will flow out of us (Luke 6:45). If we are sad, then our voices will be low and solemn. If we are angry, then harsh tones will infuse our speech. If we are filled with hope, then joyful songs from the Spirit will flood our speech. This does not mean that our days are always good, and our lives are always easy. It does mean that regardless of our circumstances, we are sealed with the Hope of Glory, and in that, we can always rejoice because of Christ (Philippians 4:4). Our positive outlook and optimistic viewpoint isn't founded in wishful thinking but in concrete faith in a God who cannot fail! May the words of our mouths always reflect the abundance of Christ in our hearts.

Sing a new song today!

December 19
SPIRITUAL STRENGTH

Ephesians 3:17-19 (ESV): *"so that Christ may dwell in your hearts through faith—that you, being rooted and grounded in love, may have strength to comprehend with all the saints what is the breadth and length and height and depth, and to know the love of Christ that surpasses knowledge, that you may be filled with the fullness of God."*

Physical strength comes from eating a healthy diet daily and exercising our muscles regularly. The same can be said for spiritual strength. We need to feast daily on the Bread of Life. It is through ingesting the Word of God that we are filled with Christ – His love, His forgiveness, His way of thinking and being. Then, fueled by the proper nutrition, we are ready to exercise our faith muscles through facing problems, trials, and difficult circumstances. As we come through each feat, we grow spiritually, becoming mature and strong in Christ.

Christ is your strength today!

December 20
THE CROSS

1 Corinthians 1:18 (ESV): *"For the word of the cross is folly to those who are perishing, but to us who are being saved it is the power of God."*

The cross … an instrument of death that God used to bring life. In human wisdom, this is foolishness. Why? Because salvation seems so unnecessary to those who do not realize they need saving. The unbelieving mind is deceived into thinking that independence from God is strength. The attitude of "I've got this" is the gateway to a self-destructive path. For those whose minds have been opened to the spiritual truth about the temporal body and the eternal soul, however, the cross is a life preserver! We cling to its power of redemption and depend on the righteousness of Christ to secure our eternity. Human logic may never rationalize the word of the cross, but it is in God that we place our unwavering faith and not our own understanding (Proverbs 3:5-6)!

Christ is your salvation today!

December 21
THE DEVIL MADE ME DO IT!

James 1:14 (ESV): *"But each person is tempted when he is lured and enticed by his own desire."*

There is a game that most every human being has played at one time or another ... the blame game! It is as old as time. When Adam and Eve disobeyed God in the Garden of Eden, Eve blamed the snake for tricking her, and Adam blamed Eve for enticing him; then he blamed God for giving him Eve! We do not like to accept personal accountability for choices that end up being less than stellar. We will even blame satan for our bad choices; after all, he is the source of all badness, right? Well, the truth is that satan is all evil, but he is far from being all-powerful! When we surrendered our hearts to Christ, satan lost the authority to rule over us. He cannot make us do anything. Satan may present the opportunity, but the choice to sin is ours alone. The Apostle James said that we sin, because we are lured away from God by evil desires in our hearts (James 1:14). The result is pain, hurt, destruction, and death (James 1:15). We can guard against temptations, though, by studying God's Word, by sharing our weaknesses with our brothers and sisters in Christ, and by gaining a greater understanding of who God is. When we stand behind the arsenal that God provides for us, we can resist the enemy. When we do sin, however, there is no need to point the finger. Just run to the open arms of God. His grace will receive you!

The Holy Spirit is your strength today!

December 22
THE MANTLE

2 Kings 2:13 (KJV): *"He took up also the mantle of Elijah that fell from him, and went back, and stood by the bank of Jordan...."*

The translation for the word "mantle" in Scripture is glorious, powerful, or worthy. The mantle represented a call to serve in a covenant relationship with God. The Prophet Elijah's mantle represented the power of God in his life and enabled him to perform miracles. When Elijah was taken away to Heaven, his mantle fell back to the earth. His young apprentice Elisha picked up the garment and carried on the anointed ministry of the prophet.

Men – God has called you to positions of leadership and authority in your homes. He has cloaked you with His glory and power, and He has anointed you as ministers. Your sons are following in your footsteps. Train them up in the way that they should go (Proverbs 22:6)! This world needs mighty men of God. If you have not been walking in your God-ordained calling as the spiritual leader of your home, go to God. Then, pick up your mantle and lead. You have young eyes upon you.

Men of God, lead your families today!

December 23

THE PRAYERS
OF THE RIGHTEOUS

James 5:16 (KJV): *"... The effectual fervent prayer*
of a righteous man availeth much."

If God is sovereign, then why do we need to pray? Have you ever wondered about this? I have. Clearly, God wants us to pray. The Scriptures tell us over and over to pray and pray often (1 Thessalonians 5:17). Jesus set the example of having an active prayer life (Mark 1:35, John 11:41-42), and He even taught His disciples to pray (Luke 11:1-13). So, how does God's sovereignty work in conjunction with the prayer of believers? God has chosen prayer to be a means by which His sovereignty works in the lives of His people. He moves on our hearts and burdens our spirits with the desires of His will. When we pray according to God's will, He hears and answers (1 John 5:14). When we don't know what to pray, He still acts on our behalf through His Holy Spirit praying for us (Romans 8:27). Either way, our act of faith and declaration of our dependence on God, motivates His heart to carry out His divine providence in our lives and in the lives of others. The most confident step you and I can take in our relationship with Father God is to pray ... and pray often!

Pray to the God who hears you today!

December 24
THE SLOW FADE

James 1:14-15 (ESV): *"But each person is tempted when he is lured and enticed by his own desire. Then desire when it has conceived gives birth to sin, and sin when it is fully grown brings forth death."*

Temptation in itself is not a sin. It is the invitation to sin. Temptation, however, does open the door to a slippery slope that if we are not careful will cause us to fall headlong into sin. The process can be so subtle and cunning. It starts with a legitimate need, a desire. Desires in themselves are not necessarily wrong. It is when we choose an illegitimate way to meet our desires that troubles occur. Our emotions tell us we are in need, and then our intellect gets involved. We convince ourselves that if we feel something, it must be true; we deceive ourselves. We allow our human logic to access our need, and we begin to rationalize ways, other than God, for satisfying it. Last, we act on the thought and yield to disobedient behavior … sin is birthed. The Bible teaches us that we are not to live by our fickle feelings (James 1:6-8) and limited understanding (Proverbs 3:5-6). Instead, we are to be rooted and grounded in the Word of God. Faith in God's sufficiency will help us to meet legitimate needs in legitimate ways (Hebrews 10:38). Faith will help us to fight against temptations, because we know that our God is enough.

Guard your heart and mind in Christ Jesus today!

December 25
TODAY IS THE DAY
OF SALVATION

2 Corinthians 6:2 (ESV): *"…Behold, now is the favorable time; behold, now is the day of salvation."*

Human beings are doers. We love to make our "to do" lists and establish our short-term and long-term plans. Some of our lives are so completely planned out that we can tell you exactly where we will be or what we will be doing six months from now! Although being good stewards of our time is admirable, the Bible warns us about placing too much confidence in our plans. The Apostle James described life as a vapor that is present today but could be gone tomorrow (James 4:4). For this reason, we need to make one thing a priority for today in our lives … salvation. We know that we have all sinned (Romans 3:23); and apart from reconciliation with God through Jesus (2 Corinthians 5:18), we are doomed to spend eternity separated from God (Isaiah 59:2; Romans 6:23). Therefore, because our days are uncertain, we cannot gamble that tomorrow will be the day we surrender our will for God's will in our lives. Make salvation a priority. Ask Jesus to be your Savior today, then all of your tomorrows will be eternally sure!

Jesus Christ is your salvation today!

December 26
THE SWORD OF TRUTH

Psalm 119: 9, 11 (ESV): *"How can a young man keep his way pure? By guarding it according to your word....I have stored up your word in my heart, that I might not sin against you."*

It is important for us to study Scripture and to get truth on the inside of us. Why? Otherwise, we will be easy prey for the deceitful tactics of satan. He loves to bait the children of God with temptations to sin. He is an expert at camouflaging destruction in appealing packaging. Satan makes the bad look really good. If we are unaware and unarmed, we will be overtaken. Jesus responded to temptations from the enemy with the Word of God. Each time satan enticed Him, Jesus attacked the deceiver with truth. The Bible describes itself as "...sharper than any two-edged sword, piercing to the division of soul and of spirit, of joints and of marrow, and discerning the thoughts and intentions of the heart" (Hebrews 4:12). The Bible is our sword of truth. With it we can fight the good fight by maintaining a surrendered heart to Christ and resisting the temptations from our enemy. The result? Satan will run from us (James 4:7)! Victory is ours in Christ.

The Word of God is your defense today!

December 27
TOWERS

Genesis 11:3-4 (NIV): *"They said to each other,*
'Come, let's make bricks and bake them thoroughly.'
They used brick instead of stone, and tar for mortar. Then they said,
'Come, let us build ourselves a city, with a tower that reaches
to the heavens, so that we may make a name for ourselves;
otherwise we will be scattered over the face of the whole earth.'"

Up until this time, there was only one language in the land. The people had become skilled craftsmen and decided to join together to build a city to display their glory. They even chose to use man-made building materials of brick and tar instead of the natural building materials of stone and tar from God. The tower represented mankind's rise and independence from God. When God observed their actions and perceived their motives, He confused the common language and caused them to be divided by different languages. Their unity was powerful, but it was being used wrongly.

Are there any towers you are building in your life today? What have you erected in your life to declare your name, your independence, and your glory? We need to be careful of the motivations of our hearts (Luke 16:15). Towers separate us from God. We need to acknowledge that our skills, talents, and resources all come from God alone. We are always dependent upon Him. When we keep our focus on God, then unity with others is a powerful force for good, and we can bring much honor and glory to the only One who is worthy.

Worship the One True God today!

December 28

TRAIN UP A CHILD

Proverbs 22:6 (ESV): *"Train up a child in the way he should go; even when he is old he will not depart from it."*

Parents wear many hats: nurse, chauffeur, cook, stylist, supervisor, and the list goes on and on. Perhaps the greatest role a parent will play in a child's life, though, is teacher. The Bible states that it is the parent's job to train a child. Much of what a child learns will not come from the words a parent speaks but from the attitudes and behaviors modeled. We need to be aware that our children are watching our lives. They may not always do what we tell them to do, but they will surely do as we do. Are we training them to be people of strength and courage with a love for God and others, or are we training them to walk in fear, rebel against God, and resent others? Remember, whatever we teach, when they are old, they will not depart from it.

Let your life teach your children about Jesus today!

December 29
TRUE BEAUTY

1 Peter 3:3 (NIV): *"Your beauty should not come from outward adornment...."*

Today's society focuses on outward beauty. In order to be considered beautiful and worthy of attention, a person must be the right height and weight, have the right color hair and eyes, wear the right kind of clothes or jewelry, and drive the right kind of car. How sad. Too many young men and women are falling prey to this lie and sacrificing personal authenticity to fit in with a fickle-minded society. We need to get back to truth! The Bible teaches us that true beauty comes from the inside. A person's integrity, character, and behavior reflects the heart, and the heart is what God is concerned with (1 Samuel 16:7). Do you want to be truly beautiful? Give your heart to Christ and allow Him to change your thoughts, behaviors, and motives. Then when other people see you, they will be drawn to the beauty of Christ in you!

Let the beauty of Christ shine through you today!

December 30

WATCH WHAT YOU WATCH

Psalm 101:3 (ESV): *"I will not set before my eyes anything that is worthless. I hate the work of those who fall away; it shall not cling to me."*

The Bible teaches us that the eye is the lamp of the body (Matthew 6:22). Whatever we set our eyes on ultimately impacts the way that we think and the way that we behave. Therefore, we need to be sober-minded and alert. Television, movies, and videos can be traps that we can easily fall into. Attractive people, off-color humor, enticing conversations, fast action scenes, and glittering sets all draw us into a fantasy world. If we are not paying attention, we can get caught up in a storyline that is glamourizing sinful behaviors. The more we watch, the more our minds become desensitized to clear cut rights and wrongs. We need to make the pledge of the Psalmist our personal declaration, "I will not set before my eyes anything that is worthless!" We need to refuse to allow those who fall away from the truth to influence us, and ultimately, the direction of our lives. Therefore, Beloved, be on guard! Choose to only set your eyes on things that honor God. We need to watch what we watch.

Guard your heart and mind in Christ Jesus today!

December 31

WE NEED GOD MORE

Exodus 33:15 (ESV): *"And he said to him,*
'If your presence will not go with me, do not bring us up from here.'"

Too often we are guilty of seeking what God can do for us or give us, rather than just seeking God Himself. How sad. We are such a people of want that we fail to see our greatest need. In this passage from Exodus, God is about to clear the way for the children of Israel to possess Canaan, a land flowing with milk and honey. He promised them this land, and God was about to make good on that promise, despite the fact that these people had been so unfaithful to Him. God told Moses that He was sending an angel to clear out all of the enemies from the land and for Moses to take the Israelites into Canaan, but God would not be going with them. The words stung Moses' ears and burned his heart. The realization that they could have all of this rich land but at the expense of God did not seem like a blessing to Moses. He cried, "No, if we can't have you, we won't go." Is that the cry of our hearts today? "God, the job, the money, the relationships, the stuff … none of this is worth anything without you!" God is our greatest need today. Without Him, our hearts and our hopes are bankrupt. In this temporal world, we must remember that earthly treasures are quickly passing away. Do not forgo the eternal love of God for the pleasure of a momentary trinket. Let us make God our treasure today. We need Him more than anything or anyone else!

Draw nearer to God today!

WILLY STEWART

Willy E. Stewart, PE, is the founder of i2. Integrated Intelligence, a consulting firm based in Raleigh, N.C. i2. Integrated Intelligence advises and equips CEOs and management with the necessary leadership, passion and tools to optimize the integration of human capital and business intelligence.

This integration enables companies to dramatically improve performance and the bottom line while remaining focused on their overall purpose and the quality of life of their employees. Mr. Stewart is formerly the president and current CEO of Stewart, Inc., a 100+ person firm, multi-disciplined engineering firm he originally founded in Raleigh in 1994. He is also the founder of the Fire Yourself Movement and author of *Fire Yourself [as your own Higher Power]*.

THERESA ALLEN

Theresa Allen serves as the Women's Ministry Director for the Haven of Rest Ministries. She is a disciple-maker for Christ; the dedicated wife and best friend of Brian Allen; and the blessed mother of Luke, Dane, and Cody. God placed a fire in Theresa's heart to minister to women at an early age. She joined the Haven of Rest Ministries team in March 2010.

Theresa has had the privilege of speaking in many churches of all denominations sharing the good news of the Gospel of Christ. She owns "The Well Life, LLC," a private counseling practice, is a licensed professional counselor – intern (LPC-I); holds a Master of Arts degree in Professional Counseling, a Bachelor of Arts degree in Communications; and is currently working towards a Doctor of Philosophy (PhD) degree in Professional Counseling. Theresa is also a licensed minister.